THE SOUL
OF HIP HOP

RIMS, TIMBS AND A CULTURAL THEOLOGY

DANIEL WHITE HODGE

IVP Books

An imprint of InterVarsity Press
Downers Grove, Illinois

InterVarsity Press
P.O. Box 1400, Downers Grove, IL 60515-1426
World Wide Web: www.ivpress.com
E-mail: email@ivpress.com

InterVarsity Press® is the book-publishing division of InterVarsity Christian Fellowship/USA®, a
movement of students and faculty active on campus at hundreds of universities, colleges and
schools of nursing in the United States of America, and a member movement of the International
Fellowship of Evangelical Students. For information about local and regional activities, write
Public Relations Dept., InterVarsity Christian Fellowship/USA, 6400 Schroeder Rd., P.O. Box
7895, Madison, WI 53707-7895, or visit the IVCF website at <www.intervarsity.org>.

Design: Cindy Kiple
Images: wheel hub: Eliza Snow/iStockphoto
        dancer: Alexander Yakolev/iStockphoto

ISBN 978-0-8308-3732-8

Printed in the United States of America ∞

Library of Congress Cataloging-in-Publication Data

Hodge, Daniel White, 1974-
  The soul of hip hop: rims, timbs & a cultural theology / Daniel
White Hodge.
      p. cm.
  Includes bibliographical references and index.
  ISBN 978-0-8308-3732-8 (pbk.: alk. paper)
  1. Rap (Music)—Religious aspects—Christianity. 2.
Hip-hop—Religious aspects—Christianity. I. Title.
  ML3921.8.R63H64 2010
  261—dc22

                                                            2009042077

P 18 17 16 15 14 13 12 11 10 9 8 7 6 5 4 3 2 1
Y 25 24 23 22 21 20 19 18 17 16 15 14 13 12 11 10

This book is dedicated,
first, to my grandmother Dede.
Her prayers and life were an example
of how to live a life for God.

I also dedicate this book to my wife, Emily,
who has been like a rock for me in my life.
We have withstood the battles and can now
begin to reap some of the new harvest.
Thank you for standing with me
in all life has to bring.

And to my daughter, Mahalia,
may you continue to be persistent,
tenacious and headstrong as you grow
into the woman God has you to be!
Keep on being Hip Hop!

CONTENTS

Language Disclaimer

Engaging a culture and its elements can be a "dirty" job. At times, elements of a culture can be crude, rude, malicious, debaucherous, ugly, mean and just straight-up nasty. This includes language. This book begins the necessary dialogue of Hip Hop's theology and therefore will deal with elements of this culture that do not look "neat" for some people. I do ask that you hang in there and listen to what is being said before casting judgment.

One such needed dialogue regards the use of the words *nigger, nigga* and *niggaz*. Some Whites feel they can use these words because they have heard them used by comedians such as Dave Chappell or read them in books such as *Roots*. These people fail to understand the history of the words or the complexity of their linguistic context. Linguists call words like these an infix; they can be incorporated into almost any sentence and used to connect other words to it. Some trace the words to their root, *Negro*, and the Spanish word for the color black. Others trace the root to the name of the African country Niger; European slave traders would add an *s* to the end of the country's name, and the word eventually morphed into the derogatory term we have now. Fast-forward to the early twentieth century and you have freed slaves beginning to morph the word once again. During the early 1900s, African Americans would use the word as a type of partnership/companionship dialect. They dropped the *er* suffix, and the word was shortened to what we now know today as *nigga*. It was sparingly used, and only among those of lower class status. Replacing the letters *er* with the letter *a* at the end of the word adds new meaning for its use among Blacks: now the word can mean friend, enemy, lover, best friend, worst enemy and even spouse. The N-word is controversial primarily because of its vulgar, racist use by many White slave owners. In 2008, the Rev. Jesse Jackson and the Rev. Al Sharpton—among many other prominent Black leaders—gathered in a ceremonial event to ban the N-word. Did it work? Well, the jury is still out.

That said, I do not have any problem with the words *nigga, niggaz, niggee, nigs* or any other N-word ending in *a*. It is part of both my heritage as an African American and my heritage as a Hip Hopper. My use of the N-word in this book is primarily to describe how other artists have used the word. I do not use the word here for jest or play—that gets too confusing, and this is not the context for that. What about when White people use the word? For example, rapper Eminem made a public statement in early 2003 that he would never use the word in his music; it was later alleged, and tapes were revealed, that he had used the word in his later years. Because he had come from the 'hood and grown up in poverty with a single mother, however, these tapes were overlooked by many in the Hip Hop community and Eminem was off the hook (so to speak; moreover, the tapes were never proven to actually be his voice). In contrast, Michael Richards (Kramer from the television show *Seinfeld*) was videotaped using the N-word flagrantly; having no real connection to African Americans or Hip Hop, Richards was severely shunned, as he should have been.

The use of this word is controversial, no doubt. Some feel that it should be outlawed and never used again, while others feel that it is acceptable used in a proper context. I would agree with the latter. While I do not enter my all-White classrooms yelling out, "Hey, how my niggas doing today?" I do use the word in other, more appropriate contexts. Moreover, if we are going to have an honest dialogued regarding Hip Hop, rap, class and race, we must engage this word head-on, with all its connotations, history and usage. The meaning of the word itself lies within the people using it and hearing it, not within the word itself. It depends on the context, but that being said, if a

White person comes up to me and says, "Hey nigga, how ya doing?" he or she had better have good running shoes on! For a more in-depth look at the N-word, I strongly suggest reading Jabari Asim's *The N-Word: Who Can Say it, Who Shouldn't, and Why.*[1]

Language is arbitrarily constructed within each society and is a reflection of many things. I do not believe in "swear words" and or "curse words." A person who has a strong command of any language can use derision, mockery, contempt and sarcasm to belittle, demean and tear down people—without ever uttering a "bad word." For some people, language considered to be offensive or labeled as "obscene" is a regular dialect and vernacular for the context and environment they inhabit, so the "bad words" actually enter into common language and even thoughtful conversations. Words contain no meanings; people do.

Still, I agree that words that have been labeled "profane" and "obscene" should not be used in every context; wisdom and discernment must be used at all times with any type of communication. However, if we are to really engage and commune with someone or something, then we must deal with the parts of culture that do not always look nice. Therefore we will commence on this journey and deal with the necessary elements of Hip Hop culture as they come. Thank you in advance for your openness and willingness to be challenged.

---

[1]Jabari Asim, *The N Word: Who Can Say It, Who Shouldn't, and Why* (New York: Houghton Mifflin, 2007).

List of Tables

List of Figures

Introduction

From the Margins of Isolation to the Main Stage

A THEOLOGICAL REFLECTION ON HIP HOP

It was rural Texas in the early 1980s—late autumn in the evening during my second-grade year. I was sitting in the back of my mom's car, riding home from one of our all-day grocery shopping trips, and I was out of tapes to listen to, so I was adjusting the knob on my boom box to find something on the radio other than country music.

This was back in the day when radios—at least the ones that were considered "cool"—were the size of a bench and required a life's fortune in D batteries. The buttons on them were so big even a giant could play tapes on them. And yes, I did say tapes.

It was at that moment that I heard the sound that would change my life forever. The lyrics, sounding like sweet melodic harmony in my ears, were coming from these seven-inch speakers. The sound was faint, coming in and out of tune. Back in those days—and especially in rural Texas—uninterrupted air space made late night a great time to pick up weird radio stations from faraway cities. The sound I heard coming in and out of my radio was the now-famous karaoke favorite "Rappers Delight" (1980), rapped by the Sugar Hill Gang. This was my first encounter with Hip Hop.

I had never heard anyone do what these guys were doing. Up until that point, I had only heard lyrics sung—never spoken—over music. I needed a minute to gather myself. "What is the big deal?" you might ask. My response is simple: it spoke to me. I did not know it then but that song was to become a staple in Hip Hop culture, part of what would become my rich cultural heritage and identity.

That song began a journey for me. I could not begin to understand the complexity of that journey, but I knew that I needed to embark on it. I wanted more. What was this strange, alien form of music? Why had I not heard it on other radio stations? Where could I get more of this? Surely there had to be more.

The film *Brown Sugar,* a great film that dances with the tension of authenticity versus commercialism, asks a poignant question that constitutes its theme: "When did you fall in love with Hip Hop?" For me, it was at that moment—my first encounter—that I fell in love with Hip Hop.

From that point on I was searching for music that spoke to me in a different way than the groups that were dominating the airwaves. Growing up in that small, rural Texas town, I realized that rap music was very much confined to obscure radio stations and satellite television networks. I tried to explain the music to my predominantly White friends, but they laughed at me. Most couldn't comprehend what I was talking about nor understand its significance: in an eclectic era that brought fame to both pop metal giants Van Halen and pop folkie Bruce Hornsby, "Rappers Delight" helped me to become more culturally aware of Black and Latin art, music, customs, lifestyles, languages, symbols, beliefs and rites of passage. I immediately identified with it.

When I first heard NWA,[1] I could not believe my ears. Were artists really allowed to say the F-word on tape? Up until that point, the most

---

[1]Niggas With Attitude (NWA), comprised of Ice Cube, Dr. Dre, MC Ren, Eazy-E, DJ Yella & The DOC, NWA ushered in the "gangsta rap era." Theirs was the first record album to require the now infamous "Parental Advisory" label. Originating out of Compton and South Central California, NWA caused much controversy with songs that discussed urban politics, societal structures, economics, sex and the gangsta lifestyle from a ghetto perspective.

scandalous lyric I had ever heard was Run-DMC's "G**d*** that DJ made my day."[2] I had to hide that from my mom! When I first heard those songs it validated the strong language in my head regarding my own life and sense of marginalization. These songs spoke to me; they used strong language because the context and environment was (and still is) strong. As Tupac once said, "How can I act like an angel when I'm surrounded by devils?" Hence, my experience, anger, thoughts and life were validated when I head these words being uttered; I was able to connect at a deeper level and realize that I was not alone. Like me, rap was coming of age.

In August 1988 my mom moved us from Texas to the Bay Area in California. That year was a hard transition for me, but Hip Hop proved to be a helpful guide for me. I was introduced to the West Coast Hip Hop sound and started my first rap group, West Coast Juveniles. I was the producer and did all of the "beats"[3] for our group. When we tried to give a concert at church (free of four-letter obscenities, I might add), we were told "There is no place for that devil music here! Get out!" It was at this moment that I determined that my "church" would be the rap music and Hip Hop community that I was involved in.

By 1988 the 'hood was rising in profile in America. Crack cocaine, gang culture, deep-seated anger among urban youth and corruption among urban police officers were all big stories. When I received my first police beating at the age of fourteen, most of the adults in my life told me "You asked for it" or "You must have done something to deserve it." Rap became for me, as Public Enemy rapper Chuck D once stated, "my CNN." When Ice Cube rapped about crooked cops on *AmeriKKKa's Most Wanted*, I could relate. When KRS-One said that the dope game runs America, I agreed. When I heard NWA state "F***

---

[2]From the Run-DMC song "Peter Piper," on the 1986 *Raising Hell* album. It is worth noting here that prior to the release of NWA's first album, other bands recorded songs with the F-word: "Add It Up" by the Violent Femmes in 1983 and even the Doors in 1967 with their song "The End." Musical artists have continually pushed the border on who can say what, and when and where.

[3]Rhythm, music or sound for each of the tracks.

the police," I cheered with all my might. That was not only my feeling; many of the people I was living in community with felt it too.

"F*** The Police," from the album *Straight Outta Compton*, was our ghetto anthem and set the tone for interactions between urban youth and the police. In the late 1980s and early 1990s, Ice Cube, Ice-T, Public Enemy, KRS-One, and Too-$hort all rapped about urban youth interacting with the police. They also warned the nation of an impending explosion that came to pass on April 29, 1992.

L.A. RIOTS AND THE 1990S

The late 1980s and early 1990s are considered the golden era for Hip Hop. Prophetic voices such as X-Klan, Tribe Called Quest, Blacksheep, Public Enemy and Jungle Brothers were speaking of the political, social, economic and educational oppression being felt in U.S. ghettos. KRS-One was a leading voice speaking about the destruction that crack cocaine was wreaking on the 'hood and the violent police beatings that were a daily occurrence. The music was alive with consciousness and social awareness. Moreover, there was a sense of unity about the collective spirit and soul of a forgotten community coming together and achieving a communal cultural voice; this, coupled with the affirming 'hood portrait that KRS-One and others had painted in their music, could be felt in many ghetto communities. Hip Hop had finally established itself as not just a musical genre but a cultural movement. People in France, China and Kenya soon caught on to Hip Hop, and Afrocentric and Latinocentric pride was "cool" and accepted. Moreover, communities were beginning to organize and demand better for their neighborhoods. I was a part of many of those movements.

Many people outside the 'hood doubted the accusations of police corruption. A common response—particularly among White people—was, "Those people are just resisting arrest. What else can a policeman do?" But we saw things a little differently. We felt as though our 'hood was being occupied by a foreign military power called the police, and they were being allowed to do almost anything to us—no one seemed to care. Then the nation saw Black motorist Rodney King savagely beaten on national television.

Once the world saw police violence, we thought we could rest easy; we actually believed that the officers would be found guilty. So when we heard the "not guilty" verdict, all of the anger exploded within us and discharged into the streets. This, the nation would see, was the last straw that any group of people could take. We took all those emotions and let them out on Korean-owned stores, White motorists, security guards and anyone who represented the White power structure we had come to despise.

The L.A. riots were a rupture of societal, economical and communal networks that had been far too long neglected in the 'hood, demonstrating the deep need in America's ghettos. Sanyika Shakur (also known as Monster Kody Scott) describes what happened on that day:

> On April 29, 1992, the world witnessed the eruption of the Crips and Bloods. The scar of over twenty years that had been tucked out of sight and passed off as "just another ghetto problem" burst its suture and spewed blood all across the stomach of America. People watched in amazement as "gang members," soldiers of the Crip army, pelted cars with rocks, sticks, and bottles, eventually pulling civilians from their vehicles and beating them. This was hours after they had routed a contingent of LAPD officers. Troop movements escalated, and Los Angeles was set ablaze. All this began on Florence and Normandie in South Central, the latest Third World Battlefield.[4]

The riots of 1992 were one of the most cathartic, spiritual and frightening events of my life. Having Korean store owners shoot at you while you look for clips to reload your AK-47 is not something that will quickly escape your mind. On the one hand, we were releasing over a decade's worth of anger, and on the other, we were destroying our own communities. Was this all worth it?

---

[4]Sanyika Shakur, *Monster: The Autobiography of an L.A. Gang Member* (New York: Penguin, 1993), p. xii.

Yes and no. That is the gray area of civil unrest. I am not saying that I approve of violence and killing, but the riots helped get some much-needed attention to the 'hood. Only after the riots were people beginning to listen.

JESUS AND THE HIP HOP PROPHETS

After seeing a good friend of mine shot in front of me seventeen times, and having detectives come to my house to investigate the credit-card fraud ring I was in, I decided I needed a change. One of two things would happen to me: I would end up like my friend, or I would end up in jail. Both of those options were not what I wanted. I knew I needed to deal with the anger inside me.

An older and much wiser man was hanging out with us at the time. We all knew that he was a pastor and that he wanted to bring change to our community. Of course, he dressed "funny" and always told "corny" jokes. We would laugh at him, but inside we knew there was something different about him. After my friend was killed, he decided to have a citywide revival (as it happens, the event would feature no elements of Hip Hop whatsoever). The first time he invited all of us to the event, we rejected his offer. Still, I knew I needed a change; more-over, I knew this man cared for me and for the culture I was a part of. I told my friend "Andre" that I would go and see what the meeting was about, just to "be nice."

A week later, I was walking down to the front of the church to receive Christ and be baptized for the third time in my life. From that point forward, I knew I would work in the 'hood with young people. Hip Hop took on a completely new meaning for me as my pastor accepted me as a part of Hip Hop culture.

For the first four years of my walk with Christ, Hip Hop was the enemy. The Bay Area was home to rapper Tupac Shakur, and many people in the community knew him and saw him as a powerful—even prophetic—voice. I saw Tupac not as a "prophet" but as a blasphemer and poor role model. The students I was working with would argue with me constantly about how Tupac was helping them in their life, but I simply could not understand what they were saying. I saw him as someone who was misled and distraught. I didn't think Tupac understood God—I never really listened to his music; I heard the first F-word and passed judgment. I went on to preach this message of judgment to many youth, going so far as to say that Hip Hop was from the devil and was not useful to the church.

TOWARD A THEOLOGY OF HIP HOP CULTURE

Hip Hop remained a friend to me even while I was not. When my wife and I were forced out of our faith community because she was White and had grown up in a different denomination, I returned to Tupac, Hip Hop and a culture I had ignored for many years. There I discovered more depth and an unexpected faithfulness in people like Tupac. I found a deeper message within the music, genre and people that were involved in the culture than I had given them credit for.

The research for this book spans from 2003 to 2007 and involves twenty-five in-depth interviews with Hip Hoppers from urban environments, conducted on their "turf" and setting. Initially for my master's thesis, my research was intended to help me better understand how the Hip Hop community defined its theology, spirituality and connection to God. When I started work on my doctorate in 2004, I expanded my research to include thirty-five semi-structured interviews with people both in and outside the Hip Hop community, focusing on specific artists like Tupac, DMX and KRS-One. I cross-analyzed our conversations with different rap albums, videos and poetry from key rap artists, making the text come "alive" and highlighting the deep connections the Hip Hop community perceives between life and God and suffering, Jesus and people, divinity and context.

In late 2007,[5] I conducted twenty more semi-structured interviews with people from the suburban context to investigate their connection to Hip Hop as well. The conclusions from these methods were then

---

[5]Between 2006 and 2008 I also conducted about fifteen nonstructured interviews with different artists, emcees and students who took my classes. These also got included in the research for this book.

linked to my current research to formulate one grand theoretical framework which forms Hip Hop's theologies. Amazingly, much of the data from 2003 remained the same in 2007, and the connection to what the artists were saying gave way to a deep sense of mission to Hip Hop culture.

To seal the deal even further, I contacted one hundred urban workers across the country—a majority of whom were African American and Latino, with a mix of Euro American and Asian respondents as well—with a survey that looked into different theological, christological and missional connections between church leaders and Hip Hop. What you will read in the pages that follow are the conclusions drawn from all this research. I will build a case for understanding what Hip Hop is about—its culture, its people and its message—spiritually, theologically, ecclesiologically and missionally.

HIP HOP'S THEOLOGY: AN OXYMORON?

Hip Hop, in the words of KRS-One, is "something that is being lived."[6] How can we box up life? How can we commercialize life and then authentically engage it? How can we turn life into a show, then actually love it? At what cost to the soul do we do such things? Hip Hop is larger than the radio, larger than commercialized artists, larger than record industry branding. It is a culture, a people, a movement, a growing community of people that live, breathe, eat, love, hate and work just as anyone else does. Hip Hop cannot be easily understood or defined. It is complex and full of narratives that would blow away even the strongest anthropologist. But as I always tell my students, we have to discuss the obvious to get to the obscure. I am suggesting we begin to deconstruct parts of Hip Hop as a larger phenomenon in order to understand the whole.

The obscure part of Hip Hop is its theology. What is it? Is Hip Hop evil, or is it misunderstood? Many Christians hear "Hip Hop" and envision loud music with rough-sounding lyrics and deep bass, low-riding pants and long white T-shirts, and ominous facial expressions

[6]KRS-One, introduction to *Ruminations* (New York: Welcome Rain, 2003).

in opposition to "God's plan." Hip Hop is as much of an enigma to many church members as is, say, Muslims or the New Age movement. Yet theology, in its basic sense, is the study of God—how God interacts, intercedes, speaks, lives, thinks, wants and is. And Hip Hop repeatedly shows God "showing up" in the most unusual and interesting places. Hip Hop theology is, in essence, a study of the Godhead (God, the Son and the Spirit) in the urban context, with a goal of better understanding God's rich and complex love for everyone (not just those who look and talk "nice") and the revelation of God through the liberation of the oppressed from the oppressor.

Kanye West, on his album *The College Dropout*, argues that God loves hustlers, pimps, killers, prostitutes and other people that society would otherwise not deal with. Tupac questions if there is a heaven for real Niggaz—changing the letter *s* to *z* to indicate class rather than individual.[7] Big Syke asks if the church can handle Hip Hoppers, while KRS-One has suggested that Hip Hoppers need to start their own church. Hip Hoppers have strong opinions about God and the church—there's no doubt about that!

While Hip Hop is not without its problems, it does not deserve the ridicule and scorn and alienation that many Christians have given to it. Hip Hop is treated as a child born out of wedlock by an unknown father (on Christmas, perhaps).

Nor does Hip Hop deserve the condescension of a quarterly "Hip Hop Sunday" that only superficially appropriates the culture without truly engaging its theological perspective. Such offerings are just a feeble attempt at reaching an entire people group and culture.

Part of the reason Hip Hop is so mysterious to people outside its culture is that its roots and religious history have both multiple and complex sources. Pastors who are trained in "classic," or modernist, hermeneutical methods struggle to make sense of Hip Hop, a theology that engages real life in real time, that respects the person Jesus

---

[7]Robin D. G. Kelly (*Race Rebels: Culture, Politics, and the Black Working Class* [New York: Free Press, 1994], pp. 207-12) suggests that Tupac's term can transcend skin color as well.

but distrusts institutional religion, doesn't efficiently or predictably systematize—which is to say it doesn't reconcile easily with traditional, modernist approaches to culture. Hip Hop cannot be defined easily. Nor can Hip Hop be "evangelized" easily. It is just too complex. Ethnomusicologist Christina Zanfagna states:

> Mainstream hip-hop percolates with unlikely and multifaceted religious inclinations. Despite its inconsistent relationship to organized religion and its infamous mug of weed smoking, drug pushing, gun slinging, and curse spewing, rap music is not without moral or spiritual content. On the flip side, religious music continues to draw upon popular music idioms—a smart mission strategy to reach today's listeners.[8]

Hip Hop explores a basic theology of life. This theological paradigm is not new. Good and evil is common subject matter for the expressions and life of urban popular culture. Andrae Crouch, Kirk Franklin and a parade of others have engaged the gray area between the sacred and the secular.[9] Hip Hop's complex theological discussion of how the profane, secular and sacred all meet at one place continues in the tradition of Black music looking for the sacred in the profane.[10] Theologian and musician Jon Spencer believes that the Black music of mass culture, while still secular, might actually present a spirituality and theology for everyday life.[11]

---

[8]Christina Zanfagna, "Under the Blasphemous W(Rap): Locating the 'Spirit' in Hip-Hop," *Pacific Review of Ethnomusicology* 12 (2006): 1.

[9]For example, artists such as Aretha Franklin, Curtis Mayfield, Stevie Wonder, and Ray Charles all featured spiritual content in their music. Ray Charles was in his time considered "profane" and "unholy," and yet his music today is heard in the foyers of many churches. Jon M. Spencer (*Protest and Praise: Sacred Music of Black Religion* [Minneapolis: Fortress, 1990], 3-34) argues that the convergence of everyday life, social commentary and praise in African American music traces as far back as the slavery era. See also Zanfanga, "Under the Blasphemous W(rap)."

[10]See Zanfanga, "Under the Blasphemous W(rap)," and Jon M. Spencer, ed., *Sacred Music of the Secular City: From Blues to Rap*, vol. 6, *Black Sacred Music: A Journal of Theomusicology* (Durham, N.C.: Duke University Press, 1992).

[11]Jon M. Spencer, *Theological Music: Introduction to Theomusicology* (New York: Greenwood, 1991), p. 9.

This is a theological paradox not just for Hip Hop but for Christians in general: Could "sin" actually produce a theological paradigm? Could debauchery actually have theological depth? Or could it be that we are more afraid than we care to admit, about dealing with the real nature of the profane? Zanfagna recognizes that "to accept this presupposes that popular culture could be a sacred place—an area in which one may encounter God even in the most unholy of places."[12] Hip Hop theology not only embraces the sacred; it dines, sleeps, laughs, cries, loves, hates and lives with the profane. To truly understand Hip Hop requires a basic theological worldview of the profane.

Even this, however, is not a new concept. Theologians and church heroes assert that God meets us first in death and despair—the hell of life. Only those who enter the "s***" (to borrow language from Martin Luther) can encounter the God of Jesus Christ. Noah—who loved him some liquor—could not wait to get off the boat and get drunk, yet we revere him and even honor his example at different points. David not only loved booty, he sold his boy Uriah out for some—but he is still cited in countless sermons and Bible studies as a man after God's own heart. Paul was a converted religious nut and continued to struggle with his "flesh," and we do not even want to begin with the story of Jonah, which ended on a real bad note when, after all he had experienced and lived through, he actually wanted the people of Nineveh to perish. Jonah was actually angered by God's forgiveness of the people; he reflects a common worldview in contemporary Christianity that people had better pay for what I've been through and for what they've done. Even Jesus embraced the profane in his context: in his encounters with Zacchaeus and the woman at the well, for example, and in his strong language directed at the Sadducees and Pharisees.

Many Christians gloss over presentations of the profane in the lives of biblical heroes, but Hip Hop says, "Man, we're dealing with it all!" Tupac's habit of calling out his own "sin" made pastors, political figures, cultural critiques, conservative zealots and even some rappers

---

[12]Zanfagna, "Under the Blasphemous W(rap)," p. 2.

extremely uncomfortable. The million-dollar question surrounding the intersection of Hip Hop and religious culture is this: How can the profane exist in communion with God?

Hip Hop scholar Anthony Pinn identifies five central themes within African American humanist traditions—five central themes that function as "a mode for religious orientation."[13] These themes likewise find expression in Hip Hop culture.

1. Humanity is understood to be fully (and solely) responsible for the human condition and the correction of its plight—especially as it pertains to social justice.

2. Supernatural claims and explanations are viewed with suspicion and even rejected. Humanity is understood to be not a deterministic created being but an evolving part of the natural environment. (This is one reason traditional evangelistic presentations often do not work on Hip Hoppers.)

3. Both religiosity and cultural production are seen as having importance, as opposed to an attitude of "just pray about it" or even worse, "just go to church." Art, music and dance actually support hermeneutical and theological understanding.

4. Individual and societal transformation is a high commitment. (This is a key aspect of all Hip Hop culture and reaches deep into its theology.)

5. Human potential and humanity's capacity for destructiveness are both recognized, along with an openness to the notion that God might intervene, at times, in the lives of humans. This results in a controlled optimism about the future.

These five elements are essential to Hip Hop's theological mantra and adjoin Hip Hop's controversial neo-secular/sacred connection.

---

[13]Anthony Pinn, "Rap's Humanist Sensibilities," in *Noise and Spirit: The Religious and Spiritual Sensibilites of Rap Music*, ed. Anthony Pinn (New York: New York University Press, 2003), p. 87. I am not suggesting that Hip Hop is entirely humanistic. However, humanism is not without some educational and theological positives.

Artists such as DMX and Tupac challenge the moral fiber of religious authorities—pastors, deacons, reverends and priests—and argue that we can have a sacred relationship with Jesus, commune with Jesus, even grow in community—without ever setting foot in a church. Tupac asks whether there is a Heaven for a "G," and DMX begins his 2003 album *Grand Champ* with illicit language and ends the album "thanking God for making me righteous."[14] This neo-secular/sacred theology does three major things for Hip Hop:

- It provides a basis for understanding life while avoiding simplistic answers to the problems of pain, distress, suffering, anxieties, and evil acts.

- It allows for everyday life, language and cultural context to be given a fair examination. Nothing is "too sacred" to talk about or deal with.

- It elevates the conversation in rap music, allowing room for lyricists to critique culture, probe deep theological questions, confront the hegemonic powers, and explore avenues for change in its musical genre.

Many artists, including Common, Mos Def, Odd Thomas and Tupac, are informed by these three theological tenets. They function as the reporters, if you will, on all aspects of life—both sacred and profane. Once again, they stand in a long tradition. The irreverent spirituality that shows up in much Hip Hop music reflects what Spencer calls theomusicology—"musicology as a theologically informed discipline."[15] Black gospel music, he argues, set a liberating tone for not only Blacks but anyone in an oppressed context; Hip Hop is its postmodern, urban equivalent, articulating liberation, authenticity and freedom from the shackles of modernity.[16]

Rap music regularly takes up this mantle of liberation from oppression. Big Syke, for example, argues that God was a killer; while he is

---

[14]DMX, "The Prayer V," in *Grand Champ* (2003).
[15]Spencer, *Theological Music,* p. vii.
[16]Ibid., pp. 35-59.

all-loving, he will take the side of the marginalized to vindicate them and kill the oppressor.[17] Just read Joshua, Deuteronomy, Judges and Genesis, and you will find Big Syke's image of God in plain view. Theologian Noel Leo Erskine sees rap theology as "intimately linked to notions of how society functions and who operates the levers of control."

> In rap theology, God takes sides and identifies with rappers in their attempt to confront violence with counter violence. Their God is the God of the Old Testament.[18]

THE HOSTILITY OF THE GOSPEL

Most Christians imagine Jesus as a mild, gentle, all loving, peaceful man who just loved everyone in a hippie sort of way. When I read the Gospels, I see a Jesus who caused much trouble, created a movement that has changed the world, spoke up for the marginalized, brought a controversial economic message to his context and ours, and left more questions than he did answers. Theologian Carter Heyward captures the essence of the Jesus so often overlooked:

> Either we overlook and ignore things that he did and said about which, if it were anyone but Jesus, we might complain (cursing and killing a fig tree?), we learn to rationalize away the biblical record (he didn't really do this), or we find positive ways of look-ing at what only appear to be negative images (he's not really belittling his mother at the wedding; he's just trying to stretch and re-image his friends' understandings of "family"). We can-not seem to bear the notion of a Jesus who didn't always do or say the right thing.[19]

---

[17]Big Syke, interviewed by Michael Eric Dyson, *Holler If You Hear Me: Searching for Tupac Shakur* (New York: Basic Civitas, 2001).

[18]Noel Leo Erskine, "Rap, Reggae, and Religion," in *Noise and Spirit: The Religious and Spiritual Sensibilites of Rap Music*, ed. Anthony Pinn (New York: New York University Press, 2003), p. 78.

[19]Carter Heyward, *Saving Jesus from Those Who Are Right: Rethinking What It Means to Be a Christian* (Minneapolis: Fortress, 1999), pp. 144-45.

Jesus' dismissive language of religious officials as "vipers" and "dogs" would have been considered profane in his context. We see Jesus telling his followers that they must eat his flesh and drink his blood (John 6:52-68), which we must remember would constitute a "sin" and great blasphemy in his context—especially for a Jewish teacher.[20] The gospel, I would suggest, is hostile.

There are multiple strong connections between Jesus' message and Hip Hop's own "hostile gospel."

- Jesus preached salvation through him and only him, without having to go through the priests and religious institutions. Hip Hoppers like Tupac make pointed distinctions between the institutional church and Jesus.

- Jesus called out injustices and had strong words for those who were in power—especially where those systems or people oppressed people. Hip Hop's message is no different. Ice Cube, for example, challenges the notion that the American government goes into every other country that needs help while not providing aid for its own within the inner city.

- Jesus chose to roll with cats who were dangerous, crude and mean—the "thugs" of his day. Hip Hop addresses the troubling question, "What do you do with the Pookies and Shaniqa's who just love to scrap?"

- Jesus chose not to use his "power" when he clearly could have. Jesus chose to allow his disciples to "get it" when he could have just implanted his message within their minds. Hip Hop in its purest form—as practiced by artists such as Immortal Technique, Mos Def and Dead Prez—reaches beyond commerce to empower and raise up its members toward greater consciousness.

- Jesus died an innocent man on the cross for the sins of humanity so that humanity would know salvation. In spirit if not in scope,

---

[20]All this is adapted from Jack Miles, *Christ: A Crisis in the Life of God* (New York: Knopf, 2001).

Hip Hop similarly looks for "good news" in the midst of—and not in willful ignorance of—the violence, injustice and sin of the world.

Hip Hop has taken theology outside the box. It is new. It is creative. It is holy. It is hostile. It is part of the narrative that we all find ourselves in—the narrative of the Bible.

THE STRUCTURE OF THIS BOOK

Hip Hop needs to be considered, engaged with and listened to in order to better understand its deep and complex theological message—which is partly rooted in Christian theology. Generalizations, knee-jerk reactions and judgmentalism have fostered a disconnect between the church and the Hip Hop community; in this book I attempt to address the need for understanding Hip Hop's theological message.

The book is divided into three "sessions." Session one lays out a historical and sociological context for the entire book, with two chapters covering a brief history of Hip Hop, its art and aesthetics, and its prophetic/philosophical connections. (For an exhaustive history of Hip Hop, I suggest Jeff Chang's *Can't Stop Won't Stop: A History of the Hip Hop Generation* and Nelson George's *Hip Hop America*.)[21]

Session two is the "meat" of the book. If you are already familiar with Hip Hop, this will be a good place to begin. It deals with Hip Hop's five main theological paradigms: theology of suffering, theology of community, theology of the Hip Hop Jesuz, theology of social action and theology of the profane.

Session three gives both practical and theoretical perspectives on dealing with, engaging in and living amidst the Hip Hop culture. The two chapters in this session help show Hip Hop's Christian connections and depth.

The Soul of Hip Hop is not about the Hip Hop church. My boys

---

[21]Jeff Chang, *Can't Stop Won't Stop: A History of the Hip Hop Generation* (New York: St. Martin's Press, 2005); Nelson George, *Hip Hop America* (New York: Penguin, 1999).

Efrem Smith and Phil Jackson do a great job of that in their book *The Hip Hop Church*. I, in essence, pick up the theological discussion that is void in much of the scholarly literature and many Christian churches regarding Hip Hop's theology. I do not intend to give a hard and fast definition of Hip Hop's theology or spirituality; that would undermine the culture's organic elements. There is much more to learn on this journey.

While I do throughout the book engage with commercial Hip Hop, I derive most of my data and information from grassroots, socially conscious, neo-positive Hip Hop. There is simply not enough material in commercial Hip Hop to develop theologies from. When I refer to Hip Hop in this book, therefore, I am talking about the largely unseen grassroots, positive, uplifting and edifying Hip Hop movement. (When I do refer to commercial Hip Hop, I will make that clear.) While "clean" rap and "Holy Hip Hop" are powerful elements of this movement, I do plan to engage the F-bombs, hood rats and "crap" that even the so-called positive rappers talk about.

This book is for anyone wanting a deeper, more challenging and awakening look at Hip Hop. I do not pretend to offer a comprehensive presentation of Hip Hop's theology. However, I do open the door for a broader discussion and lay out some rudimentary concepts that are both necessary and vital for Christians to missionally deal with Hip Hop culture as a whole.

SESSION ONE

A Bird's-Eye View of Hip Hop

People always ask me, "Yo, Mos what is happening with Hip
Hop," I tell them what ever is happening with us, if we smoked
out then hip-hop is going to be smoked out, if we are fine
then hip-hop is going to be fine, people be talking about hip-
hop as if it is some type of giant sitting on the hill side, "WE ARE
HIP-HOP," so the next time you wondering where hip-hop is
going, ask yourself where am I going, what am I doing.

MOS DEF, *BLACK ON BOTH SIDES*

Mark Slobin and Jeff Todd Titon contend that "every human society has music. Music is universal; but its meaning is not."[1] Music is all
over the Bible, beginning in Genesis 4:21 where Jubal, the second son
born to Lamech and Adah, is considered to be the inventor of musical
instruments and the "father of all who play the harp and flute." Music
became an essential part of training in the schools of the prophets (1
Samuel 10:5; 19:19-24; 2 Kings 3:15). Music is employed powerfully
to convey messages throughout the Bible; music brought down walls,
caused King David to dance till his clothes fell off, provided a back-

---

[1]Mark Slobin and Jeff Todd Titon, "The Music-Culture as a World of Music," in
Worlds of Music, ed. Jeff Todd Titon, J. T. Koetting, D. P. McAllester, D. B. Reck and
Mark Slobin (New York: Schirmer Books, 1984), p. 1.

drop for parties that Jesus attended, and helped people mourn the death of loved ones—including the death of Jesus.

Music today is no different. Music sets moods, it creates atmospheres, it can transcend you into another time and dimension, and its very rhythm can return you to the same place or taste you were experiencing when you first heard that particular song.

Music is powerful. Therefore, it is no surprise that rap is such a powerful medium for so many people. As Murray Forman has noted,

> Hip-hop has evolved into one of North America's most influential youth oriented forces. It provides a sustained articulation of the social partitioning of race and the diverse experiences of being young and black or Latino in North America.[2]

When DJ Jazzy Jeff and The Fresh Prince won the first rap Grammy in 1989, the entire music industry was changed. America would waver on its acceptance of rap for many years to come, but as of now, Hip Hop and rap remain a powerful social and musical might in the shaping of American pop culture. Hip Hop's three foundational components (see table 1) have not changed much throughout the years.

Table 1. Hip Hop's Foundational Components

Foundational Component	Elements of the Component
Morals and Beliefs	Relevance Respect/nonjudgmentalism Equality Authenticity
Art and Custom	Clothes Tagging Dance Language
Liberation	Restoration of life, community and the self. Self-awareness Questioning authority Providing new answers to people who have been betrayed by traditional authorities.

[2]Murray Forman, *The 'Hood Comes First: Race, Space, and Place in Rap and Hip-Hop* (Middletown, Conn.: Wesleyan University Press, 2002), p. 3.

So, if Slobin and Titon are right that a culture's meaning is embedded in its music, and if Mos Def is right that Hip Hop is people and people are Hip Hop, then it's imperative that we begin by examining the people and music of Hip Hop as it has come of age both historically and aesthetically. Hip Hop's theology did not begin in a void. A rich historical community gave birth to it.

Back in the Day

TRACING THE ORIGINS OF HIP HOP

*A*s I entered the student lounge at Pasadena City College, I quickly realized it would be hard to find a seat. The room was filled with young, eager students under the age of twenty. They embodied a sense of unity that one could only understand if experienced personally.

The students did not even notice my entrance. Most were so captivated by the speaker that no one really took notice of my tardiness. I could hardly believe that all these young people—mostly though not exclusively from an urban background—were sitting and listening so attentively, so respectfully, to the speaker. Most adults assume that people from this age group don't listen to or care for older folk. But this day was different. These young students were captured by the speaker's message.

The speaker was none other than KRS-One, one of the founding fathers of Hip Hop culture. KRS-One (given name Lawrence "Kris" Parker) was one of the original emcees out of the Bronx during the early 1980s, and is a renowned scholar and teacher of Hip Hop "Kulture." KRS-One had everyone in that room clinging to each word of his message of love and peace, like that found in the Bible, particularly the New Testament. He spoke about pain, suffering, economic injustice, the war in Iraq, political injustices and God. The crowd devoured every word of it. *Wow,* I thought, *Hip Hop does all of this!*

KRS-One ended his time with a call to growth and critical think-ing among the next generation. He could have taken an altar call, and many of the four hundred students gathered there would have come to know Christ a little better.[1] At the end of his time, he was engulfed by requests for autographs and pictures. To the crowd's delight, he gladly accepted most of their requests.

Here was a Hip Hop king that had been around when the culture was birthed in the Bronx. A popular radio personality in the mid 1980s, he is still captivating a younger generation—without even "performing." How did all of these young people identify so well with KRS-One? How did this forty-plus year old man connect so well with this new generation? What is this Hip Hop culture, as KRS-One per-ceives it, that attracts so many young people?

The main reason for such a strong identification with KRS-One and these young people can be summed up in one word: *authenticity.* Ethnomusicologist Bonnie C. Wade links authenticity to knowledge: "Authenticity is also thought of as residing in a person who has ac-quired the knowledge that permits him or her to perform authenti-cally." To the value of knowledge I would add values of realism, open-ness, transparency and honesty—both to the self and to others. Awareness of tradition and creation of music that allows for consen-sus around meaning culminates in music that is rightly described as authentic. Hip Hoppers such as KRS-One cultivate this process, and KRS-One's persona emanates this definition. Young people intuitively know and understand this. Hip Hop culture is, in fact, founded on authenticity.[2]

---

[1]KRS-One is part of the Five Percenters, "an idiosyncratic mix of black nationalist rhetoric, Kemetic (ancient Egyptian) symbolism, Gnosticism, Masonic mysticism, and esoteric numerology" (Felicia M. Miyakawa, *Five Percenter Rap: God Hop's Music, Message, and Black Muslim Mission* [Bloomington: Indiana University Press, 2005], p. 23). While Five Percenters part from Christian orthodoxy in various ways, they have a lot to offer philosophically, and they do a lot of ministry that is commend-able. For more on Five Percenter theology, including their perspective on Jesus, see Miyakawa, *Five Percenter Rap*, pp. 23-37.

[2]Bonnie C. Wade, *Thinking Musically: Experiencing Music, Expressing Culture* (New York: Oxford University Press, 2004), pp. 142-45.

KRS-One's life and theological worldview come from Hip Hop, and Hip Hop is KRS-One. I am intrigued by this symbiotic relationship. What is Hip Hop culture? How did it come about?

WHAT IS HIP HOP CULTURE?

Hip Hop is not easily defined. Still, we have to put some nuts and bolts to what we are discussing. Within any culture are norms, values, shared traditions, shared beliefs and identity.[3] A good definition of *culture* comes from Ting-Toomey and Chung: "A learned meaning system that consists of patterns of traditions, beliefs, values, norms, meanings, and symbols that are passed on from one generation to the next and are shared to varying degrees by interacting members of a community."[4]

The Temple of Hip Hop, run by KRS-One and his team, define Hip Hop as

the name of our collective consciousness and inner-city strategy toward self-improvement. In its spiritual essence, Hiphop cannot be (and should not be) interpreted or described in words. It is a feeling. An awareness. A state of mind. Intellectually, it is an alternative behavior that enables one to transform subjects and objects in an attempt to describe and/or change the character and desires of one's inner being.[5]

In this definition we begin to see what some in the culture mean when they say they "feel" the music or they "are" Hip Hop." Authenticity is fundamentally important to Hip Hoppers. Ice Cube is no less

---

[3]Myron Lustig and Jolene Koester, *Intercultural Competence: Interpersonal Communication Across Cultures* (New York: HarperCollins College Publishers, 1996), pp. 32-38.

[4]Stella Ting-Toomey and Leeva C. Chung, *Understanding Intercultural Communication* (Los Angeles: Roxbury, 2005), p. 376.

[5]Wade, *Thinking Musically.* For a broader definition see Tricia Rose, *Black Noise: Rap Music and Black Culture in Contemporary America* (Middletown, Conn.: Wesleyan University Press, 1994), pp. 1-20; Nelson George, *Hip Hop America* (New York: Penguin, 1999), pp. 1-33; and Bakari Kitwana, *The Hip Hop Generation: Young Blacks and the Crisis in African-American Culture* (New York: Basic Civitas, 2003).

Hip Hop, with his father and mother both having degrees and living a seemingly privileged life, than is KRS-One, with his more difficult background. Hip Hop culture transcends wealth or poverty to emphasize an authentic lifestyle.[6] My definition of Hip Hop, adapted from a definition from pastor Phil Jackson, is this:

> Hip Hop is an urban subculture that seeks to express a lifestyle, attitude or theology. Rejecting the dominant culture, it seeks to increase social consciousness, cultural awareness and racial pride. Rap music functions as the vehicle by which the cultural messages of Hip Hop are sent, and the industry by which Hip Hop culture is funded and propagated.

Some argue that commercial rap and Hip Hop are one and the same, but the two are separate, as detailed in figure 1.[7]

There are a variety of styles of rap music, all of which fit under the cultural umbrella of Hip Hop, but each of which has developed its own particular norms and values. William Perkins states:

> When the genre first appeared in the late 1970's, culture and music critics falsely predicted a quick demise, but rap music grew and flourished, simultaneously reshaping the entire terrain of American popular culture. Even rap music's hyped commercialization cannot dampen its tough, raw, hard-core street essence. Rap music's most powerful safeguard has been its uncanny ability to reenergize itself, to remain "true to the game," in the words of one of Ice Cube's most important rhymes.[8]

---

[6]See Michael Eric Dyson, *Between God and Gangsta Rap* (New York: Oxford University Press, 1996); Rose, *Black Noise;* Tricia Rose, "A Style Nobody Can Deal With: Politics, Style, and the Postindustrial City in Hip Hop," in *Microphone Friends: Youth Music and Youth Culture,* ed. A. Ross and T. Rose (New York: Routledge, 1994); William Eric Perkins, ed., *Droppin' Science: Critical Essays on Rap Music and Hip Hop Culture* (Philadelphia: Temple University Press, 1996).
[7]See Garth Alper, "Making Sense out of Postmodern Music?" *Popular Music and Society* 24, no. 4 (2000): 1; and Elizabeth Blair, "Commercialization of the Rap Music Youth Subculture," *Journal of Popular Culture* 27, no. 3 (1993): 21-46.
[8]Perkins, *Droppin' Science,* p. 1.

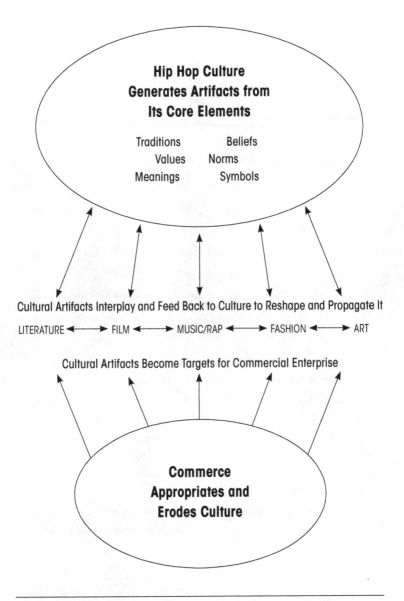

Figure 1. The differences between Hip Hop culture and commercial Hip Hop

Each area can at any time be in the forefront, but it takes a major event to shift the focus from one subgenre to another. For example, the "party-rap" mode of the early 2000s overtook gangsta rap upon the murders of Tupac Shakur and Biggie Smalls. Each area in figure 2 represents one of the strong subgenres of rap I've identified in over ten years' worth of study. Each is supported and given life by unique sounds that carve out its musical landscape. The six key sounds that contribute to these subgenres are

1. West Coast sound: thick, heavy bass lines

2. East Coast sound: lyric-driven with a lot of samples

3. Dirty South sound: centered on the "hook" or chorus line; featuring strong bass lines and, at times, erratic-sounding drum lines

4. Third Coast rap sound: similar to Dirty South but with a more "Southern" beat

5. Bohemian/Jamaican sound: influenced by Jamaican music

6. Reggaeton sound: a blend of salsa, cumbia and West Coast sound; Latin-flavored

The smooth/R&B/soul subgenre, made popular by artists such as Ne-Yo, Mary J. Blige and Bryan McKnight, technically doesn't feature "rapping." Nevertheless, it possesses strong Hip Hop connections similar to other rap subgenres and subscribes to many of the foundational elements of Hip Hop culture. Hip Hoppers use the multidimensional language of music to identify and speak with each other. The subgenres keep growing, and I would predict that in ten years, this wheel will be twice as large.[9]

Scholar Angela Nelson sees in rap music the repetition of a pattern: like other black musical forms in the United States, rap is fueled and

---

[9]Ralph Watkins (*The Gospel Remix: Reaching the Hip Hop Generation* [Valley Forge, Penn.: Judson Press, 2007], p. 7) suggests eleven types or genres of rap music: East Coast rap, West Coast rap, dirty South rap, third coast rap/Houston, political rap, jazz rap, bohemian rap, Reggaeton rap, Holy Hip Hop, Midwest rap, and party/booty rap.

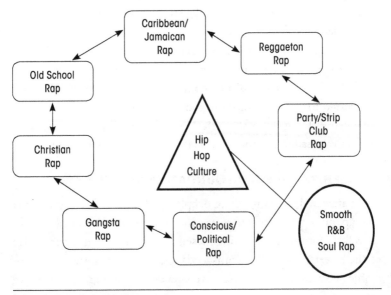

Figure 2. The subgenres of rap music

shaped by the experience of racial oppression. "Contemporary rappers, like early bluespeople, are responding to the 'burden of freedom,' in part by relaying portrayals of reality to their audiences through their personal experiences."[10] As the main medium of Hip Hop culture, rap has offered definition, value, understanding and a shared language and linguistic form to ghetto communities, which are often otherwise characterized by social isolation, economic hardship, political demoralization and cultural exploitation. Rap takes on forms other than music, including poetry, preaching, lecturing, inspirational messages, even simple conversations between two people about life. Not limited to merely Black or Brown people, rap esteems the ghetto poor experience as valid and real. This is seen in the 2003 film *8-Mile*; rapper Eminem is given a safe haven, a "home," within

[10]Angela Nelson, "Theology in the Hip-Hop of Public Enemy and Kool Moe Dee," in *The Emergency of Black and the Emergence of Rap*, ed. J. M. Spencer (Durham, N.C.: Duke University Press, 1991), pp. 51, 56.

the community of "The Shelter." (The film *8-Mile* will be discussed in greater detail in a later chapter.)

At the same time, rap as a musical form has functioned as an economic engine, making some artists and corporations a lot of money. While fueling Hip Hop culture, commercial rap also leaves Hip Hop vulnerable to commodification and a dilution of its message. The same genre that gave us the lyrical complexity of Biggie Smalls also gave us Vanilla Ice and the early 90s group "The Rapping Grannies."

HIP HOP'S TEN FOUNDATIONAL ELEMENTS

What attracted so many young people to KRS-One that day was not just rap music. Hip Hop offers its adherents community and a voice—as well as, for many (including myself), a safe, productive alternative to the streets.[11] Hip Hop transcends age, political status, socioeconomic status, social standings, even gender,[12] offering an alternative source of identity and social status for young people in a community that had abandoned them.[13] One interview subject told me that rap music helped him through many nights in which he felt lost and abandoned by all, including "church folk."

KRS-One has said that when he first started out, he wanted a place to hold spoken-word nights, poetry hours and concerts. When he approached Christian churches, he was quickly told to leave. Somehow, these church folk suspected, this new emerging culture was not "of God."[14] So from the onset, there was opposition to Hip Hop from the church. The Nation of Islam and the Five Percenters, by contrast, of-

---

[11]On the communal form that Hip Hop presents, see Dyson, *Between God and Gangsta Rap;* Adreana Clay, "Keepin' It Real: Black Youth, Hip-Hop Culture, and Black Identity," *American Behavioral Scientist* 46, no. 10 (2003): 1346-58; KRS-One, *Ruminations* (New York: Welcome Rain, 2003) for this discussion. Ronald Jemal Stephens, "The Three Waves of Contemporary Black Music," in *The Emergency of Black and the Emergence of Rap*, ed. J. M. Spencer (Durham, N.C.: Duke University Press, 1991), pp. 25-40.

[12]See the 1997 film *Ryme and Reason,* dir. Peter Spirer, Miramax.

[13]Tricia Rose, *Black Noise: Rap Music and Black Culture in Contemporary America* (Middletown, Conn.: Wesleyan University Press, 1994), p. 34.

[14]Taken from an interview with KRS-One around 1990.

fered Hip Hop a warmer reception and have since been shown appreciation in lyrics from artists such as Common, Nas and Tupac.

Hip Hop culture has ten foundational elements to it:[15]

- DJing and Turntablism
- Breaking, Break Dancing and B-Boying
- Graffiti
- Break Beats
- Emceeing
- Street Knowledge
- Street Language
- Street Fashion
- Entrepreneurialism
- Knowledge of God and Self

Any one of these ten areas may interact or overlap with each other. For example, an emcee can also be a beat-boxer that keeps the show moving while others are break dancing. But each has its own tradition to it.

DJing and *turntablism* refer to the study and application of music production and broadcasting.[16] Unlike the traditional disc jockey, however, Hip Hop DJs interact artistically with recorded music by cutting, mixing and scratching songs. Popularized by Kool DJ Herc, Afrika Bambaataa, Jazzy Jay, Grand Master Flash, Grand Wizard Theodore, Kool DJ Red Alert, DJ Cash Money, Marley Marl, Brucie B, Chuck Chillout, Kid Capri, Afrika Islam and Jam Master Jay, practi-

---

[15]While I am aware that scholars such as Anthony Pinn (*Why Lord?* [New York: Continuum, 1995], pp. 125-32) and KRS-One (*Ruminations,* pp. 211-63) give alternate and longer definitions of Hip Hop culture, I have condensed these down into the traditional nine foundational elements. Definitions adapted from <www.templeof hiphop.com>, accessed May 21, 2005.

[16]Also see Juliana Snapper ("Scratching the Surface," *European Journal of Cultural Studies* 7, no. 1 [2004]: 9-25) in which she discusses the culture and art behind turntablism, a mentality and culture that is unique to Hip Hop culture.

tioners of this style are known as turntablists, mixologists, grand-masters, mixmasters, jammasters and funkmasters.

The study and application of street dance forms is commonly called *breaking, break dancing* or *B-Boying,* and now encapsulates the once-independent dance forms up-rockin', poppin' and locking, jailhouse or slap boxing, Double Dutch, Electric Boogie and Capoiera[17] martial arts. The practitioners of traditional breaking are called B-Boys, B-Girls and Breakers. Commonly referred to as freestyle street dancing, breaking moves are aerobic and acrobatic. James Brown was a leader in the development of the dance, which was later popularized by artists such as the Nigga Twins, Dennis Vasquez–the Rubber Band Man, Rock Steady Crew, Pee Wee Dance, the N.Y.C. Breakers and the Breeze Team. Michael Jackson's style of dance during the "Thriller" era would be characterized as breaking.

Graffiti is the study and application of color, light and handwriting. Forms of this art include Bombin' and Taggin', which involves placing a name or logo on a wall to represent yourself, your community or your gang. Practitioners are known as writers, graffiti writers, graffitists, and graffiti artists. They rate themselves on their ability to write, and/or draw a good story. Many go on to become graphic artists, fashion designers, photographers and motion picture directors. Popularized by Taki 183, Phase 2, Kase 2, Cope 2, Tat's Cru, Presweet, Iz the Wiz, Seen, Quik, O.E., Revolt, Dondi, Zephyr and Futura 2000, the medium is variously called aerosol art, life art, pieces, burners, graf and urban mural.

The study and application of body music—creating rhythmic sounds with various parts of the body, particularly the throat, mouth, and hands—is called *break beats.* Its practitioners are known as human beat-boxes or human orchestras. Earlier versions of this musical expression included handbone, or hambone. However, modern beatboxin' is an imitation of early electronic drum machines. The genre was popularized by Doug E. Fresh, Biz Markie, The Fat Boyz, DMX,

---

[17]Also derived from Brazil in street dancing.

Greg Nice, Bobby McFerrin, Emanon, Click the Super Latin, K-Love and Razell.

The study and application of rap, poetry, and divine speech is called *emceeing* but often referred to as rappin'. The emcee directs the crowd by rhyming in rhythmic spoken word. The word *emcee*, an abbreviated form of "master of ceremonies," refers to the host of an event, which early Hip Hoppers modified to encourage crowd participation. Today, the emcee seeks to be a master of the spoken word, and so often, in addition to performances, emcees deliver lectures and other forms of public instruction. Emcees rate themselves on their ability to rock the party, speak clearly and tell a good story. Emceeing and its antecedents were made popular by people such as Cab Calloway, Coke La Rock, Busy Bee Starsky, Cowboy, Melle Mel, Grandmaster Caz, Kool Moe Dee, Rakim, Big Daddy Kane and Muhammad Ali.

The study and application of life, society, culture, religion, theology, spirituality and the self in the context of Hip Hop is referred to as *street knowledge*. The ability to "spit" knowledge in rhymes is imperative in understanding where an emcee or rapper is coming from; similarly, artists who don't display knowledge and creatively communicate their historical, societal context are derided as unoriginal, "phony" or "fake." KRS-One, Tribe Called Quest, Dead Prez, Tupac, DMX, and Eminem are notable artists who issue deep and complex street knowledge.

With any cultural form comes its own structure of language. *Street language* distinguishes Hip Hop culture from other cultures and musical genres. Words such as "busta," "mamma jamma," "marinate," "nine" and "whassup" derive from common English words and follow a structure of nine patterns, labeled by Geneva Smitherman as "African American language": (1) the "r" sound is dropped from the end of a word (e.g., "busta"); (2) hard consonants are dropped from the end of a word (e.g., "cold" becomes "coal"); (3) emphasis is placed on the first syllable of a word (e.g., "PO-leece" for "police"); (4) vowel sounds are modified (e.g., "think" and "ring" are spoken as "thank" and "rang"); (5) time is indicated by context, not by verb tense (e.g., "Mary do anythang she want to"); (6) the verb *be* is used to indicate continuous action or frequently recurring activity (e.g., "they be up to no good"; "where you be at?"); (7) the soft "th" sound is replaced by a harder "d" sound at the beginning of words or phrases (e.g., "da bomb"); (8) words ending with "th" are instead ended with an "f" sound (e.g., "wif" instead of "with"; note that "Def Comedy" or "Def Jam" are modifiers of "deaf"); (9) "Is" and "are" are often contracted in sentences (e.g., "Whad up?").

Baggy pants, loose fitting clothing, long silver necklaces, and baseball caps slightly turned to one side are just a few of the examples of *street fashion* in Hip Hop. Major department stores such as Macy's, The Gap and Old Navy have adopted street fashion in some form. Brand Nubian was one of the first groups to begin wearing the "baggy fit," along with others that included Spice 1 and MC Hammer.

Hip Hop's roots are in *entrepreneurialism*. The culture started as rap artists actively promoted themselves and built loyal followings. Sean Puffy Combs and Jay Z each have their own clothing label, record company and recording studios. The self-reliant spirit of Hip Hop is, however, developed within a supportive community.

Knowledge of God and of self are important values and fundamental elements of Hip Hop culture. Hip Hop is rooted in spirituality: feeling the beat, moving your mind to a higher elevation, connecting with a community in song and dance, building up one another and even relationship with God are disciplines and practices woven throughout the history and culture of Hip Hop. Some have argued that more violent and hedonistic trends in Hip Hop culture are evidence that it has left its spiritual roots, but at its base, Hip Hop is undeniably spiritual. Through rap, Hip Hop culture links to an oral African tradition that also connects with jazz and Black gospel music.[18] While much of the church is leery of rap music, Christina Zanfanga reports that "performers and listeners of hip-hop claim to un-

---

[18]Howard Odum, *The Negro and His Songs: A Study of Typical Negro Songs in the South,* 36 vols. (Westport, Conn.: Negro Universities Press, 1968). See also Eileen Southern, *The Music of Black Americans,* 2nd ed. (New York: W. W. Norton, 1983).

dergo ecstatic experiences—proof that spirituality resides in so-called profane expressions as well."[19]

Tricia Rose notes that Hip Hop culture

> emerged as a source for youth of alternative identity formation and social status in a community whose older local support institutions had been all but demolished along with large sectors of its built environment. Alternate local identities were forged in fashions and language, street names, and most important, in establishing neighborhood crews or posses.[20]

HIP HOP, THE CHURCH AND THE POST-INDUSTRIAL SHIFT

Hip Hop was born into the dysfunction we now call the ghetto,[21] whose postindustrial conditions reflect the shift detailed by Daniel Bell from an industrial to a postindustrial society.[22] The middle economic section of urban communities collapsed, displacing many and unemploying thousands. Hip Hoppers managed to find meaning in the misery and pain of inner-city living.

> Hip-hoppers joined pleasure and rage while turning the details of their difficult lives into craft and capital. This is the world Hip Hop would come to represent: privileged persons speaking for less visible or vocal peers.[23]

The church helped shape many of Hip Hop's roots. The call and response of the pastor, and the sense of community developed in the Black church are reflected in the values of the DJ or the emcee. More-

---

[19]Christina Zanfagna, "Under the Blasphemous W(Rap): Locating the 'Spirit' in Hip-Hop," *Pacific Review of Ethnomusicology* 12 (2006): 3.

[20]Tricia Rose, *Black Noise: Rap Music and Black Culture in Contemporary America* (Middletown, Conn..: Wesleyan University Press, 1994), p. 34.

[21]Also see Tricia Rose, "A Style Nobody Can Deal With," in *Microphone Friends,* ed. A. Ross and T. Rose (New York: Routledge, 1994), where she also describes the postindustrial living conditions in which Hip Hop culture was formed.

[22]Daniel Bell, *The Coming of a Post-Industrial Society: A Venture in Social Forecasting* (New York: Basic Books, 1973), pp. 47-118.

[23]Dyson, *Between God and Gangsta Rap,* p. 177.

over, the Black church helped form the worldviews of many of today's
Hip Hop legends and remains a cornerstone for many. A survey of Hip
Hop's foundational decades shows the societal, cultural and theologi-
cal themes that helped to form Hip Hop's theology.

Hip Hop developed in the early 1970s in the South Bronx,[24] where
DJs would play disco, funk or reggae dub records while a "master of
ceremonies" would handle the verbal interchange with the crowd. DJs
such as Kool DJ Herc and Pete Jones began to draw huge crowds at
clubs and block parties. Hip Hop rhythms and breaks began to
emerge, and craftsmanship began to extend beyond the turntables to
other things such as emceeing and B-Boying.[25]

Several developments in the 1970s helped shape Hip Hop's foundation:

- P-Funk, the foundational sample for many rap songs to this day,
  fused together disco, soul and an early form of rap. It had many
  spiritual nuances and connotations. George Clinton and Parlia-
  ment are the most notable P-Funk artists.

- Soul music emerged as a response to R&B. Stevie Wonder, Marvin
  Gaye, Ray Charles, Aretha Franklin, Donna Summer and many
  others gave breath to this rich music tradition and served as "street
  pastors" for many of their listeners.[26]

- The late 1970s was the end of a disco era of music that Hip Hoppers revolted against, because it quite simply did not address any of
  the real issues that Hip Hoppers were going through and made
  "fun" seem universal.

- The Black church was growing. Black theologians like James Cone
  were emerging to help argue for a contextualized gospel message
  for Black people. A cornerstone during the Civil Rights movement,

---

[24]Jeff Chang, *Can't Stop Won't Stop* (New York: St. Martin's Press, 2005), p. 3.
[25]Cheryl Keyes, *Rap Music and Street Consciousness* (Chicago: University of Illinois
Press, 2002), p. 40.
[26]Michael Eric Dyson, *Open Mic: Reflections on Philosophy, Race, Sex, Culture and
Religion* (New York: Basic Civitas, 2003).

the Black church was beginning to be seen as an authoritative figure for not just Blacks but those who were most acutely poor. In form, music and lyrical content, it laid foundational elements to the communal orientation that Hip Hop took.

Meanwhile, as Tricia Rose states,

> Cities across the country were gradually losing federal funding for social services, information service corporations were beginning to replace industrial factories, and corporate developers were buying up real estate to be converted into luxury housing, leaving working class residents with limited affordable housing, a shrinking job market and diminishing social services.[27]

The devastation of the postindustrial shift on cities was evident in the 1970s, and the Hip Hop culture that began taking shape in those years was undeniably linked to it.

"Until 1979," William Eric Perkins writes, "rap was a key component of a flourishing underground culture in the Bronx and upper Manhattan, where parties went on all night in seedy nightclubs or the music was played in schoolyards and small public parks."[28] Despite a growing following, very few early Hip Hop music groups released records. Of the groups that did, most never enjoyed significant commercial success on the airwaves, since rapping was seen as a musical novelty. At the time, it was not as much of a concern, because so much of their efforts were focused on live performance. Emcees would "battle" each other for prize money.[29]

Even in its early forms, Hip Hop was about community, with artists such as Melle Mel giving voice to a group of people that had no

---

[27]Rose, *Black Noise*, p. 27.

[28]William Eric Perkins, ed., *Droppin' Science: Critical Essays on Rap Music and Hip Hop Culture*, Critical Perspectives on the Past (Philadelphia: Temple University Press, 1996), p. 9.

[29]Although difficult to find through conventional retailers, live recordings of these jams do exist. They are known as "battle tapes." Nancy Guevara, "Women Writin' Rappin' Breakin'," in *Droppin' Science: Critical Essays on Rap Music and Hip Hop Culture*, ed. W. E. Perkins (Philadelphia: Temple University Press, 1996), p. 55.

voice, questioning authority, recovering empty answers and providing spiritual guidance for its members. This emphasis on empowering the powerless would carry on throughout the explosive growth Hip Hop experienced in the years to come.

Hip Hop was in its teens by the 1980s, and witnessed its greatest growth during this decade. The concept of *representin'*—letting the world know who you are—came to form as television shows such as *Different Strokes, The Cosby Show, Different World, The Fresh Prince of Bel Air* in different degrees and forms pulled back the curtain separating mainstream culture from Hip Hop. The nation was being "warmed up" for what was to come.

1980 ushered in the Reagan era. Major social programs such as community outreach, welfare and social security were scaled back considerably. I remember my grandmother's social security check being cut when in 1984 Reagan announced on television that "communities should help their own." During his first successful presidential campaign, Reagan had coined the term "welfare queens," reflecting a profound prejudice against the urban poor.[30] The "trickle down economics" intended to replace cut social programs never really reached the 'hood.

Social commentary became an increasingly common feature of Hip Hop. In 1982 Grandmaster Flash, with Melle Mel, dropped the song "The Message," a cultural sample of 'hood life:

Broken glass everywhere
People pissing on the stairs, you know they just
Don't care
I can't take the smell, I can't take the noise
Got no money to move out, I guess I got no choice
Rats in the front room, roaches in the back
Junkies in the alley with a baseball bat
I tried to get away, but I couldn't get far

---

[30]Reagan was not the president for the 'hood. While this book does not allow the space for a full discussion, the 'hood was victimized by the interrelated crack cocaine epidemic and Iran-Contra scandal that took place under the Reagan administration. Hip Hop veterans understand this and still lament about this dark decade.

Cause the man with the tow-truck repossessed my car
Don't push me, cause I'm close to the edge
I'm trying not to lose my head
It's like a jungle sometimes, it makes me wonder
How I keep from going under.

In 1984, Run DMC dropped the song "Hard Times":

Hard times spreading just like the flu
Watch out homeboy, don't let it catch you
P-p-prices go up, don't let your pocket go down
When you got short money you're stuck on the ground
Turn around, get ready, keep your eye on the prize
And be on point for the future shock.

Songs like these offered a critical counterpoint to the jingoistic enthusiasm of Reagan's America. In the face of claims of prosperity from mainstream culture, Hip Hop made note of several alarming social trends:

- Homelessness was the norm for many 'hood families.

- Many mental institutions were forced to close due to budget cuts.

- Inner-city crime reached an all-time high.

- With an increase of gang activity, local governments formed gang task forces, many of which became corrupt.

Meanwhile, the landscape of popular music was changing, a development that would open doors for Hip Hop artists.

- In 1980 Kurtis Blow signed with Mercury Records—the first B-Boy to be featured on a major label.

- MTV debuted on August 1, 1981.

- In 1987, NWA created the West Coast sound with their album *NWA & The Posse*. Ice-T played a major role in this, along with a lesser-known MC Hammer.[31]

---

[31]Personal interview with Hip Hop icon Davey D. See also Andrew Blake, "Making Noise: Notes from the 1980s," *Popular Music and Society* 21, no. 3 (1997): 32-34.

- In 1989, NWA released "F*** the Police" in response to police beatings.

- Also in 1989, DJ Jazzy Jeff & The Fresh Prince were given a
  Grammy award for "Parents Just Don't Understand." Rap music
  became a "legitimate" music genre in mainstream pop culture.

- The song "Self-Destruction" was released in 1989 by a broad group
  of East Coast rappers to address ghetto violence and Black-on-
  Black crime.

The ground was now set for an explosion of Hip Hop culture. Murray Forman writes, "Hip-hop was saturating the media spaces of the
mainstream press and, of greater consequence, television, gaining un-
precedented attention throughout North America."[32] Urban youth
joined pleasures with suburban youth, and the attraction to Hip Hop
culture was suddenly unanimous and multiethnic.[33]

THA 1990S

The period between the late 1980s and about 1993-1994 is known as
Hip Hop's "Golden Age."[34] Prior to 1991, Hip Hop had been largely
an East Coast phenomenon. But the 1990s saw the rise of the West
Coast. West Coast rap artists were developing a more melodic sound,
and the now infamous drum machine Roland TR-808 created a deep
sounding bass drum which was heard in almost every mini-truck
with a sound system. Dr. Dre's agenda-setting album *The Chronic* was
Rolling Stone magazine's number one album for four weeks in 1993.
Steve Huey from AMG Music wrote of this release, "With its stylish,

---

[32]Murray Forman, *The Hood Comes First* (Middletown, Conn.: Wesleyan University
Press, 2002), p. 214.

[33]See Daniel Hodge, "Can You Hear Me Calling: Hip Hop/Gangster Culture & the
Future Urban Church," thesis (Pasadena, Calif.: Fuller Theological Seminary, 2003);
Bakari Kitwana, *The Hip Hop Generation: Young Blacks and the Crisis in African-
American Culture* (New York: Basic Civitas, 2003); and S. Craig Watkins, *Repre-
senting: Hip Hop Culture and the Production of Black Cinema* (Chicago: University
of Chicago Press, 1998).

[34]As heard in my interviews, and in the documentaries *Letter to the President* (2003),
and *Rhyme & Reason* (1997).

sonically detailed production, Dr. Dre's 1992 solo debut . . . established his patented G-funk sound: fat, blunted Parliament-Funkadelic beats, soulful backing vocals, and live instruments in the rolling baselines and whiny synths."[35] Young people outside the black community were buying the album and going to concerts.[36] Hip Hop culture was being represented in the mainstream. The numbers proved it.

By now, Hip Hop's protest and praise movement was in full swing. Most artists were speaking deep knowledge about sociological issues, politics, economics, Jesus and everyday life. This era saw the rise of rap groups such as A Tribe Called Quest, Black Sheep, Das EFX and Arrested Development, as well as solo artists like Ice Cube, Dr. Dre, Snoop Dogg and Tupac. Also emerging in the early 1990s was "Hoodie films." While there had been other films on Hip Hop—*Krush Groove* (1985), *Breakin'* (1984) and Charlie Ahearn's classic *Wild Style* (1983)—none received the notoriety, publicity and awards of *Boyz in the Hood* (1991).[37] I had a spiritual moment seeing Ice Cube on screen in *Boyz in the Hood;* it was as though I could say, *Man, Hip Hop has made it!* Other "Hoodie films" of the early 1990s included *New Jack City* (1991), *Menace II Society* (1993) and *Belly* (1994).

Meanwhile, two major issues were affecting rap music's momentum: sampling and explicit lyrics. Sampling—featuring elements of previously released songs in new, original music—had long been practiced in Hip Hop. It hadn't been a legal concern during that time, since for many years rap had not been considered "music" by the Academy of Music. But in the early 1990s rap became a commercial behemoth; suddenly, with songs like Ice Cube's "Jackin' for Beats" sampling liberally and gaining a broad hearing, there was money to be made and an intellectual property debate worth engaging. Record labels Priority and Def Jam each won important cases that allowed rap

---

[35]Steve Huey, review of *The Chronic* by Dr. Dre, taken from <www.allmusic.com/cg/amg.dll?p=amg&sql=10:gbfuxq95ldae>.

[36]Forman, *Hood Comes First,* pp. 252-55.

[37]See Watkins, *Representing,* and Melvin Donalson, *Black Directors in Hollywood* (Austin: University of Texas Press, 2003), for a more comprehensive discussion of this very important development.

artists to pay royalties and other fees in exchange for sampling music. This set of rules remains true to this day.

Freedom of speech issues certainly should have been in play when "F*** The Police" came out, but rap was not established enough to earn that much official scrutiny. Then in 1990, 2-Live Crew's fourth album, *Banned in the USA*, gained widespread attention with explicit lyrics about women and sexuality. The reality of the 'hood scared many in Middle America; panic ensued when rap music began being sold in the suburbs. Many in Congress feared that rap would "corrupt" children's morals.[38] Nevertheless, 2-Live Crew won an important Supreme Court decision in 1994 under the Free Speech amendment.

On March 3, 1991, George Holliday videotaped Rodney King being beaten by four White officers in the Los Angeles Police Department. KTLA television aired the tape, showcasing the police brutality reflected in music by KRS-One, Ice-T, Ice Cube, NWA and many others. On April 29, 1992, a jury of ten Whites, one Latino and one Filipino acquitted officers Koon, Wind and Briseno of the beatings. Within hours, riots ensued around the country. Ice Cube, in his album *The Predator* (1992), rapped about the riots:

> Not guilty, the filthy, devils tried to kill me
> When the news get to the hood the niggaz will be
> hotter than cayenne pepper, cuss, bust
> Kickin up dust is a must
> I can't trust, a cracker in a blue uniform
> Stick a nigga like a unicorn
> Born, wicked, Laurence, Powell, foul
> Cut his f***in' throat and I smile
> Go to Simi Valley and surely
> somebody knows the address of the jury

---

[38]See Eileen Southern, *The Music of Black Americans*, 2nd ed. (New York: W. W. Norton, 1983); the backlash against rap in the 1990s was remarkably similar to White America's first encounter with jazz, blues and even Black gospel music. Anecdotally, I would play several songs from 2-Live Crew in my own youth group to frame our discussions of sexuality. The conversations were amazing!

Many would see these lyrics and only see the anger. And in fact, by 1996 the Crime Bureau had released a statement warning the public of a new breed of "super predators"—urban Black males. Many new laws were created to keep these "animals" behind bars. Many churches simply "moved out" of the 'hood. But Ice Cube's song and others like it reflected back to White America decades of injustice and political misrepresentation, when brutal police beatings took place regularly and no one would believe anyone from the 'hood.

Nevertheless, violence became part of the hallmark of rap music in the mid-1990s. On September 13, 1996, West Coast artist Tupac Shakur died of gunshot wounds from a drive-by shooting. Less than a year later, on March 9, 1997, East Coast rapper Biggie Smalls was killed in Los Angeles by drive-by shooting. Both artists had been at the forefront of a bitter feud between the coasts. Many record industry engineers, producers and executives were being killed during this period. During this "dead era"[39] major labels began to decrease their social/political rap releases, turning instead to less "dangerous" or violent "party rap" artists such as Nelly and Trick Daddy.

Here are some other important events for Hip Hop during the 1990s:

- Public Enemy releases their third and most critically acclaimed album, *Fear of a Black Planet,* in 1990.

- September 10, 1990, marks the release of the television series *The Fresh Prince of Bel-Air*, starring Will Smith and profiling the convergence of White suburban and Black urban America in a digestible way.

- Tupac Shakur's debut film *Juice* is released in 1992.

- Eminem begins his run in 1997. Wiggas, wankstas and the "White Rapper" become more legitimate.

- By the end of 1999, Nelly's debut album *Country Grammar* takes party/strip-club rap to the airwaves.

---

[39]As described during an interview with Joan Morgan and Davey D.

With the rise of party/strip-club rap, the denigration of women—particularly Black women—became hailed as not only acceptable but also humorous. Commercial Hip Hop grew exponentially after Nelly's album *Country Grammar,* as major record labels sought out sound-alike artists over authentic, true, honest, unique talent. Intent on selling records and making money, the record industry determined that a positive rap album sells two hundred thousand copies, whereas a rap album that talks about "Big Booty Hos" sells two million. This has larger implications about the overall tone of a society in which records that talk about women in such derogatory terms would sell so well, but that is not the scope of this book. In any event, the end of the 1990s saw the decline of prophetic Hip Hop in the public sphere.

RACE AND CLASS

No discussion on Hip Hop would be complete without a look into two of its hottest topics: race and class. Race and class have come to shape much of what rappers talk about. From the lavish home apparels of 50 Cent's house to the humble beginnings of David Banner, class is widely talked about in rap music. But what makes the discussion interesting is that often when young, chiefly male, urban youth of color discuss race and class, they are quickly labeled as antagonistic, aggressive, hostile and even dangerous. As Michael Emerson and Christian Smith remind us, "A major problem in understanding race relations in the United States is that we tend to understand race, racism, and the form for racialization as constants rather than as varables. This view has grave implications."[40] So artists such as Bruce Spring-

---

[40]Michael Emerson and Christian Smith, *Divided by Faith* (New York: Oxford University Press, 2000), p. 8. For example, people hear "racism" and think of a KKK member or a neo-Nazi skinhead, but more vicious, poisonous, venomous racism comes from people who are churchgoers, people who believe they are moral, and people who are completely ignorant to both their ethnic and cultural heritage and the ethnic and cultural heritage of those who are not in power. By that I mean the kind of racism that sustains a system in which Black and Latino men today earn less than what a White male did in 1963. This statistic is found in James Waller, *Face to Face: The Changing State of Racism Across America* (Cambridge, Mass.: Perseus, 1998), where he discusses at length the strong disparities between people of color and Whites in America.

steen and U2 are allowed to freely and openly critique American society and are even invited to the White House, and angry lyrics from songwriters such as Nirvana's Kurt Cobain are hailed as representing the cries of a generation. Meanwhile, "Cop Killer" scribe Ice-T and groups like Public Enemy are denigrated as "un-American" or, even worse, "terrorists."

Rap offers a view of race and class from the streets, showing the impact of racism and classism on a large segment of the American population. Race, class and Hip Hop are nearly synonymous for many rappers, including Odd Thomas, a White Southern California Holy Hip Hopper, whose music etches an authentic urban landscape and argues for justice and peace in the streets.

So it should come as no surprise when rappers talk about the severe inequalities which exist within the 'hood today, when rappers like Kanye West make provocative statements such as "George Bush doesn't care for Black people."[41] Much truth is contained in such statements and critiques, and it should not be easily dismissed.

THE 2000S

The Gen Y generation grew up with rappers like Snoop Dogg, Dr. Dre, Tupac and Will Smith. Gen Y knows all too well the failed promises, empty political solutions, false hope and ultimate failed promises of the years since the civil rights movement. Hip Hoppers saw firsthand the devastating social policies that wreaked havoc on the urban family and made racism and classism acceptable at the expense of urban dwellers. So when NWA dropped the song "F***

---

[41]This controversial statement was made by Kanye West during a fundraiser for the victims of Hurricane Katrina. Many defended Bush, pointing to the presence of minorities such as Condoleezza Rice and Colin Powell in his cabinet. But Kanye was summing up a racist system that benefits those in power (e.g. White culture) while ignoring the cries of poor, underclass and underrepresented people. While President Bush is not a KKK member or neo-Nazi, we can see the impact of the "racialization" depicted in Emerson and Smith's *Divided by Faith* in the trail of destruction left by Katrina. For more on this, see Michael Eric Dyson, *Come Hell or High Water: Hurricane Katrina and the Color of Disaster* (New York: Basic Books, 2006), chap. 2.

the Police" it became a Hip Hop national anthem and is still played loudly to this day.

Hip Hop has gone through a series of transformations—from social movement (1970s), to marginalized political movement (mid-1980s), to mainstreamed entertainment genre and political movement (early 1990s), to a violent bicoastal clash (mid 1990s), to a celebration of hedonism (2000s). In 2004 and again, to greater effect, in 2008, Hip Hop provided a soundtrack for political change: "Vote or Die" was an ultimately unsuccessful effort by Hip Hop mogul Diddy to increase voter registration and galvanize the urban vote for Democratic presidential candidate John Kerry. In 2008, Will.I.am of the Black Eyed Peas cemented Barack Obama's iconic status and heralded his presidential victory by setting his words to music in the award-winning "Yes We Can."

Meanwhile, "Black America" is no longer monolithic. Michael Eric Dyson distinguishes two classes of Black Americans today: the Afristocracy versus the Ghettocracy. The Afristocracy is the "upper-middle class blacks and the black elite who rain down fire and brimstone upon poor blacks for their deviance and pathology,"[42] while the Ghettocracy consists of "the desperately unemployed and underemployed, those trapped in underground economies, and those working poor folk who slave in menial jobs at the edge of the economy."[43] These two classes go to verbal war with each other, with people like Bill Cosby representing the Afristocracy while rappers like Ludacris and 50 Cent speak for the Ghettocracy. Since Hip Hop is mainly made up of that Ghettocracy that Dyson discusses, and the church is more often grouped with the Afristocracy, it is no wonder that Hip Hoppers reject the values, norms, beliefs and language laid out by the church.

The late 1990s saw the rise of three personas, particularly for Black

---

[42]Michael Eric Dyson, *Is Bill Cosby Right? Or Has the Black Middle Class Lost Its Mind?* (New York: Basic Civitas, 2005), p. xiii.
[43]Ibid., p. xiv.

males, in mainstream American pop culture.[44] The *race man* persona locates itself in the politics of advancement primarily, though not exclusively, of Black people. The image is carried over from the Civil Rights era: an individual who can lead. Todd Boyd sees the concept of the race man as "applicable to African American cultural producers as well. Musicians, artists, and entertainers were celebrated or criticized for their ability to provide positive images."[45] Bill Cosby represents this persona, along with former United Nations ambassador and mayor of Atlanta, Andrew Young.

The *new Black aesthetic* is a persona whose context is the inner city. President Obama would fit the persona of the new Black aesthetic, as does filmmaker Spike Lee, whom Boyd describes as "the perfect example of this new generation, having attended Morehouse, the citadel of the Black male bourgeois, and the highly regarded New York University film school."[46] Rev. Calvin C. Butts is another example.

Characteristics of this persona[47] include speaking up about injustices, going to college, attaining an education in a known university, getting ahead, and doing your best to represent the Black race. Still, this suggests a notion of middle to upper-middle-class socioeconomics.[48] You need to have some money to go to college, and most in the inner city do not have that type of money. This persona

---

[44]These concepts are derived from Todd Boyd, *Am I Black Enough for You?* (Bloomington: Indiana University Press, 1997), pp. 13-37. The Black male image and Black youth are the foundational piece to Hip Hop culture when it emerged within the inner city. Hip Hop has embraced many different ethnicities, but overall, the Black image, particularly the Black male persona, is still referred to when Hip Hop culture is discussed (e.g. Michael Eric Dyson, *Between God and Gangsta Rap,* and *Holler If You Hear Me* [New York: Basic Civitas, 2001]; Kitwana, *Hip Hop Generation*; Andreana Clay, "Keepin' It Real: Black Youth, Hip-Hop Culture, and Black Identity," *American Behavioral Scientist* 46, no. 10 (2003): 1346-58; Hodge, *Can You Hear Me Calling?*

[45]Boyd, *Am I Black Enough for You?* p. 19.

[46]Ibid., p. 25.

[47]This image is not totally gone; Pearl Stewart's study on Black universities ("Unparalleled Challenges," *Diverse Education,* March 2004) reveals that many feel that Hip Hop is a negative influence, and some are arguing to ban the music and fashions.

[48]Ibid., p. 26.

fits a more "cultured" or "civilized" Black; one not necessarily from the ghetto.[49]

The *nigga*[50] as a persona is "a return to an older form of Black masculinity in popular culture, but rejuvenated relative to the circumstances of contemporary culture."[51] The film *Menace II Society* captured this image well: "Old Dogg was America's worst nightmare: Young, Black and don't give a f***!" This is the "in your face," restless rebel that many urban youth identify with. For the "nigga," identification with the 'hood is more important than a "formal" education. "Gangsta rap, with its origins on the West Coast, specifically addresses the worldview of the truly disadvantaged."[52] Many older Boomers have issues with this image; they see it as troublesome and negative. Tupac was the first and still is the primary spokesperson for this persona: one that embodies the positive and the negative, while embracing education and social activism.[53] The Rev. Jeremiah Wright, whose pastorate drew media attention during the Obama presidential campaign, is another example.

In 2006 many key figures in the Afristocracy, among them the Revs. Al Sharpton and Jesse Jackson, held long public discussions, ultimately recommending a ban on the word *nigga*. Much of the Hip Hop community saw this as neither relevant nor significant. "Older Black folk . . . don't really know what's going on in the 'hood, they done lost their connection with us. . . . We gon' keep using the word with or without their approval."[54]

---

[49]Rap groups such as Public Enemy, X-Clan, and Professor X are representative of this image but do not encompass all of the attributes.

[50]The term *nigga* also takes on a class-conscious state as argued by Robin D. G. Kelley, *Race Rebels: Culture, Politics, and the Black Working Class* (New York: Free Press, 1994), pp. 183-227. I will be discussing Kelley's use of the word *nigga,* as it has a significant relationship to how certain Hip Hoppers use it too.

[51]Boyd, *Am I Black Enough for You?* p. 30.

[52]Ibid., p. 34.

[53]This is what Richard Middleton calls "locating the people from within the music." The nigga image, gangsta and political rap genres speak to and for the people (Martin Clayton, Trevor Herbert and Richard Middleton, eds., *The Cultural Study of Music* (London: Routledge, 2003), pp. 251-54. Therefore it is imperative to listen to their stories—they are just as valid as, say, Noah's story of drunkenness.

[54]Interviewee response, 2008.

The term *nigga* is not just about race. Imani Perry sees it as "in some ways an extension of the idea of the black [in] everyman, and it has become a public word in hip hop."[55] While the term is racialized—the infamous *nigger*—nigga can even encompass Whites, Latinos, women, Europeans and people living in inner cities.[56] We will cover this a little more in chapter four.

The race man and the new black aesthetic are more "friendly" personas to many within the urban church (especially the Black church), whereas the nigga persona is primarily seen as a thug/hoodlum/killer/mugger/gangster—ultimately separate from God. This creates tension, and yet as Mark Anthony Neal has noted, there is a deep and strong intellect among people from a post-soul perspective. The nigga persona offered important, significant commentary on the tumultuous Reagan/Bush 1980s, the devastating effects of crack cocaine on their communities and the rise of Hip Hop as cultural capital. Neal calls this the "Post-Soul Intelligentsia":

> a generation of black thinkers in large part distanced from the nostalgia that pervades the civil rights generation, but who as young adults and teens experienced the terror of the Reagan and Bush (Sr.) years armed with distinct social and cultural, albeit often nostalgic in their own right, memories of the traditional black public sphere.[57]

Within these three personas lies an even deeper phenomenon known as the post-soul era.[58] The Civil Rights generation tends to

---

[55]Imani Perry, *Prophets of the Hood: Politics and Poetics in Hip Hop* (Durham, N.C.: Duke University Press, 2004), p. 142.

[56]For a great study and discussion on the word *nigga,* see Kelley, *Race Rebels.*

[57]Mark Anthony Neal, *Soul Babies: Black Popular Culture and the Post-Soul Aesthetic* (New York: Routledge, 2002), p. 104.

[58]To gain a broader sense of the post-soul era, I suggest reading Mark Anthony Neal's *Soul Babies.* Neal breaks down the history of the post-soul aesthetic and names its distinctives within Black culture and Hip Hop. Neal gives a great examination of what it means to live within a post-soul, post-civil rights, and in a post Reagan-Bush (Sr.) era. Nelson George (*Post-Soul Nation* [New York: Penguin, 2005]) is also largely known for coining the term "Post-Soul" era.

see the post-soul person as immoral, disrespectful, irreverent, and "secular." The post-soul person tends to view the Civil Rights generation person as old school, out of touch, hierarchal and extremely judgmental. This has caused much turmoil between the two personas and for ministers working from a Civil Rights generation perspective; it only deepens the misunderstanding when you add in theology and religion.

We now shift our discussion to the soul and post-soul context and its relation to Hip Hop. While much as been written in regards to postmodernism, there has been very little that connects it back to Hip Hop and the soul era and post-soul era. This is where we come in.

2

Hip Hop & the Post-Soul Matrix

The post soul-era is better understood by first understanding what the "soul era" was about. Soul culture integrated a religious worldview into the marketplace and the public sphere, producing such artists and public figures as Marvin Gaye, Aretha Franklin, Jackie Wilson, Sam Cooke, Donnie Hathaway, James Baldwin, Sidney Poitier and Lena Horne. Nurtured in the womb of the church and religious culture, the soul era was characterized by an optimism that sought to work with existing power structures to bring about necessary change.

The soul era was etched with faith and religious overtones that marked its norms and values. In many ways overlapping the worldviews and values of the Civil Rights movement, the soul era also rooted its understanding of Christ and morality in the King James Version of the Bible— Christ steeped in tradition, unyielding views of theology, and rigid fundamentals that tend to not produce integrated and transparent people.

The post-soul era,[1] by contrast, developed its identity and values outside the church environment and, as Otis Moss states, "nursed from the breast of market forces and morally ambiguous political ideology."[2]

---

[1]Mark Anthony Neal contends that the post-soul era could be feasibly documented in its emergence with the rise of the 1980s and the Reagan Right; because of this, Neal argues, Reagan's policies further helped to instigate the advent of Hip Hop music and culture, as Hip Hop became the most visible site of an already hostile and oppositional urban youth culture (Mark Anthony Neal, *Soul Babies: Black Popular Culture and the Post-Soul Aesthetic* [New York: Routledge, 2002], pp. 102-3).

[2]Otis Moss, "Real Big: The Hip Hop Pastor as Postmodern Prophet," in *The Gospel Remix: Reaching the Hip Hop Generation*, ed. R. Watkins (Valley Forge, Penn.: Judson Press, 2007), p. 111.

The truth is that many people of color, especially youth, are fighting for survival and attempting to gather meaning out of this strange land called America. With the increase of police repression, demonization of people of color, introduction of crack cocaine, and the de-industrialization of urban centers, black people find themselves at a crossroads. Old tactics and strategies of change are now obsolete.[3]

So Hip Hop finds itself caught in a fierce battle to be heard and understood by its parent generation. Table 2 lists some key elements of difference between the soul era and the post-soul era. These areas are by no means conclusive and exhaustive, yet they give us a place in which to begin to better understand why Hip Hop helps to usher in post-soul tendencies. Moreover, Hip Hop begins new didactic conversations in regards to Christology, salvation and the kingdom of God.

Rap groups such as Public Enemy and NWA gave voice and breath to Hip Hop's post-soul aesthetic. Strongly criticized for their take on

Table 2. The Differences Between the Soul Era and the Post-Soul Era

Soul Era	Post-Soul Era
Absolutist: final answers, universal truths, firm boundaries	Open truth: culture and context are important; majority thinking
Linear reasoning	Circular, triangular and visual reasoning
Hierarchal; ordered power structures	Group-centered; power is equally distributed
Individualism is valued	Community-based while still allowing for individual creativity and expression
Answers are solid and conclusive; everything can be explained.	Uncertainty; everything does not have to have an answer; respect for ambiguity and mystery
Racial; ethnicity and class are clear categories	Postracial, postclassist

[3]Ibid., p. 113.

many social problems, these two groups also put a face to much of rap music that still exists today. While their critique was lost within the commercialization of the post-soul era, their "style"—Black, exotic yet scary, dark, "in your face"—still characterizes Hip Hop for many onlookers, bringing billions of dollars to many corporations and caricaturing large sections of the Black community. The post-soul era's commercialization has made it "ok" to niggarize the suburbs, as in the film *Malibu's Most Wanted.*

My interviews and other research have uncovered four taxonomies of responses to post-soul Hip Hop.[4] There are some real disconnects in perceptions between young people in general, urban youth, Christian youth and youth workers. If not taken seriously, these disconnects can turn into a complete break.

My research focused on youth workers with at least one year's experience. Broadly, Hip Hop is perceived by such youth workers as all about sex; most were preoccupied with the prevalence in contemporary rap of the F-word and discussion of body parts. Most such youth workers have separated themselves from "worldly" Hip Hop since they were "saved," seeing Hip Hop culture as selfish and populated by the "lovers of self" identified by the apostle Paul in Galatians 5 and elsewhere. They feel that Jesus would disapprove of Hip Hop culture—unless it's explicitly "Christian," or the vague category "used for the Lord." They feel that young people need to "get over" Hip Hop, keeping the spirits in the music out of their heads and instead staying connected to the Lord.

Urban and even suburban youth who listen to rap music and identify themselves with Hip Hop are much more positive toward Hip Hop than their youth workers. The contend that Hip Hop gives them a voice and helps them interpret the world around them. Adults—especially Christian adults—are too critical of it; hip hop can influence

---

[4] I identified these taxonomies by compiling of all my interviews using what is called grounded theory to find and examine text patterns and consistencies. I have broken down each category by using the themes that came up during the interview process with each person.

you, but you have to make your own decisions about how it will influence you. In any event, Hip Hop is a reality of their daily lives.

Christian youth—active in their church for at least a year and explicitly identifying themselves as Christian—by contrast are not in touch with current Hip Hop culture. They love Jesus and feel that they've been delivered from old worldly patterns, which includes the music of Hip Hop. They are, however, "open" to forms of outreach to non-Christians that link to Hip Hop culture.

STREET YOUTH ON HIP-HOP

Meanwhile, "street youth"—young people in an urban context not connected to a church and not professing a faith—find God in the music of Hip Hop. Such music and lyrics "keep it real." While they don't care for church as they've encountered it, they do express love for Jesus, and they report that they would change their cultural habits—including the music they listened to—if someone they respected and who understood them were to ask them to make a change. In short, they're open to the outreach of the church.

In other words, street youth see God showing up in their music; youth workers see Hip Hop at best as a "tool" to reach but not to keep youth. The attitudes among street youth are consistent with a post-soul worldview, which finds God in almost every facet of life. Christian youth by contrast see Hip Hop as their "other life," characterized as "worldly."

HIP HOP AND POSTMODERNITY

While I am not going to give an exhaustive study regarding the very important relationship between Hip Hop and postmodernity, it does deserve some discussion. Modern social theory sought a universal, historical and rational foundation for its analysis and critique of society.[5] Postmoderns have rejected such foundationalism and tend instead to be relativistic, nonrational and nihilistic. Postmoderns be-

---

[5]"For Marx, that foundation was species-being, while for Habermas it was communicative reason." George Ritzer, *Sociological Theory,* 5th ed. (New York: McGraw Hill, 2000), p. 604.

lieve that the foundations being handed them tend to favor some groups and downgrade the significance of others, giving some groups power and rendering other groups powerless.[6] The postmodern age is a re-enchantment of the "forest" of life, society, the human experience, even theology, God and Jesus. For postmoderns, the "forest" is a mystery, something that cannot be managed, predicted or produced, let alone controlled by one "foundation," such as White power brokers dictating what is "right" and "wrong." Postmoderns are, for the most part, very spiritual. The spirituality may not always be in line with Christian beliefs and practices, but it is spiritual nonetheless and presents an open door to discuss Christ—the first "postmodern," if we look at his life carefully (more on this in the chapters to come).

Russell Potter argues that Hip Hop and rap were among the leading agents for postmodern culture to develop; indeed, rap was the music for the postmodern generation.[7] The music became the philosophical base for Hip Hop artists, questioning authority with no remorse, standing with, not over people. Hip Hop is also about expression and individuality infused in community; just go to any true Hip Hop concert and you'll see that the focus is on the spectacular, inviting each person in attendance to reach a higher level of knowledge. Any culture that focuses on the spectacular might be termed transcendent, and postmoderns and Hip Hoppers are no different—searching for the experiential and the transcendent in contemporary culture, from hyperreal theme parks to "profane" rap music.

Hip Hop has four key postmodern elements to it:

1. Restoration. The goal of Hip Hop culture, especially in many spoken word venues, is that the authentic self be restored and built up from its broken state.

---

[6]See Ritzer, *Sociological Theory,* p. 610; Russell Christopher White, *Constructions of Identity and Community in Hip-Hop Nationalism with Specific Reference to Public Enemy and Wu-Tang Clan,* Ph.D. dissertation (Hampshire, U.K.: University of Southampton, 2002), p. 200.

[7]Russell Potter, *Spectacular Vernaculars: Hip-Hop and the Politics of Postmodernism* (New York: State University of New York Press, 1995).

2. Self-awareness. For Hip Hoppers, to be self-aware simply means to go deeper into who you are as a person while continually being transparent and open to new ideas. This is nothing new for Christians either. Jesus challenges us to probe deeper and ask the hard questions by giving us multifaceted parables and complex statements about his gospel message.

3. Power, control and institutions. Most of the people I interviewed who agreed that no matter the type of rap genre, "questioning authority" still remains widespread. Hip Hop continues to ask the question, "Whose authority/power/institution should we follow? And what makes them right?"

4. Recovering empty answers. Hip Hop is about making some "right" in a world that is not "right." Rap artists such as Tupac, Ice Cube, Chuck D, Eminem and David Banner challenge the broken promises given by politicians, church officials and other people in control. A crucial scene in the film *Freedom Writers* (2007) takes place when students ask why they should "respect" the teacher. Was it simply because she was a teacher—in charge, having institutional authority? The students then proceeded to break down their life and struggles and how so many "adults" had let them down.

Hip Hop culture speaks for those who need a voice in the public sphere. Many urban youth do not have this "voice." Rap music and Hip Hop culture provide that outlet and medium in which to argue, love, hate, yell, whisper, chill, eat, sleep, walk, talk, confide and build community in a postmodern world. This function of Hip Hop culture is not articulated by many living in the 'hood; it is more felt than talked about. But suburban youth are looking for that transcendence too. The postmodernism of Hip Hop gives meaning, voice and connection to a widespread community—Black, Brown and White, urban and suburban, wealthy and poor alike.[8]

---

[8]See Garth Alper, "Making Sense out of Postmodern Music?" *Popular Music and Society* 24, no. 4 (2000): 1; Raymond D. S. Anderson, *Black Beats for One People: Causes and Effects of Identification with Hip-Hop Culture,* Ph.D. dissertation (Vir-

Cornel West notes three significant changes in American culture that gave rise to the postmodern.[9] The first is the displacement of European models of culture. Europe had been the locus of "high culture," the self-styled universal subject of culture, defining culture itself as the last "refuge," in the spirit of nineteenth-century British critic Matthew Arnold. In contrast to high culture, which consisted of the fine arts, classical music and gourmet dining, was the low culture of the urban world, which embodied folk and popular music, abstract art and sur-

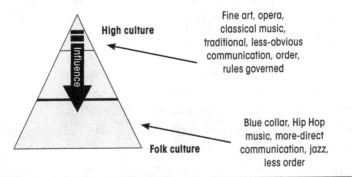

Figure 3. High culture influencing folk culture

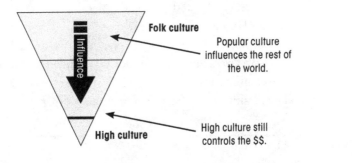

Figure 4. Folk culture influencing high culture

ginia Beach, Va.: Regent University, 2003).
[9]These three points are adapted from Cornel West's essay "The New Cultural Politics of Difference," in *Out There: Marginalization and Contemporary Culture,* ed. Russell Ferguson, Martha Gever, Trinh T. Minh-Ha and Cornel West (Cambridge, Mass.: MIT Press, 1990), pp.19-38.

vival skills (all attributes unsuitable for gentlemen). By the 1960s Europe was displaced and the low was no longer being influenced by the high; the cultural tables were shifting (see figures 3 and 4).

Meanwhile, the United States had emerged as a world power. Through the means of slavery and the rise of capitalism during the nineteenth century, America grew economically and socioeconomically, ultimately becoming the center of global cultural production and circulation. "This emergence is both a displacement and a hegemonic shift in the definition of culture—a movement from high culture to American mainstream popular culture and its mass-cultural, image-mediated, technological forms."[10]

Soon to follow was the decolonization of the third world.[11] The world was becoming its own person, bit by bit, and no one place could claim the center of cultural hegemony. Inner-city America thus became a distinct cultural center point, as urban areas were "decolonized" by White culture, and Black culture became prominent.[12] Dick Hebdige identifies three "negations" that can be perceived in Hip Hop culture.[13]

1. Against totalization. Hip Hop culture is not in favor of one grand story or "metanarrative." Rap music calls out the faults and errors of the previous and current generation's dogma on success, life, theology, love, hate, gender and sex. The belief that was given to many in the Hip Hop generation—just work hard and you will succeed—is confronted in the passionate lyrics of artists such as Tupac and Eve. We are each created uniquely and individually, yet we require the community of others; this is a large part of Hip Hop culture and its ensuing attraction to many urban youth.

---

[10]Stuart Hall, "What Is This 'Black' in Black Popular Culture," *Social Justice* 20 (1993): 21-22.

[11]Cornel West, *Prophetic Thought in Postmodern Times: Beyond Eurocentrism and Multiculturalism*, vol. 1 (Monroe, Maine: Common Courage Press, 1993), pp. 122-23.

[12]Also look into James Cone (*Black Theology and Black Power,* 5th ed. [Maryknoll, N.Y.: Orbis, 1997], chap. 6), how the rise of the "suffering Jesus" came into play and how that played out in Black culture and the urban gospel message.

[13]Dick Hebdige, "Postmodernism and 'the Other Side,'" in *Cultural Theory and Popular Culture: A Reader*, ed. J. Storey (London: Pearson Prentice Hall, 1998), pp. 374-81.

2. Against teleology. Hip Hop culture is against the "final word" from scholars and professionals that explain the origins and existence of the earth, God, religion and humanity. Rap music calls out the monopoly of rich White males that have dominated most of Western Culture to this day.[14] Hip Hop culture increases the span of knowledge and brings back mystery. For many urban youth, this distancing from the former generation is a relief; this is one reason why so many urban youth are entrepreneurs and are seeking alternative employment.

3. Against Utopia. The harsh realties of the inner city force young people to question whether there really is a God that allows such despair. Hip Hop culture calls out the lie that hard work equals success, and ushers in the realty of ghetto living.

Hip Hop is postmodern in its questioning of absolute truths and absolute authority, and its deep belief in community.[15] And yet, while many Hip Hoppers reject "absolute truth," they embrace the absolute Christ. This is because Jesus, when seen without the stained lens of Christian dogmatic tradition, is acceptable and embraceable to them. Hip Hoppers identify with a Jesus that can relate to them. Jesus is needed in the 'hood, and postmodernity opens up new paths to him from outside the church, while Hip Hop culture offers a theologically transcendent outlet.

Many Christians are dubious about that proposition. But I ask you, didn't Jesus say the same thing? We'll explore that question in session two.

---

[14]See Mark Anthony Neal, "Sold Out on Soul: The Corporate Annexation of Black Popular Music," *Popular Music and Society* 21, no. 3 (1997); Mark Gottdiener, "Hegemony and Mass Culture: A Semiotic Approach," *American Journal of Sociology* 90, no. 5 (1985): 979-1001.

[15]Scott Lash, "Postmodernism as Humanism? Urban Space and Social Theory," in *Theories of Modernity and Postmodernity*, ed. B. S. Turner (Thousand Oaks, Calif.: Sage Publications, 1990); Jean-Francois Lyotard, *The Postmodern Condition: A Report on Knowledge* (Minneapolis: University of Minnesota Press, 1984); Ioanna Kuçuradi, "Rationality and Rationalities Within the Framework of the Modernism-Postmodernism Debate," *Diogenes* 51, no. 2 (2004): 11-17; J. Andrew Kirk, "Following Modernity and Postmodernity: A Missiological Investigation," *Mission Studies* 17, no. 1 (2000): 217-39.

SESSION TWO

The Theology of Hip Hop

There is good biblical evidence that God not only suffered in Christ, but that God in Christ suffers with his people still. . . . It is wonderful that we may share in Christ's sufferings; it is more wonderful still that he shares in ours.

JOHN R. W. STOTT, *THE CROSS OF CHRIST*

Hip Hop's theology encompasses three tasks every new theological movement must accomplish, as articulated by Herbert Edwards, a Black theologian who shaped Black theology in the 1970s.[1] According to Edwards, any theological movement must

- prove the inadequacy of previous and existing theologies for the present crisis
- demonstrate its own adequacy for the present moment
- establish its continuity with normative expressions of the faith

Hip Hop addresses the crisis of urban America and begins to seek spiritual answers connected to Jesus, while challenging the institutionalized church and questioning the centralization of power in pastors to bring about a higher involvement with God. Hip Hop prophets

---

[1]Herbert Edwards, "Black Theology: Retrospect and Prospect," *Journal of Religious Thought* 32 (1975): 46-59.

such as Tupac, DMX, Lauryn Hill and Mase establish a new adequacy for this postmodern era, offering a new view of (and path to) Jesus from outside the church. This movement finds its theological continuity with thirteenth- and fourteenth-century African theology, where God is felt, heard, seen and connected with through spoken word, dance, community and meditation.

The irreverent spirituality in Hip Hop music has formed its own *theomusicology,* "musicology as a theologically informed discipline."[2] The sacred, profane, and urban elements alike are all brought before God; rappers become what Dyson calls "natural theologians."[3] The fact that Hip Hop music is theologically rooted is no coincidence. Hip Hop is about liberation from the shackles of modernity. As Black gospel music had a liberating tone, Hip Hop likewise offers postmodern youth a new and "meatier" image of Jesus.[4]

Hip Hop theology presumes that God "shows up" in unusual and interesting places. Thus Hip Hop theology is, in essence, the study of the Godhead in the urban context, to better understand God's rich and complex love for everyone (not just those who "look nice" and "talk nice"), and the revelation of God through the oppressed being liberated from the oppressor.

---

[2]Jon Michael Spencer, *Protest and Praise: Sacred Music of Black Religion* (Minneapolis: Fortress Press, 1990), p. vii.
[3]Michael Eric Dyson, *Holler If You Hear Me: Searching for Tupac Shakur* (New York: Basic Civitas, 2001).
[4]See Tricia Rose, *Black Noise: Rap Music and Black Culture in Contemporary America* (Middletown, Conn.: Wesleyan University Press, 1994).

3

Pain, Misery, Hate & Love
All at Once

A THEOLOGY OF SUFFERING

I remember the period well. It was the months following the 1992 L.A. Riots. We were young, full of energy, and having borne witness to the destructive forces that tore our community apart, we wanted to change the direction of the 'hood.

So what did we do? We organized gangs, nonprofits and people with like-minded worldviews to create something that had never been done, a gang truce.

A fifteen-city organizational effort involving gang leaders, community organizations and rappers like Tupac, the then lesser-known Snoop Dogg and former members of NWA, as well as people who wanted to see a change from the violence of the 1980s, put together posters, banners, flyers and events that helped put a message of peace out in the community. Large gangs like the Crips and the Bloods came to park BBQ's to celebrate the newfound peace. MTV covered many of the events.

For the first time it seemed as though urban peace was beginning to take shape. I was truly amazed. Especially being as angry as I was after the Rodney King trial verdict, I was beginning to see some change that I could be a part of.

We decided that each city needed to take their concerns to City

Hall. We had hoped to file for a "state of emergency" to begin receiving federal funds to clean up our 'hoods and begin to restore our families. So we put together documents, papers, statistics, and firsthand accounts of what was happening in our communities. We knew it would be hard, but we also knew that we had a legitimate case. By now, it had been almost two years without a gang-related shooting.

Our first five attempts to talk with our mayor went unheeded. The next fifteen attempts, we were told, "Oh, you just missed him." Finally, on our twentieth attempt to reach someone in city council, someone who supposedly had the mayor's "ear" gave us about five minutes before cutting us off: "What exactly are you all doing here? Don't you have some drive-by to do? Why are you wasting the mayor's time?"

His statements floored us all. But we persisted and began to explain our success in five cities. His response, "We don't entertain a bunch of thugs in the mayor's office, I suggest you get off these premises before we call the cops and have you forcibly removed." At this point, we were a little hot under the collar and demanded to see his supervisor, to which he responded, "Let me make this perfectly clear: *We don't care!*" He walked away as security guards escorted us off the premises with a warning that if we ever set foot on these premises again, we would be arrested like "the dogs you are."

Yes, that happened.

Most of the groups in other cities faced similar reactions from their local government. Some were even arrested, given violations to their current parole and sent back to prison for conspiring with known gang members. Within months, the media hype from the 1992 riots dimmed, and it was business as usual in the 'hood. Only now the younger generation was even more pessimistic about organizing and social justice.

I was stunned. I did not know what to do. I went to tell my pastor about what had happened; he looked at me as if I were just crazy to even be thinking about such a thing. He reminded me of how I needed to pick my pants up when I was in church, and that my language and attitude could have been a lot better. Moreover, he also reminded me that if we had just prayed harder, God would have opened up those doors for us.

Hip Hop was my only solace at the time. I have come a long way since those dark days, but one thing remains true. In those days, rap music was my christological light.

Pain, suffering, and misery are nothing new to the human experience. It is part of life that we all suffer at some level. We all know that it's not true that the more money you have, the fewer problems you have. But you would not know it from the American media. Against a backdrop of romanticized suffering as portrayed by Hollywood, Tupac sought to shine a more journalistic light on the urban context of so much pain:

> It's like, you've got the Vietnam War, and because you had reporters showing us pictures of the war at home, that's what made the war end, or that s*** would have lasted longer. If no one knew what was going on we would have thought they were just dying valiantly in some beautiful way. But because we saw the horror, that's what made us stop the war.
>
> So I thought, that's what I'm going to do as an artist, as a rapper I'm gonna show the most graphic details of what I see in my community and hopefully they'll stop it quick. I've seen all of that—the crack babies, what we had to go through, losing everything, being poor, and getting beat down. All of that. Being the person I am, I said no no no no. I'm changing this.[1]

While much suffering is messy, confusing, dirty, dark and just plain miserable, some suffering looks "neater." Most of the "rich" experience a "higher level" of mild pain. Suffering in the 'hood looks a lot different. Hip Hop aims to give that suffering its due attention.

SUFFERING IN THE HIP HOP CONTEXT

Hip Hop defines suffering in five ways:

- suffering because of circumstances that you cannot control (e.g., financial hardships, family drama, physical ailments, mental disabilities)

---

[1]Tupac Shakur, Afeni Shakur, Jacob Hoye, Karolyn Ali and Walter Einenkel, *Tupac: Resurrection, 1971-1996* (New York: Atria Books, 2003).

- suffering for a cause you believe deeply in (e.g., sociopolitical issues, social justice concerns, racial matters)
- suffering because of who you are (e.g., resentment directed at you due to your personal prosperity or prestige)
- suffering as a result of something you have done or something someone has done to you (e.g., mistakes, life errors or difficult relationships)
- suffering as a result of social, political or spiritual oppression (e.g., persecution or marginalization due to your worldview or belief system, at an individual or systemic level)

These five suffering contexts are extremely fluid. For example, DMX talks about the struggles of forgiveness in his song "Look Thru My Eyes."

Lost all control, my shoulders hold a lot of weight
Just like first I'm sold an eight, then told it's not an eight
But then it's out of state, and it's too late for changes
    to be made
That's what I get for f***ing with strangers in the shade
This is it, that nigga's got to give me a place
For the same reason that fate, chose to give me away
Take away hate, now I'm supposed to love the one that
    cursed me
The one that wouldn't give me a cup of water when
    I was thirsty
It was always him versus me, but now I gotta teach him
Personal feelings put aside, cuz now I gotta reach him
What I'd like to do is turn my head, like I don't know him
But it seems like I've been called on to show him
So I'ma show him
And if you never met me, then you've no right to judge me
I've got a good heart but this heart can get ugly[2]

[2]DMX, "Look Thru My Eyes," from the album *It's Dark and Hell Is Hot* (1998).

DMX here challenges his listeners to see life is full of paradoxes—struggles that result from a mixture of "personal feelings" and personal affronts ("the one that cursed me"). This is only one example of DMX exploring suffering because of social, political and spiritual oppression. In the song "Prayer III" he states:

Let us pray
Lord Jesus it is you, who wakes me up every day
And I am forever grateful for your love. . . . This is why I pray
You let me touch so many people, and it's all for the good
I influenced so many children, I never thought that I would
And I couldn't take credit for the love they get
because it all comes from you Lord;
I'm just the one that's givin it
And when it seems like the pressure gets to be too much
I take time out and pray, and ask that you be my crutch
Lord I am not perfect by a longshot—I confess to you daily
But I work harder everyday, and I hope that you hear me
In my heart I mean well, but if you'll help me to grow
then what I have in my heart, will begin to show
And when I get goin, I'm not lookin back for NOTHIN
Cause I will know where I'm headed, cause I'm so tired
    of the sufferin
I stand before you, a weakened version of, your reflection
Beggin for direction, for my soul needs resurrection
I don't deserve what you've given me, but you never
    took it from me
because I am grateful, and I use it, and I do not, worship money
If what you want from me is to bring your children to you
my regret is only having one life to do it, instead of two
Amen[3]

Here, we see DMX turning to God, finding a sense of vocation in

---

[3]DMX, "Prayer III," from the album . . . *And Then There Was X* (1999).

his processing of circumstantial suffering. The rap group The Outlawz paints a picture of suffering that is in a sense self-inflicted:

> I know this young nigga who love to keep his gun in his pants
> 14, little Ant will snatch your s*** to enhance
> He lost his moms at a early age, pops was cracked out
> His brother ran a drug house where they slept with they
>   Mac's out
> And where we from, f*** them basketball teams
> And your neighborhood PAL cause it's all about makin cream
> He stayed dirty, copped a clip for thirty
> He'd rather be sellin drugs early instead of young, black and
>   nerdy
> He had his hard hat, born ready for war
> This young nigga heart's gone and I saw this before
> He lived day by day, prey by prey, stray by stray
> Blunted on Chancellor Ave. 380 hallway
> He bought a AK and I know he gon' sway, it ain't no d*** way
> That this young nigga can turn his life around, mang
> Now where is God when you need him, he's internally bleedin
> Little Ant's barely breathin but he gotta stay eatin
> So he robs again but this time he all smoked out
> He put his finger on the trigger and let the death fly out
> Some man got hit, he's layin on the pavement stiff
> Blood drippin from his face and he drownin in it
> Now what a surprise that little Ant can't come around
> That it's his own man dead on the ground
> Dead on the ground[4]

Here pain and suffering result from someone making poor choices
and decisions. The song echoes with a call to "turn from your ways"
because if you do not, then the resulting consequences could be unfa-
vorable for you. There are echoes, however, of suffering as a result of

---

[4]The Outlawz, "Lost And Turned Out," from the album *Neva Surrenda—The Rap-A-
Lot Sessions* (2002).

forces and problems you cannot control, suffering from social, political and religious oppression.

For rappers like Bizzy (former member of Bone Thugz-N-Harmony), suffering is often beyond our control; life is hard in the 'hood and can force you to do things you never imagined possible.

> Puttin' a pistol to my brain, one second before I squeeze
>   since I'm
> A gangster, I'ma put myself on my knees, I'm to many
>   suicide I'm
> Sick, of feelin' depressed, and I'm stressed out like a mothaf*****
> I can't even rest, I smoke weed, drink liquor just to ease
>   the pain
> They used to tell me that God was cryin' whenever it'd rain, I
> Grew up without my momma and my father, just me and my
>   sisters, and
> They split us all up with the foster, I've been molested and
>   I learnt
> About love, I don't respect women, now I'm just sinnin',
>   nigga row
> I'm livin', how long may this survive like this, if it's
>   Heaven and
> The Abyss you will fry to the crisp now drinkin', and
>   drinkin' and
> drinkin'
> And smokin' and smokin' and thinkin' and thinkin' want a
>   little bit
> More and more a my mind still slip a, it's ridiculous, can't take
>   it, come on
> Save me I'll take death everybody's so all worked up[5]

Bizzy is dealing with deep social shortcomings like the foster care system and economic depravities, as well as individual shortcomings and missteps. He was molested, a deep and dark secret that many do

---

[5]Bizzy, "Blow you Away," from the album *Bone Brothers* (2005).

not reveal. Bizzy is crying out with his pain, much like David does in Psalm 69:1-3:

> Save me, O God,
> for the waters have come up to my neck.
> I sink in the miry depths,
> where there is no foothold.
> I have come into the deep waters;
> the floods engulf me.
> I am worn out calling for help;
> my throat is parched.
> My eyes fail,
> looking for my God.

Another dimension of pain and suffering comes when someone close to you has done ill toward you. Lauryn Hill discusses this well in her song "When It Hurts So Bad." Here, Hill discusses the pain of loving someone who has not loved back:

> I loved real, real hard once
> But the love wasn't returned
> Found out the man I'd die for
> He wasn't even concerned
> I tried, and I tried, and I tried
> to keep him in my life (to keep him in my life)
> I cried, and I cried, and I cried
> but I couldn't make it right
>
> But I, I loved the young man
> And if you ever been in love
> then you'd understand
>
> That what you want might make you cry
> What you need might pass you by
> If you don't catch it (if you don't catch it)
> (if you don't catch it)[6]

---

[6]Lauryn Hill, "When It Hurts So Bad," from the album *The Miseducation of Lauryn Hill* (1998).

Pains within intimate relationships are another essential element of suffering for the Hip Hop community. Mary J. Blige, queen of the R&B rap genre, sings about horrific relationships; in so doing she offers listeners suggestions on how to avoid the pain she has experienced. In songs like "Each Tear" ("You're much more than a struggle that you go through / You're not defined by your pain, so let it go") Blige is able to transcend her own experience and then empower her listeners so that they too can make it through rough times.[7]

HIP HOP AND PASTORAL CONCERN

In essence, artists like Blige, Hill, DMX and Tupac (whom many of my interview subjects consider a "martyred saint") become the pastors for their generation.[8] In the song "Heavy in the Game" we find Tupac conflicted about having to sell drugs, but his life circumstances demand that he survive:

> I'm just a young black male, cursed since my birth
> Had to turn to crack sales, if worse come to worse
> Headed for them packed jails, or maybe it's a hearse
> My only way to stack mail, is out here doin dirt
> Made my decisions do or die, been hustlin since junior high
> No time for askin why, gettin high, gettin mine
> Put away my nine, cause these times call for four-five sales
> cause life is hell and everybody dies
> What about these niggaz I despise—them loud talkin cowards
> shootin guns into crowds, jeapordizin lives
> Shoot em right between them niggaz eyes, it's time to realize
> follow the rules or follow them fools that die[9]

Without glorifying or excusing it, Tupac puts some context to this lifestyle. Continually mistaken for valorizing violence, in fact the

---

[7]Mary J. Blige, "Each Tear," from the album *Stronger with Each Tear* (2009).

[8]Michael Eric Dyson, *Holler If You Hear Me: Searching for Tupac Shakur* (New York: Basic Civitas, 2001).

[9]Tupac Shakur, "Heavy in the Game," from the album *Me Against the World* (1995).

overwhelming majority of Tupac's lyrics actually talk against violence
and dubious lifestyles.

> Everybody's tryin to make the news, niggaz confused
> Quit tryin to be an O.G. and pay your dues
> If you choose to apply yourself, go with the grain.[10]

In this respect, Tupac and artists like him are assigning meaning to
suffering, and pointing a way forward for those who suffer—actions
that are highly pastoral in nature. Christina Zanfagna suggests that
claiming your suffering actually makes you more alive:

> To claim your suffering in the moment, to truly feel it and accept
> it, is a powerful act of self-attestation. As DMX, 2Pac and others
> illustrate, suffering is a catalyst for a certain spirituality, a way
> to come to terms with deep-soul anxiety or alienation, and a
> possible route to freedom.[11]

Further, E. T. Long sees the experience of suffering as "a boundary,
a limit to our ordinary experience of ourselves as beings in the world
in relation to other persons and things where being and becoming
seem closely linked."[12] Marian Maskulak argues that dealing with suffering is essential for moving forward in the Christian faith.[13] Jürgen
Moltmann goes so far as to claim suffering as central to Christianity.
"At the centre of Christian faith is the history of Christ. At the centre
of the history of Christ is his passion and his death on the cross."[14]

Kathleen O'Connor sees an important moment of spiritual growth
in the questioning that emerges during times of extreme hardship,
questioning that is often quickly characterized in the Christian community as "backsliding" or walking away from the faith. "When faith

[10]Ibid.

[11]Christina Zanfagna, "Under the Blasphemous W(Rap): Locating the 'Spirit' in Hip-Hop," *Pacific Review of Ethnomusicology* 12 (2006): 8.

[12]Eugene Thomas Long, "Suffering and Transcendence," *International Journal for Philosophy of Religion* 60 (2006): 140.

[13]Marian Maskulak, *Theology Today,* January 2008.

[14]Jürgen Moltmann, *The Way of Jesus Christ: Christology in Messianic Dimensions* (San Francisco: HarperSanFrancisco, 1990), p. 151.

in God comes under such intensive assault," she writes, "how can recovery take place and life begin anew? It seems impossible, for the ancient bonds of community turn to menacing uncertainty, and the community of faith itself appears destined to disappear. . . . To revive, people must maintain some continuity with their ancient story."[15] Many Hip Hoppers turn to rappers for that "ancient story"—what Louis Stulman calls "the symbolic super structure" of their narrative.[16] Rappers such as Tupac, DMX, Biggie, Common, Nas, and Ice Cube relate the suffering in their subject matter to this symbolic super structure, weaving the micronarratives in each song with what Jürgen Moltmann calls "the apocalyptic sufferings of Christ."[17] This is not done in an irreverent or blasphemous way. Far from it. Tupac raps:

> I'm fallin to the floor; beggin for the Lord to let me in
> to Heaven's door—shed so many tears
> (Dear God, please let me in)
>
> Lord, I've lost so many years, and shed so many tears.
> I lost so many peers, and shed so many tears
> Lord, I suffered through the years, and shed so many tears.
> God, I lost so many peers, and shed so many tears[18]

Tupac is crying out to Jesus in his suffering and asking him to let him in to heaven, to take away his pain.

When listening to songs which dealt with pain and suffering by artists such as The Outlawz, Ice-T, Tupac and DMX, 95 percent of my interviewees—even those who did not subscribe to the Christian faith—made connections between the songs and Jesus, seeing Jesus as himself a sufferer. Many respondents mentioned having a "real-life experience" when listening to such music, suggesting that many people just want their struggle validated—not fixed or figured out, just

[15]Kathleen O'Connor, "Lamenting Back to Life," *Interpretation* 62, no. 1 (2008): 35.
[16]Louis Stulman, *Order Amid Chaos: Jeremiah as Symbolic Tapestry* (Sheffield, U.K.: Sheffield Academic Press, 1998).
[17]Moltmann, *Way of Jesus Christ*, pp. 151-212.
[18]Tupac Shakur, "So Many Tears," from the album *Me Against the World* (1995).

listened to. Such spiritual engagement of suffering in Hip Hop is in line with much of the Black spiritual tradition, in which individual singers would speak, collectively, for the entire community's sufferings. Anthony Pinn traces this theology of suffering in the songs of American slave communities.

> In the mind of the slave, the interconnectedness between their condition, God, Christ, and heaven implied a concrete and contextual response to the problem of evil. God, through Christ, made victory out of human suffering. One way or another, they knew their life would mirror Christ's life and that they would be free in heaven.[19]

Pinn observes the communal nature of such songwriting: "Although these spirituals, for the most part, were created by individuals, they narrated the community's collective physical and psychological experience and development."[20]

In this way, Hip Hop is similarly connected to the blues, jazz, soul and Black gospel. Sampling from these genres is one of the many ways Hip Hop artists pay respect to older generations.[21] This tradition of exploring the spirituality of suffering culminates in Tupac's theological message: Keep ya head up, cuzz someday we gonna be free in heaven!

HIP HOP, SUFFERING AND THE BIBLE

Hip Hop's five suffering contexts are connected to different biblical characters as well. Jeremiah, Paul, Job, and Jesus all experienced the suffering contexts in which Hip Hoppers go through daily.

Jeremiah, for example, spends chapters 11-20 reflecting on lament, pain and suffering as he reflects on the aftermath of destruction. Jer-

[19]Anthony Pinn, *Why Lord? Suffering and Evil in Black Theology* (New York: Continuum, 1995), p. 32.
[20]Ibid., p. 23.
[21]Zanfagna, "Under the Blasphemous (W)rap," pp. 2-5.

emiah wants God to vindicate him (15:15-16).[22] Kathleen O'Connor sees the confessions of Jeremiah as "prayers for people mired in loss and play[ing] a major role in the theological and spiritual process of healing."[23] Jeremiah is quite open with his issues and brings them before God (see chapter 11). But what is more interesting about Jeremiah is that he is able to connect with Hip Hop's suffering contexts one and five; Jeremiah wants God to take out his enemies:

> But, O LORD Almighty, you who judge righteously
> and test the heart and mind,
> let me see your vengeance upon them,
> for to you I have committed my cause.

O'Connor states, "The confessions portray Jeremiah as a character with strong confidence in his own understanding of his suffering and with trust in his power to name and influence his relationship with God."[24] Still, by chapter 12 we see the prophet struggling with God's dealing with the "wicked." In Jeremiah 12:1 we actually see Jeremiah questioning the justice of God:

> You are always righteous, O LORD,
> when I bring a case before you.
> Yet I would speak with you about your justice:
> Why does the way of the wicked prosper?
> Why do all the faithless live at ease?

Most pastors would condemn Hip Hoppers for such a straight-

---

[22]This is similar when Hip Hoppers want justice in their communities but find none.
[23]O'Connor, "Lamenting Back to Life," p. 34.
[24]Ibid., p. 40. O'Connor also suggests that the prayer in Jeremiah 11 is a form of "deceptive flattery." "[Jeremiah] names God as one upon whom he can rely, one who will even the scales against his enemies because of their mutual relationship of devotion and absolute loyalty. But this is a set up, an ironic claim that Jeremiah contradicts immediately" (ibid., p. 40). In the following chapter Jeremiah feels hopeless because "no matter what he says, God will claim to be in the right. He cries out to a God who is beyond reach, unavailable, indifferent to human testimony even from the chosen servant" (ibid., p. 40). This type of flattery, deception, and ensuing contradictions are no different for Hip Hoppers or any other God-fearing human as well—they are part of a healthy Christ-following relationship.

forward confrontation of God, yet Jeremiah gets a free pass.[25] O'Connor sees the prophet's question emerging out of "his decision to challenge God's management of the world, a decision he arrives at from observing how the wicked prosper and the treacherous flourish."[26] This very human question of God's methods and motives is in fact a healthy spiritual discipline; O'Connor recognizes that such complaints "keep communication with God alive in the midst of destruction and despair."[27] In that respect Hip Hoppers, through the art that emerges out of the five suffering contexts mentioned earlier, are providing a forum for serious spiritual reflection.

Another significant story of suffering is found in the book of Job. Many scholars have had trouble interpreting the complex matrix of meanings in Job regarding suffering, pain, human affliction and God's response. Two questions dominate in the Hip Hop context: Why would God stand by and allow all of these afflictions to fall upon Job? And if God is all powerful and wise, why does he allow people like Job to complain for so long (in Job's case, thirty-eight chapters) before stepping in?

Liberation theologian Gustavo Gutiérrez reads Job and raises some important questions regarding human suffering and the nature of God.

> Can human beings have a disinterested faith in God—that is, can they believe in God without looking for rewards and fearing punishments? Even more specifically: Are human beings capable, in the midst of unjust suffering, of continuing to assert their faith in God and speak of God without expecting a return? Satan, and with him all those who have a barter conception of religion, deny the possibility.[28]

---

[25]Many of the pastors I interviewed in 2004-2005 suggested that rappers who question the justice of God in light of the prosperity of the wicked were "complaining and whining" and should instead concentrate on "praising God."

[26]O'Connor, "Lamenting Back to Life," pp. 40-41.

[27]Ibid., p. 34.

[28]Gustavo Gutiérrez, *On Job: God-Talk and the Suffering of the Innocent*, trans. Matthew J. O'Connell (Maryknoll, N.Y.: Orbis Books, 1987), p. 1. Gutiérrez makes

If Job had been a rapper, he would have gone platinum after his triumphal return to the stage. Here are the facts:

- Job has all of the riches.
- The devil hates on him.
- The devil takes everything from him.
- Job is in pain.
- His baby-mamma leaves him.
- Job's boys let him down and actually contend that Job is a "sinner" incurring the wrath of God.
- Job lives in the ghetto and complains about it.
- Job does everything but curse God.
- God comes at the final hour and replenishes Job.
- Job's life is restored to ten times greater than before.

Three possible paradigms are applied to Job's context:[29]

1. Suffering is divine retribution. "Job, you must have done something to deserve this!" It is common for many Christians to see suffering in this category.

2. Suffering is divine chastening. "Job, God is going to teach you something important from this." Job's suffering is able to serve the "better good" of humanity and we are able to gain some type of benefit from his suffering.

3. Suffering is only temporary. "Job, you've lost perspective—in the end, everything's going to be all right." Many Black religious traditions subscribe to this paradigm, and thus it becomes easy to minimize pain in the context that it is only "temporary." But what hap-

---

the connection between the book of Job and the Latin struggle. His discussion deals with the language of Job, the Jesus of Job, and how Job's life is not that much different from ours. I agree and would add that the Hip Hop community connects with Gutiérrez's work too.

[29]Adapted from James T. Butler's syllabus for "The Book of Job" (Sacramento, Calif.: Fuller Theological Seminary, 2002).

pens when the suffering is life-long, part of an ongoing social oppression, connected to political tyranny or a consequence of physical disabilities?

While all of these three paradigms can be true at different times, it is too simplistic to narrow down suffering into only these three categories. And yet many churches have done this very thing. So many devotees of Hip Hop culture look outside the church for artists to take up the question and really wrestle with it. Job is a complex book and does not offer any absolute answers in regards to suffering other than to say, it happens to all of us and that it is OK to question, argue, even yell obscenities to God. In the end, the symbolic superstructure asserts, our experiences of suffering give us communion with God.

DEATH AND HIP HOP

While many Christians would claim to have absolute knowledge of what is going to happen to them and their loved ones after they die, there still seems to subsist a wide variety of theologies and philosophies about it. Many people, not just Christians, see death in many different ways. These mechanisms for coping with death carry right over into Hip Hop culture:

- using technology to "flee" or escape from death[30]

- denying death by simply not talking about it[31]

- looking to "solve the riddle" of death in medicine[32]

- using metaphors to deny the reality of death, as when morticians display dead bodies as "sleeping"[33]

---

[30]Elisabeth Kübler-Ross, ed., *Death: The Final Stage* (Englewood Cliffs, N.J.: Prentice-Hall, 1975).

[31]Philippe Aries, *Western Attitudes Toward Death: From the Middle Ages to the Present,* trans. P. M. Ranum (New York: Knopf, 1974).

[32]Sherwin Nuland, *How We Die: Reflections on Life's Final Chapter* (New York: Vintage, 1993).

[33]David Chidester, *Patterns of Transcendence: Religion, Death, and Dying* (Belmont, Calif.: Wadsworth, 1990).

- "removing death as a reality from ordinary experience and creating a 'buffer' between the living and the dead"[34]

Some scholars see race as a factor in how death is perceived. James Perkinson states, "People racialized as 'black,' for instance, give evidence of the highest disease and mortality rates, whereas society's dominant 'white' community lives longest."[35] Writer Amiri Baraka has stated that during slavery days, Black people perceived death as a gateway to freedom, a bridge to a better life. Many street Hip Hoppers tell me that death is just a rite of passage; the afterlife has to be much better than their current existence.

Consequently many rappers welcome death. This itself can be a survival mechanism, however. Peter J. Paris observes that "the practical meaning of life in the midst of the actual experience of suffering and the existential threat of death is the subject matter of survival theology."[36] Such survival mentality gives people hope of another day; death is only the next part to life. Moreover, Elijah Anderson suggests that the cultural "code" of the young person prioritizes respect, honor and power over life—must be adhered to as it relates to death. In other words, "if I gotta die" for respect, "I will"; respect means that much.

Cornel West sees a powerful current of nihilism among youth in the inner city. Some young people have already dismissed life as of no value; consequently, death is welcomed as better than what is in front of them. For other Hip Hoppers, though, death is a mystery. For many it is seen in one of seven ways:

1. a transition into another dimension

2. a place of rest

3. unknown and therefore feared and rarely discussed

---

[34]James Perkinson, "Rap as Wrap and Rapture: North American Popular Culture and the Denial of Death," in *Noise and Spirit: The Religious and Spiritual Sensibilities of Rap Music*, ed. Anthony Pinn (New York: New York University Press, 2003), p. 133.
[35]Ibid.
[36]Peter Paris, *The Spirit of African Peoples* (Minneapolis: Fortress Press, 1995), p. 48.

4. an event that leads to greater enlightenment and consciousness

5. a better place than the current location

6. a chance to commune with God

7. the end—death and nothing more

The most noted rap group to begin a serious discussion on death is Bone Thugs-N-Harmony. Their song "Tha Crossroads" begins with a call to consciousness: a life on the streets will only lead to bad consequences. Moreover, the group asks the all-important question "Whatcha'gon do when you can't run no more?" The first lyric states:

> Let's all bring it in for Wally, Eazy sees uncle Charlie
> Little Boo, God's got him and I'm gonna miss everybody
> I only roll with Bone my gang look to where they lay
> When playing with destiny, plays too deep for me to say
> Lil' Layzie came to me, told me if he should decease well
>   then please
> Bury me by my grand-grand and when you can, come
>   follow me.

Rapper Bizzy's granddad is in heaven. Bizzy wishes to be buried next to him so that they can spend their physical death together. Rapper Layzie continues "Crossroads" with

> God bless you working on a plan to Heaven
> Follow the Lord all 24/7 days, God is who we praise
> even though the devil's all up in my face
> But he keeping me safe and in my place, say grace
> For the case to race with a chance to face the judge
> And I'm guessing my soul won't budge
> Grudge because there's no mercy for thugs
> Oh what can I do it's all about our family and how we roll
> Can I get a witness let it unfold
> We living our lives to eternal our soul aye-oh-aye-oh.[37]

---

[37]Bone Thugs-N-Harmony, "Tha Crossroads," from the album *E. 1999 Eternal* (1995).

Here Layzie encourages his listeners to have a relationship with God, to work on their "plan" for entry into heaven and to see death as only a gate into another dimension. The video to this song brings the lyrics alive. Beginning with a Black funeral in a church, we see grieved parents sitting in front of a church, when all of a sudden a man wearing black leather comes down the front of the aisle. Only the mother of the lost one sees him. The man dressed in black—presumed initially to be death itself—lifts the spirit of the young man out of the casket and carries him out. The mom is beside herself, and yet with one glance from death, she stops yelling and crying. All of this is taking place while the song "Mary Don't You Weep" is being sung—an old Negro spiritual sung during death ceremonies.

Initially, we are not sure the intentions of this ominous figure. The video continues showing death taking lives, one by one, as the artists continue asking the question of all Hip Hoppers: "What-cha'gon do when you can't run no more?" He even takes a baby, much to the protest of its parents. The crossroads only becomes more apparent near the end of the video. We see death going up a long mountain; following him are the souls of the people he has touched—all silhouetted in white. (In this group is the groundbreaking rapper Eazy-E, who died not long after the original release of "Tha Crossroads.") At the top, Bone Thugs-N-Harmony are singing, bearing witness to death bringing up all of these souls. The video then shows that death is not all that scary; still carrying the baby he took, the man drops his black jacket, revealing his wings and then leading people to heaven.

Bone Thugs-N-Harmony here contend that we will meet our loved ones at the crossroads and wind up in a better place. This is just one rap group's rendition of what death and heaven might actually be like. Different artists will have different interpretations.

In Hip Hop, everything is contextualized. Death is valued, feared and even glamorized in the ghetto. Dyson writes:

> The sheer repetition of death has caused black youth to execute
> funeral plans. In its response to death, black youth have reversed

perhaps the emblematic expression of self-aware black morality. Martin Luther King Jr.'s cry that "every now and then I think about my own death." They think about it constantly and creatively. With astonishing clinical detachment, black youth enliven King's claim that he didn't contemplate his death "in a morbid sense." They accept the bleak inevitability of death's imminent swoop—which, in truth, is a rejection of the arbitrariness we all face, since death to these youth is viewed as the condition, not the culmination, of their existence. Black youth tell funeral directors to portray their dead bodies with a style that may defeat their being forgotten and that distinguish them from the next corpse.[38]

In his song "Death on Every Corner," Tupac depicts death as a regular event in the ghetto:

I see death around the corner, gotta stay high while I survive
In the city where the skinny niggas die
If they bury me, bury me as a G nigga, no need to worry
I expect retaliation in a hurry
I see death around the corner, any day
Tryin to keep it together, no one lives forever anyway
Strugglin and strivin, my destiny's to die
Keep my finger on the trigger, no mercy in my eyes.[39]

Tupac continued to rap about the horrors and pleasures of death. On one track you might have him rapping about the horrible death of a friend, while on the other he is rapping about the joy of finally being free.

For most Hip Hoppers, death is a time to rest, a time to finally be out of the hell called the ghetto. Tupac states, "Don't feel bad for the people that died, Feel bad for the folk that gotta stay behind. They the ones still in hell. The person who's dead is now at peace, and in joy,

[38]Dyson, *Holler If You Hear Me*, p. 227.
[39]Tupac Shakur, "Death on Every Corner," from the album *Me Against the World* (1995).

finally resting."[40]

This is one of the many reasons why Hip Hoppers have a hard time letting go of a rapper like Tupac. When I lecture on Tupac, the two most common questions I get are "Do you think Tupac is in Heaven?" and "Do you think Tupac is still alive?" Eazy-E, Biggie, Left-Eye, Aaliyah and others were all revered, but Tupac stands out. His prophetic voice and ability to connect to the despicable, depraved, immoral, disreputable elements of life have made Tupac both a spiritual icon and a prophet for his generation. Tupac even called himself an urban missionary, claiming that while Jesse Jackson was up at the White House, he was actually being a "reverend" to the 'hood. Many want to believe Tupac is still alive and in Jamaica somewhere, in part because Tupac is seen as someone able to identify with their suffering and pain, someone who actually experienced the same thing they were experiencing; someone who could connect them with God and Christ; someone who could see into future events and speak into lives through his music.

Tupac's canonization notwithstanding, death for rappers typically is thought of as the "final event." Christina Zanfagna states, "Unlike Biggie Smalls and Mobb Deep, AZ (and Nas as well) does not necessarily see death as the gateway to spiritual liberation. Rebuking the possibility of an afterlife, he must take his pleasures in the material world and get 'high' before he goes below."[41] So the immediate takes priority, because the afterlife is the end. Death is the final frontier and must be respected, even venerated. Record companies take on names like "Death-Row"; words like "Immortal" get their fair treatment and open discussion.

JESUS' CONNECTION TO HIP HOP'S SUFFERING

Jesus' life—and the theme of suffering running throughout—serves as a connection point to Hip Hop culture. Jesus, for example, had a baby-mamma. An unmarried woman with child could only mean one

---

[40]Shakur et al., *Tupac: Resurrection*, p. 80.
[41]Zanfagna, "Under the Blasphemous (W)rap," p. 6.

thing—someone's been dippin' in the field! I have often had to run intercession between fathers and their pregnant daughters. Those are rough times, and they would have been rough for Mary as well. Jesus was conceived in all spiritual righteousness, but the societal implications were scandalous. One can only imagine the amount of gossip that took place during that time. Joseph would have been, in Hip Hop language, straight trippin' with Mary when he heard that she was pregnant. What are people going to say? How was Joseph to maintain his reputation in the community with a wife that was pregnant before they were married? It took a prophetic dream to convince Joseph that Mary was OK to marry (Matthew 1:18-25).

Beyond the conditions of his birth, Jesus did not have a good relationship with the officials of his time, a point that many Hip Hoppers can relate to. Rev. Al Sharpton did a Christmas skit on *Saturday Night Live* where he and two other actors played the Wise Men, making their way by camel to visit the infant Jesus; they were pulled over by Roman soldiers for "Driving While Black." This is just one example of Hip Hop identification with Jesus' story as it relates to the authorities. The Gospels are full of identifiable stories. In fact, the chief—King Herod—tried to have him killed as a baby. "A king of the Jews? Not in my 'hood!" bellowed Herod. As an adult, Jesus had to contend with haters challenging him on all kinds of matters, including who to pay taxes to (Matthew 22:15-22). Never at a loss for words, Jesus called them out using a word that carried much weight during his day: *hupokrinomai*, or "hypocrite." In Jesus' day, this word was considered graphic, profane. We do not typically think of Jesus having a "foul mouth," yet we find Jesus several times using profane language for his context (more on this in chapter six).

When Hip Hoppers find out that Jesus was a "rebel" within his context, Jesus' image goes up five notches.[42] Some of his most pointed,

---

[42]This is, partly, because the image of Jesus has been primarily seen as soft, timid, "turn the other cheek." For others still, this is because Jesus has been painted as a White person who is so "holy" one cannot reach him without following strict rules laid out by people who have little to no understanding of how Hip Hoppers are.

direct and harsh language was directed toward religious people. In John 2:13-20 we find Jesus in Jerusalem during the Passover. Finding the temple being defiled, Jesus goes off. He creates a "scourge of cords" that he uses to "drive out" people selling items in the temple. Several commentaries note that this whip Jesus made was part of the Roman tradition to publicly punish people. Could you imagine if this had been someone from the Hip Hop community doing the same thing? Couldn't Jesus have just spoken with these people? Did he have to overturn tables and whip people? After all, violence only begets violence.

Many Christians would not even dream of putting forth such questions about Jesus, yet rappers like DMX are held in contempt of Christ for even thinking about it. Could it be that some Hip Hoppers who have been labeled "profane" might in fact have godly motives for their words and actions?

This hints at another point of identification between Jesus and the Hip Hop community. The church of Jesus' day did not understand or relate to him. Likewise, KRS-One has said that often the Christian church has not understood Hip Hop. Many rappers like Immortal Technique are shunned by churchgoers because of his illicit and very graphic lyrics. Many Christians see KRS-One as a "new ager" and one who is "not representing Christ very well."[43] Jack Miles gives an excellent treaty of Jesus as a "crisis in the life of God"—a blasphemer in his context and time period, in the eyes of religious officials. Jesus flagrantly violated the Sabbath,[44] refused to condemn an adulteress[45] and gave new commandments such as kindness to strangers.[46] Jesus was thus a problem and a theological paradox—something to consider as we look at contemporary prophetic artists like Tupac.

One of the key elements of Hip Hop culture is loyalty, and so one of Jesus' boyz (Judas) doing him in is particularly scandalous to the Hip Hop community. Jesus predicted this betrayal several times. In

---

[43]Quotes taken from my interviews with people in the church.
[44]Jack Miles, *Christ: A Crisis in the Life of God* (New York: Knopf, 2001), pp. 145-47.
[45]Ibid., pp. 152-59.
[46]Ibid., pp. 178-84.

John 6:70-71 we find many of Jesus' disciples leaving him because his message was too much to handle; Jesus asks the Twelve if they too will leave. Simon Peter replies by asking a question, "Where will we go? You are who we follow!" to which Jesus replies: "Have I not chosen you, the Twelve? Yet one of you is a devil!" The text goes on to indicate that Jesus was speaking specifically about Judas. Most people would have taken out Judas right there. But Jesus suffered with Judas even longer, all the while knowing what his intentions were. Jesus would have even forgiven Judas if Judas would have had the sense to look beyond himself.

Given his experiences of disloyalty, most notably with Judas, Jesus is able to relate to those who have been betrayed by people close to them, such as Hip Hoppers who have had loyalties broken by crewmembers. Moreover, Jesus died on a cross for all of humanity, so Hip Hop artists, while not rising to the level of atonement, can see in Jesus a point of identification in his suffering at the hands of others for something he's doing for them.

In Jesus' day, crucifixions were for people whom the Romans wanted to make an example of, or for the hardened criminal who deserved such a harsh sentence. Jürgen Moltmann states:

> According to Roman law, execution through crucifixion was the punishment designed to deter against the political order of the Roman empire, or the social order of the Roman slave-owning society. Jesus was publicly executed together with two Jewish insurgents, who had been arrested for revolt.[47]

To see Jesus up there might have caused some confusion for those who had thought he was going to save the world. Even the disciples doubted Jesus' mission. In Luke 24 we find two such disciples walking with the resurrected Jesus, unaware that it was him (v. 16), talking about how they had "hoped" Jesus would have been the redeemer of Israel (v. 21). Jesus then has to break down for the

[47]Moltmann, *Way of Jesus Christ*, p. 163.

disciples what his suffering really meant:

> He said to them, "How foolish you are, and how slow of heart to believe all that the prophets have spoken! Did not the Christ have to suffer these things and then enter his glory?" And beginning with Moses and all the Prophets, he explained to them what was said in all the Scriptures concerning himself. (Luke 24:25-27)

For Hip Hoppers, this means Jesus not only knows about pain, suffering and death; he can actually be with you in the process of all of it. Jesus is both a divine person in whom we can confide in, and also someone who was "flesh" and "human" who suffered as the writer of Hebrews exclaims:

> Therefore, since we have a great high priest who has gone through the heavens, Jesus the Son of God, let us hold firmly to the faith we profess. For we do not have a high priest who is unable to sympathize with our weaknesses, but we have one who has been tempted in every way, just as we are—yet was without sin. Let us then approach the throne of grace with confidence, so that we may receive mercy and find grace to help us in our time of need. (Hebrews 4:14-16)

The event on the cross connects Jesus with the five contexts of Hip Hop sufferings and thus make him Hip Hop. And yet in Western American culture, suffering is typically seen as resulting from having done something "wrong" in the eyes of God. So to hear a bunch of low-class rappers talking about their pain must suggest that they have brought it on themselves.[48] Carter Heyward argues that suffering originates in two universal areas, the first of which being "the suffering steeped in the unfinishedness of creation."[49] In other words, we all have trials and tribulations that come in different forms. For example, natural disasters are a

---

[48]Of course, this perspective is not applied to events like the September 11, 2001, terrorist attacks. It is hard for many U.S. citizens to admit the country might have some responsibility to bear in the events that led to 9/11.

[49]Carter Heyward, *Saving Jesus from Those Who Are Right: Rethinking What It Means to Be a Christian* (Minneapolis: Fortress Press, 1999), p. 23.

part of an unsettled world. Did the victims of Hurricane Katrina in 2005 "bring on" their own suffering? No, of course not. But they did suffer.

The second kind of suffering Heyward discusses is the "broken-ness of creation."[50] In other words, there are "bad" people in the world and "bad" things will happen to us all if we live long enough. The same crime element that exists in the 'hood also exists in suburbia; suburbia just knows how to "dress it up" better. For Hip Hoppers, and humans in general for that matter, it is hard to understand this element of suffering. One thinks immediately of the old-time question," Why does God let bad things happen?"

Heyward is careful to note that "in real, everyday life [these realms of suffering] are never mutually exclusive. Both are ancient, tenacious realms with roots that reinforce and strengthen each other."[51] Bringing us back to Jesus and the cross, James Cone argues that Jesus had to go to the cross not just for the salvation of humanity but also to connect with the suffering of every person on earth.[52] The prophet Isaiah even proclaims in regards to Jesus:

> He was despised and rejected by men,
> a man of sorrows, and familiar with suffering.
> Like one from whom men hide their faces
> he was despised, and we esteemed him not.
>
> Surely he took up our infirmities
> and carried our sorrows,
> yet we considered him stricken by God,
> smitten by him, and afflicted.
>
> But he was pierced for our transgressions,
> he was crushed for our iniquities;
> the punishment that brought us peace was upon him,
> and by his wounds we are healed. (Isaiah 53:3-5)

---

[50]Ibid., pp. 24-25.
[51]Ibid., p. 23.
[52]James Cone, *God of the Oppressed* (New York: Seabury Press, 1975), pp. 160-61.

James Cone further states:

> Jesus' death was a sacrifice. Thus the reality and the depth of God's presence in human suffering is revealed not only in Jesus' active struggle against suffering during his ministry but especially in his death on the cross. The cross of Jesus reveals the extent of God's involvement in the suffering of the weak. God is not merely sympathetic with the social pain of the poor but becomes totally identified with them in their agony and pain. The pain of the oppressed is God's pain, for God takes their suffering as God's own, thereby freeing them from its ultimate control of their lives. The oppressed do not have to worry about suffering because its power over their lives was defeated by God. God in Christ became the Suffering Servant and thus took the humiliation and suffering of the oppressed into God's own history.[53]

Taken together, the image we then have of Jesus becomes identifiable to 'hood culture.

LISTENING TO THE SPIRITUALITY IN A HIP HOP NARRATIVE OF SUFFERING

While artists like Tupac become the archetype for rap artists seeking to discuss street theology, and rap music dealing with pain and suffering offers community and potential hope for youth seeking solace and identity, well-known pastors like Bishop T. D. Jakes argue that "in the absence of strong unity in our community, these entertaining voices have been mistaken for the messiahs of a generation who has lost their way and desperately needs a compass that directs them beyond a lyric that excites them."[54] Other pastors that I interviewed exclaimed, "Rap represents a generation that is under the judgment of Christ. Sure they suffer; God is trying to get their attention."[55] Others contend that rappers like Tupac represent a "generation that has stomped on God's

---

[53]Ibid., p. 161.
[54]T. D. Jakes, interview with Dyson, *Holler If You Hear Me,* p. 208.
[55]Taken from an interview in 2005.

law and moral authority." One pastor even told me that it is not enough to simply listen to the "pain" of the song; we must move beyond that to the "liberating power of Jesus."[56]

But whose narrative and story is "morally correct"? As Noel Erskine states, are we "circumscribing prophecy"?[57] While I agree that not all rap and Hip Hop culture is "holy" or "sacred," certain rap songs do produce, as Ralph Watkins describes, "a God-conscious awareness . . . defined by explicit referencing to God and Jesus within the context of questions related to the ultimate questions of life and being."[58]

More important, the narrative of suffering is extinguished for the Hip Hop community when pastoral figures devalue its stories of suffering. As Dyson states, such dismissal "slights the initiative and ingenuity of poor black youth who filled a leadership vacuum with artistic expression."[59] If we are to follow strict religious paradigms for spirituality and the search for God, then we run the risk of losing an entire generation.

Bishop Jakes and the many other pastors that I interviewed are not completely incorrect. We do have to critically evaluate the message of rappers, along with being able to decisively assess the differences between sheer entertainment and christological worth—particularly during this party/strip-club rap era. Yet, as Dyson argues, there are countless sacred narratives that are hardly distinguishable from rap.[60] From Jeremiah to Jonah, the Psalms, Job, Paul, and even Jesus, "we must not forget that unpopular and unacceptable views are sometimes later regarded as prophetic."[61]

---

[56]Taken from an interview in 2005.

[57]Noel Erskine, "Rap, Reggae and Religion," in Noise and Spirit: The Religious and Spiritual Sensibilities of Rap Music, ed. Anthony Pinn (New York: New York University Press, 2003), p. 79.

[58]Ralph Watkins, "Rap, Religion and New Realities: The Emergence of a Religious Discourse in Rap Music," in Noise and Spirit: The Religious and Spiritual Sensibilities of Rap Music, ed. Anthony Pinn (New York: New York University Press, 2003), p. 185.

[59]Dyson, Holler If You Hear Me, p. 208.

[60]Ibid., pp. 208-9.

[61]Ibid., p. 209.

What is the pain and suffering being felt by a particular rapper or community? Does it have merit? Is it just complaining? Even if so, is the complaining valid? These are just some of the questions I pose when listening to rap songs. Listening, for many Christians, means waiting for an end to a person's monologue before offering advice. The Hip Hoppers I have interviewed all agreed that what they needed was not pity, advice or even a solution—just someone to listen. Far too many times the suffering and pain of each person was whittled away by simplistic resolutions and belittling comments. One interviewee told me, "Christians are the worst! They never listen, they always too busy wantin' to give you answers fo everythin' man. I just don' need that all the time, you know what I mean? I just need someone to listen to me, ya know what I'm sayin'? that's for real."[62]

Hip Hop's theology of suffering brings about self-awareness and restoration within a person.[63] If we are able to listen to the pain in these narratives, we may actually learn something from it and actually take away a deeper understanding of the person telling us about it. But we must remain quiet long enough to actually grasp something from another person's experience. One thing Hip Hoppers will not stand for very long is inauthentic gestures and demeaning suggestions.

I suggest we begin connecting with the symbolic superstructure of suffering within the Hip Hop matrix. It is deep. It is complex. It is a sea of mystery that can easily overwhelm. However, it is also a part of the narrative of Hip Hop, and therefore part of the narrative of Christ.

---

[62]Taken from an interview in 2006.
[63]Efrem Smith and Phil Jackson, *The Hip Hop Church: Connecting with the Movement Shaping Our Culture* (Downers Grove, Ill.: InterVarsity Press, 2005), pp. 118-21.

4

Where Are My Dawgs At?

A THEOLOGY OF COMMUNITY

When I was in high school, my mom and I lived in a cramped one-bedroom apartment. The place was just large enough to accommodate my twenty-two pound cat, Milo, and us. It was one of those apartments where you had to go through the bedroom to get to the bathroom; and we shared the one bedroom, so I would often wake her up.

If I had more than three people over, there was simply no room for them to sit down. We were the last apartment on the west side of the building, so we could make some noise and not have to worry about neighbors complaining, but they did anyway. Because my friends had to take the stairs to get to the apartment, everyone would know when they were coming; they had the uncanny habit of stomping up every stair to notify me of their arrival.

Saturday nights were the time to connect with friends and extended family. We would reflect together on the previous week, social conditions, politics, relationships, economics and, of course, Hip Hop. We were an eclectic, multiracial group: my friend Sam was Filipino; my friend Ali was Black mixed with some Caribbean and Native American; my friend Kavicka was a mix of Irish and Scottish; Nancy was Korean and White; Wha King was Nigerian and Black; Rob was

Korean and Black; Cherie was Black and Chinese; Shawn was Black. And I was, and still am, Black and Mexican. Saturday nights were a time of community for all of us.

For three years it was a day that we would all rarely miss. We would meet at my place soon after sunset. If the mood was right, we would just chill out and watch movies or listen to music. But often we would pile into Sam's GMC Astro van and take a ride down to the boardwalk. Sometimes we would terrorize tourists.

The boardwalk in the Monterey Bay was not your typical multicultural fair. It was quite often filled with people who looked at us as lowlifes. So one day Sam decided that we should play into that stereotype. He suggested that while walking down the street as a group, we should all simultaneously and aggressively reach into our jacket pockets when passing tourists to give them "something to talk about." This worked like a charm. As we passed unsuspecting tourists in a group, we would all reach into our jacket pockets and give them quite a fright. We would then, of course, walk away laughing as if to say, "See, not all of us are criminals."

I know, I know. We could have spent our time a lot better, but hey, I was a teenager. A lot of us do crazy things when we are that age.

One of the biggest opponents to my hanging with this community was my church community. At the time I was attending a church youth group, and the people in the group called my friends "bad influences," "bad seeds" and "sinners." Why would a Christian hang out with such people?

At first, I tried to hide the fact that I was hanging around my friends. But when I blew off youth group to go with my friends on Saturday night, I would typically get caught at the bowling alley or boardwalk. My church community did not understand my relationship with my friends. It was rare that my friends would negatively talk about my church community, but my church saw my relationship with them as not "glorifying God." My church community even tried an intervention with me to "cast out" the spirit of the world. When I would go through rough times, my church community would often blame my friends as the cause of those problems; meanwhile, my friends would provide communal support for me.

My church group would constantly talk with my mom, trying to get her to make me leave my friends. That did not work either. Saturday nights would come, and we would do our same routine much to the disapproval of my church community. Sure, my friends were not perfect. Sure, my friends and I did some things that bent one or two laws. And sure, my friends and I were not always "pure." My friends and I would also get into arguments; it was not as if our relationships were perfect. But that is what you do in community: live life together. And more important, they were more church to me than my church was.

The number one argument that my church community had about my friends and I was the fact we all listened to rap music. Rap, in the church's eyes, was evil and needed to be avoided at all costs. It was of the world and had no part in the church. At the time, Ice Cube's first solo album, *AmeriKKKa's Most Wanted*, had dropped. The language alone was enough to convict me of sin in my church's eyes.

I wish there could have been more congruity between my church community and my friends. I think there were a lot of opportunities for both groups to learn from each other. Moreover, from a youth pastor's perspective, there was a huge opportunity to minister to not only one student but a whole tight-knit group. Instead, the church decided to build walls between us and God. God was made out, by the church, to not care for us unless we were all dressed up, spoke right, never used foul language and followed every commandment in the Bible—including some Levitical codes.

Those were the days though. It was. The late 1980s and early 1990s were a great time for Hip Hop. Hip Hop was in its teens and having fun. Hip Hop was being defined and redefined, including its understanding of community. Space and place are fundamental elements for Hip Hop. Street names, area codes and city names provide the Hip Hop community meaning, identity and community in an environment that has vastly left them unknown.

Theologically speaking, community is everything. Most Bible stories happen in the context of community. Even Jesus' birth took place in a communal setting. Salvation happens in community and with people. Western Eurocentric theology has given us a more individualistic view of salvation and community,[1] but the idea that we can "do it by ourselves" and "pull ourselves up by our own bootstraps" not only undermines the gospel, it is practically impossible. Yet many churches continue to insist that we can go at salvation, missions, evangelism and our personal walk with Jesus without a supporting community.

For Hip Hoppers, life is done in community. Whether those communities are small, large, medium, one or two people, sixty or one hundred, community is still occurring. Church happens in that community; the presence of God is not only felt but experienced.

SPACE, PLACE AND IDENTITY WITHIN HIP HOP

Community happens in spaces. Spaces have places. And within those spaces and places there is a thing called identity.

Identity helps to shape who we are. Identity refers to the reflective self-conception or self-image that we derive from family, gender, cultural, ethnic and individual experiences during multiple and complex socialization processes. There are several forms of identity, including

- social identity

- personal identity

- ethnic identity

- cultural identity

Identity in community therefore takes on many different shapes. How our social construction of identity is realized will influence how we interact with different spaces and the people within those spaces.

---

[1]See John William Drane, *The McDonaldization of the Church: Consumer Culture and the Church's Future* (Macon, Ga.: Smyth & Helwys, 2001); Zygmunt Bauman, *Liquid Modernity* (Malden, Mass.: Polity Press, 2000).

For example, if we were brought up in a conservative evangelical Christian home, our parents may have taught us that the world outside the house is "sinful" and "wicked." Our friends may have reinforced that belief, as did the media outlets we used. Our pastor may have confirmed that the "world" is in fact scary and should be avoided; our educational systems may also have supported that conviction. Our social construction of identity would thus tend toward social anxiety. We might avoid conflict at all costs, have passive-aggressive tendencies, see the world through only one or two lenses, restrict our socialization to people of "our own kind," see "the world" as needing "salvation," and view "strangers" as potential enemies and/or threats.

Meanwhile theologians such as Harvey Cox or Ray Bakke would argue that "for the urban Christian and pastor there can be no throwaway real estate because 'The earth is the Lord's, and everything in it' (Ps 24:1), and that includes every 'hood."[2] Any number of places are rendered sacred for Hip Hoppers—places where Jesus "shows up"—including

- concerts
- spoken-word event venues
- recorded rap music
- dancing
- small groups
- battle raps

Murray Forman observes that in Hip Hop "space is a dominant concern, occupying a central role in the definition of value, meaning, and practice":

A highly detailed and consciously defined spatial awareness is one of the key factors distinguishing rap music and hip-hop

---

[2]Ray Bakke, *The Urban Christian* (Downers Grove, Ill.: InterVarsity Press, 1987), p. 63.

from the many other cultural and subcultural youth formations currently vying for popular attention.[3]

When I lived in the Monterey Bay area, many of my friends had t-shirts featuring the area code "408" as well as having it tattooed on their arms, legs, neck, stomach and other body parts. When the silicon revolution hit during the early 1990s and everyone began getting multiple phone lines, the area code for our area changed from 408 to 831. But even when those area codes changed, people were still identifying themselves with 408. It was not about the "change" or even the physical numerical code. It was about space and place and the identity that ensues with that. Geraldine Pratt writes, however, that identity is also created by crossing boundaries into different spaces, producing a sharpened sense of consciousness; social inequalities become "visible through travel," as when one goes from the 'hood into a suburban space.[4] Imani Perry contends that "good music often has a beauty identifiable across the boundaries of nation and culture. And yet a musical composition, and musical forms in general, have identities rooted in community." Thus Hip Hop's suburban audience grows, yet Hip Hop retains an urban identity.[5]

---

[3]Murray Forman, *The 'Hood Comes First: Race, Space, and Place in Rap and Hip-Hop, Music/Culture* (Middletown, Conn.: Wesleyan University Press, 2002), p. 3. The dimensions of this book restrain me from going deeper into the complex, multifaceted, yet intriguing conversation regard spatial awareness. Forman argues that space takes on several elements including apparatus domination, hegemonic order and the bounding of subjects within that space (pp. 1-34). For further insight see Henri Lefebvre (*The Production of Space* [Oxford: Basil Blackwell,1991], pp. 24-26) as he discusses how space is "produced." David Harvey ("From Space to Place and Back Again: Reflections on the Condition of Postmodernity," in *Mapping the Futures: Local Cultures, Global Change*, ed. J. Bird, B. Curtis, T. Putnam, G. Robertson and L. Tickner [New York: Routledge, 1993]) concludes that spaces can be used for power and manipulation, and Harvey Cox (*The Secular City: A Celebration of Its Liberties and an Invitation to Its Discipline* [New York: Macmillan, 1965]) details the complexity of urban space and how spirituality exists in many of those places.

[4]Geraldine Pratt, "Grids of Difference," in *Cultural Studies: An Anthology*, ed. M. Ryan and H. Musiol (Malden, Mass.: Blackwell, 2008), p. 158. Bell hooks (*Yearning: Race, Gender, and Cultural Politics* [Toronto: Between The Lines, 1990]) agrees with Pratt's assessment.

[5]Cf. Imani Perry, *Prophets of the Hood: Politics and Poetics in Hip Hop* (Durham, N.C.:

Space in the 'hood is very important. Gangs set their territory by space. Families relegate themselves to a certain square mile and never leave that space. Urban neighborhoods are "sectioned" off by city officials, and rap artists identify themselves with the "space" they are from.[6] In the film *8 Mile*, characters were distinguished and categorized by which area code they were from. B-Rabbit (played by Eminem) calls out Papa Doc by showing that he was from an area code that had nothing to do with the 'hood. Tupac was known for his upbringing in Marin City, California, an area known for being "hard" and "mean." Compton became an important identifier in the West Coast rap scene with recordings by DJ Quick ("Jus Lyke Compton") and NWA (the album *Straight Outta Compton*).[7]

Anderson contends that respect, a strong part of the code of the streets, has a role in the identity formation of teens within their space.

> Typically in the inner-city poor neighborhood, by the age of ten, children from decent and street oriented families alike are mingling on the neighborhood streets and figuring out their identities. Here they try out roles and scripts in a process that challenges their talents.[8]

Street corners thus become spatial corners in which not only identity formation is taking place, but also socialization skills.[9] It can then be assessed that one becomes a "product of their environment" and the socialization within that environment helps to shape the overall person's identity. With identity so important to the genre, and the genre so conducive to identity formation, Hip Hoppers are often able

---

Duke University Press, 2004), pp. 11, 38-57.

[6]Davarian Baldwin, "Black Empires, White Desires: The Spatial Politics of Identity in the Age of Hip-Hop," in *That's the Joint! The Hip-Hop Studies Reader*, ed. M. Forman and M. A. Neal (New York: Routledge, 2004), p. 160.

[7]Forman, *Hood Comes First*, pp. 193-98.

[8]Elijah Anderson, *Code of the Street: Decency, Violence, and the Moral Life of the Inner City* (New York: W. W. Norton, 1999), p. 68.

[9]Ibid., pp. 69-72.

to identify one another with very little interaction.[10]

Church, therefore, can happen in the unorthodox spaces where Hip Hoppers find themselves and one another: concerts, spoken-word venues, street corners, malls, battle raps or face-to-face conversations become sacred ground, in contrast to the contrived settings of churches using Hip Hop as "bait" or as a novelty act for special events. We can begin to see the postmodern in this concept.[11]

People form their collective identity in a four-ring process I call the spatial identity formation model (see figure 5).

Figure 5. The spatial identity formation model

[10]See Melissa August, Leslie E. Brice, Laird Harrison, Todd Murphy and David Thigpen, "Hip-Hop Nation: There's More to Rap Than Just Rhythms & Rhymes," in *Common Culture: Reading & Writing About American Popular Culture*, ed. M. Petracca and M. Sorapure (Upper Saddle River, N.J.: Prentice Hall, 2001); Raymond D. S. Anderson, *Black Beats for One People; Causes and Effects of Identification with Hip-Hop Culture*, Ph.D. dissertation, (Virginia Beach: Regent University, 2003). For Hip Hoppers, these means of reorganization can be broken down into several categories—relevant, respectful and authentic—as a way of identifying each other within the community of Hip Hop.

[11]Murray Forman discusses that spatial discourse coheres around the concept of the 'hood; this concept is manifested in what is called "Gangsta Rap" or "West Coast" rap. This is an important special element that Forman argues is a pivotal point for Hip Hoppers (*Hood Comes First*, pp. 191-92).

Each sphere represents a different culture, context or social construction, and comes with its own set of cultural patterns and history. There is much overlap in the different spheres. From the center comes our level of spatial identity for whichever social group we are a part of. Several factors influence our level of spatial awareness:

- family dynamics
- family communication
- education
- worldview/take on life
- personal origins
- personal sense of spatiality
- theological training

Total strangers can go to a concert and connect with each other in a way that outsiders will not be able to understand. Spatial identity is why the actor Martin Lawrence coined the now famous term "It's a Black thang, you wouldn't understand!" People in that spatial arena "understand" the statement, while outsiders remain confounded.

IDENTITY AND THE SELF IN THE POST-SOUL HIP HOP WORLD

Identity in the soul era of the 'hood was embedded in public figures such as Martin Luther King, Cesar Chavez, the Black Panther Party, Malcolm X, and Angela Davis. They came to define for the soul era what a public figure "should" be. For the post-soul urbanite, however, identity takes on different dimensions. Todd Boyd argues that Hip Hop culture is this current generation's Civil Rights Movement, their voice and vehicle to the public sphere. "Hip-hop has always placed great worth on making connections to a larger historical sense of the culture, thus the lofty status accorded to the idea of an 'old school.'"[12]

---

[12]Todd Boyd, *The H.N.I.C.: The Death of Civil Rights and the Reign of Hip Hop* (New York: New York University Press, 2003), p. 124.

If the city was the catapult of modernism, as suggested by Scott Lash, then the city has been the catapult for the postmodern, post-soul era.[13] Ghetto values continue to be marketed to the masses. Baggy pants, initially a ghetto style, originated when released prisoners would keep their oversized prison outfits, because they could store a great deal of concealed objects. Baggy pants made their way into stores like the Gap and the Limited. Now, almost anyone can identify themselves with the "Loose Fit."

Drive down Slauson or Vernon Avenue in L.A. You will see a mural of graffiti art that identifies one's name, ranking, talent and position in society. In the film *Wild Style*, artists would sit in a certain corner of the Bronx just to watch the subway train go by so that they could see their name, art, and new artists pass them by on the train.[14] Graffiti was introduced to Los Angeles through the movies *Wild Style, Beat Street* and *Style Wars*. Lacking the New York subways, the L.A. answer was to "bomb" or paint freeways and use empty lots as outdoor studios with rotating exhibits of wildstyle pieces.[15]

The modern mind saw "broken English" as deviant and "bad." But with the rise of Hip Hop culture and music, the language of the ghetto has made its way into everyday conversation.[16] Twenty years ago it was uncommon for a White man to say, "You go girl!" But in postmodern America, it is common. Table 3 shows the evolution of terms

[13]Scott Lash, "Postmodernism as Humanism? Urban Space and Social Theory," in *Theories of Modernity and Postmodernity*, ed. B. S. Turner (Thousand Oaks, Calif.: Sage Publications, 1990), p. 31.

[14]Tricia Rose, "A Style Nobody Can Deal With: Politics, Style, and the Postindustrial City in Hip Hop," in *Microphone Friends: Youth Music and Youth Culture*, ed. A. Ross and T. Rose (New York: Routledge, 1994), p. 101. Often, Graffiti artists use nicknames and/or aliases because public graffiti is illegal and no one really wants to be caught. Urban pseudonyms such as Snoop Dogg, Ice Cube, Ice-T, and even Dr. Dre cover up formal names such as Clarence, Calvin, and Andreas.

[15]Ruben Martinez, "Going Up in L.A.," *LA Weekly*, February 5, 1998 <www.laweekly.com/1998-02-05/news/going-up-in-l-a/>.

[16]Cf. Russell Potter's discussion about Hip Hop vernacular and the postmodern revolution in speech (*Spectacular Vernaculars: Hip-Hop and the Politics of Postmodernism* [New York: State University of New York Press, 1995], pp. 55-79).

from the modern to postmodern era.[17] Similarly, the Blaxploitation
films of the 1970s helped make it possible for vulgarities to become
mainstream.

Table 3. Post-Soul Urban Language Differentiations

WORD	SOUL CONTEXT	POST-SOUL CONTEXT
God	Deity	Person (New York Context)
Down	Literal sense	Are you with me?
Love	Marriage/ Family	Sexual
Dub	To make a copy of	Two vowel sounds together or two letters back to back. J-Dub would be Jason Double.
Hood	Head Covering	Community/ Ghetto
Freak	A weird person	Someone who is not only open with sexuality, but is open to the public about it as well
Pimp	Street thug	Someone who dresses nice, got it going on, and has nice things
Pimpin	Street thugs with prostitutes	Living large with money
Jackin	Messing up, using a person	Taking someone else's stuff
22's	Guns	Rims
Hustle	Street thugs	To make money and survive

Soulists like Delores Tucker, Jesse Jackson and Bob Dole had so
much trouble with Hip Hop lyrics because they did not understand
the revised root meaning of such words and could not comprehend
the cultural significance. The postmodern Hip Hopper utilizes micronarratives, not a macronarrative, to make sense of their world.[18]
Hip Hop and the post-soul worldview gives voice to the voiceless, demands justice and gives way to micronarratives for the people; the

---

[17]Language is a primary source of identity in any society. For postmodern urban youth,
how you talk and present that verbal tone, will dictate to them exactly how authentic
you are, and "real" you are about their life and with life in general.
[18]Jean-François Lyotard, *The Postmodern Condition: A Report on Knowledge* (Minneapolis: University of Minnesota Press, 1984), pp. 32-34.

individual urban youth responds to this with open arms.[19] The tribal narrative of the urban post-soul era has the wind at its back and is dominating the contemporary landscape.

Within the soulist worldview, the self then becomes what Stanley Grenz calls "The Self-Focused Self,"[20] a derivative of the Enlightenment that has engulfed parts of the Hip Hop community.

The elevation of individual autonomy in the Enlightenment led to an atomistic understanding of the social realm that viewed the individual as the source of social institutions as well as of society itself. Society, therefore, was a collection of autonomous, independent selves, each of whom pursues his (and sometimes her) own ends, albeit within the context of some overarching wider harmony. . . . The modern self is the self-created and self-sufficient above the vacillations and shifting relationships that characterize day-to-day living.[21]

Some Hip Hoppers feel that in order to "make it" in the business realm, one must be "self-sufficient" and "self-reliant." While part of that is true—to a degree to which if someone has a dream, then they are typically responsible in seeing that dream come true—there is a part of that worldview which leaves out authentic community and separates that individual from societal interactions despite being, as Grenz contended, still in pursuit of the overarching "wider harmony." Thus, though your neighbor might be eight inches away from you, you will not know him or her, because in the city we are to remain anonymous. This is what Zygmunt Bauman describes as strangerdom.

---

[19]Christopher Tyson explores the generation gap between the Civil Rights generation and the Hip Hop generation, suggesting new ideologies of Hip Hop culture and music and how the two generations can mend (*Exploring the Generation Gap and Its Implications on African American Consciousness* [New York: Urban Think Tank, 2001]).

[20]Stanley Grenz, *The Social God and the Relational Self: A Trinitarian Theology of the Imago Dei* (Louisville, Ky.: Westminster John Knox, 2001), p. 99.

[21]Ibid., p. 99.

Strangers are likely to meet in their capacity of strangers, and likely to emerge as strangers from the chance encounter which ends as abruptly as it started. Strangers meet in a fashion that befits strangers; a meeting of strangers is unlike the meetings of kin, friends, or acquaintances—it is, by comparison, a mismeeting. In the meeting of strangers there is no picking up at the point where the last encounter stopped, no filling in on the interim trials and tribulations or joys and delights, no shared recollections: nothing to fall back on and go by in the course of the present encounter.[22]

In such an environment, Bauman recognizes, "loving your neighbor" is made difficult.[23]

Bauman also illustrates the kind of conversation that characterizes urban postmodern industrial community—the talk is small, usually centered on self-autonomous achievement and typically about sex, some new monetary conquest, lifestyle, and/or sports. The conversation is shallow, brief and forgetful: "How are you?" and other American idioms have no substantial meaning. Rap songs are no different: commercial Hip Hop has grown untamed in this consumerist environment.

The commercialization of the Hip Hop community roughly began during the mid to late 1990s when media moguls such as Warner Music Group, NBC and Fox realized that they could make money off urban struggle. Television shows like *New York Undercover, The Martin Lawrence Show, The Fresh Prince of Bel Air* and even *The Cosby Show* made Black culture popular and paved the way to a post-soul industrial community, in which capitalism and globalization have made an impact on the vitality of urban space.[24] There is not a corner in South Central L.A.

[22]Zygmunt Bauman, *Liquid Modernity* (Malden, Mass.: Polity Press, 2000), p. 95. "Strangerdom" refers to the element of unknown human bodies. Your neighbor is eight inches from your head, but you will never know them, because it is the city, and in the city, you must maintain that anonymity.

[23]Zygmunt Bauman, *Liquid Love* (Malden, Mass.: Polity Press, 2003), pp. 77-84.

[24]On another level, such television shows also gave White America front-row seats into the lives of Blacks and the urban community. It is part of the many reasons why

that does not have some type of transglobal trademark. Herbert Schiller suggests that corporate logos are being distributed to youth and teens all around the world, consequently squelching the individual opinion.[25] Production companies in fact manipulate individual opinion in order to make a buck. Community forums are made available for most television shows, films and even rap groups. "Ordinary" people are there free to complain, voice concern, comment on programming and give a piece of their mind to anyone who happens by the site. Ricky Ross, former drug dealer turned community activist, observes that in such an environment, talent and thoughtfulness take a back seat.

> It's all about packaging and marketing. Talent is no longer a requirement. Sources like BET, MTV, MySpace, and others dictate who will make it and who will fail. . . . Now, being the most talented rapper or MC, or even the best producer is no longer important.[26]

Rappers like 50 Cent, Snoop Dogg, Jay Z, Nelly and The Game, by celebrating hedonism rather than exploring the serious sociopolitical trends covered by their predecessors, embody a certain element of this cultural trend. But many Hip Hop moguls, such as Eminem, Ice Cube, Tupac, Dead Prez, Common, KRS-One and Queen Latifah, have continued to cultivate space for authenticity and depth. The Hip Hop soul singer Gina Rae produces a climate at her concerts that evokes a surreal, spiritual experience for the participant and listener. Gina connects with God through song, dance and spoken word, and the spatial identity brings in people that connect not only with Gina but with the larger community of soul Hip Hop and find a Christ transcended in this communal experience.

White kids love Hip Hop (Bakari Kitwana, *Why White Kids Love Hip-Hop: Wankstas, Wiggers, Wannabes, and the New Reality of Race in America* [New York: Basic Civitas, 2005]).

[25]Herbert Schiller, *Culture Inc.: The Corporate Takeover of Public Expression* (New York: Oxford University Press, 1989), p. 124.

[26]Ricky Ross, "The Rise & Fall of the Rapper & Rap Music" <http://freewayenterprise.ning.com/forum/topics/2417957:Topic:144>.

Even within commercial rap, Jesus is still present. He might be packaged up, blinged out, and rolling in an Escalade to be sold to the highest bidder, but nonetheless, he is still present within the industry of Hip Hop community.

THE JESUS OF COMMUNITY IN HIP HOP

Commercialization aside, Hip Hop continues to connect with the poor, downtrodden and marginalized of society. Christologically speaking, this was what Jesus did too. It is what Jürgen Moltmann describes as "the messianic mission of Christ" where Jesus was a person in social relationships.

> As we have seen, Jesus lived in mutual relationships with the poor and the sick, sinners, and the men and women who had been thrust out of society. It was in his reciprocal relationships with the faith of the people concerned that the miracles of the messianic era came about. It was in his reciprocal relationships with the men and women disciples who followed him that Jesus discovered his messianic secret. We have to look more closely at his life in the context of these social relationships, for we can only understand the life-histories of men and women in the light of their relations with other people, and the communities to which they belong.[27]

I find it interesting that Moltmann discusses how we need to get to know Jesus in the context of social relationships. This is a stark difference from the Western individualist gospel message we receive in many of our churches. For Jesus, it was about, as Jack Seymour has put it, finding the "God in the peoples of God."[28] Jesus looked beyond people's flaws and imperfections, entrusting his message to people who would not always get it right, who in fact changed the world in which we live today.

---

[27]Moltmann, *Way of Jesus Christ,* pp. 145-46.
[28]Jack Seymour, "Meeting God in the Peoples of God," *Religious Education* 96, no. 3 (2001): 267-69.

Jesus' social relationships were some of his most important interactions. Many of the valuable lessons Jesus taught were learned in
community. For Hip Hop, it is no different; Hip Hoppers learn, grow,
worship, love, argue and see Jesus through social relationships.

In Mark 3:34 we find Jesus telling his people that whoever does
"his will" is part of his community: "Whoever does God's will is my
brother and sister and mother." In Matthew 12:46 the word *family* is
replaced by *disciples,* but even the process of discipleship was done in
community and among others; the root of the word means "pupil" or
"learner." Further, the word *brothers* in verse 33 can connote connec-
tivity. For Jesus, it meant being connected to him not just in spirit but
in community as well.

Jesus became space, place, and identity for many who did not have
that or could not have it. In Mark 6:33-44 we find Jesus feeding the
multitudes. "When Jesus landed and saw a large crowd, he had compassion on them, because they were like sheep without a shepherd. So
he began teaching them many things." Moltmann asserts that "the
'multitude' are the poor, the homeless, the 'non-persons.' They have
no identity, no voice, no power and no representative."[29] Jesus became
hope and vision for people that had none. It is no surprise when Hip
Hop also becomes this type of christological incubator for many who
are also "harassed," who have been displaced, marginalized or broken by hardships in life.

In Mark 8:34-38, Jesus calls the community to discipleship, encouraging the crowd to follow him and giving the basic plan of salvation.
Jesus becomes our representative as we represent him. For Hip Hop, a
simple rap song or video can be such a representative: the listener or
viewer is able to see in the images or lyrics not just him- or herself but
the community of which he or she is a part. Through this newfound
community in Hip Hop, the struggle of our lives is given greater meaning. "His [Jesus'] 'compassion' is not charitable condescension. It is
the form which the divine justice takes in an unjust world."[30]

---

[29]Moltmann, *Way of Jesus Christ,* p. 148.
[30]Ibid., p. 149.

Moltmann observes Jesus' "reciprocal" relationship with his people. Jesus' life was constructed around that reciprocity. He was not concerned with making himself look good; he was about the other person—not just building them up but building his gospel in them. While Hip Hop is not an end to salvation, it does provide a similar reciprocity that builds people up, helps its members out and points to Jesus through creative forms within its art. Hence, Hip Hop is like Jesus to many urban post-soulists. So those of us who want urban post-soulists to know Jesus, need to know Hip Hop.

What becomes problematic for some Christians is the notion that Jesus would even be in places like a club, rap concert, and/or event that was not centered around some church. Some Christians cannot see beyond the four church walls and the programs that run it. So, finding Jesus in these irregular and nontraditional places will be hard to understand. Still, even in these nontraditional spaces, community is happening. And, if we really believe that God is Alpha and Omega, omnipresent, "all-seeing," might Jesus be in that smoke-filled strip club trying to talk to the inhabitants there?

Jesus did not avoid these tough problems engaging community. He knew that within community nothing is perfect. Community within Hip Hop is not some utopian place where everyone gets along and hugs each other until they are blue in the face. The Hip Hop community has arguments, fights, loves, hates, despises, embraces, encourages and lifts up. The Hip Hop community is real and transparent, but in that community there exists the ability to grow with others and learn from others. Jesus' community during his time was no different. Jesus' world was not utopian either, but many Christians are simply unable to see that aspect of Jesus' community. We continue to want a G-rated savior in an NC-17 world.

Being able to interpret, comprehend, analyze, and then digest messages is all part of the ever-important skill of listening. It is not always easy—particularly when certain elements of Hip Hop are loud, vulgar and oversexualized, or when they tear down people and exhibit extreme pride or lust. I can understand why so many "church folk" find rap offensive and just ugly to listen to. I really do. Listening in those types of situations is not an easy task. Still, when I find myself offended and/or my own levels of indignation rising, I ask myself, *Am I missing anything here? Could God be speaking in the midst of all of this?* More important, I ask how I can engage this community that seems to think, feel, believe, and act this way in which I do not approve of. That, for me at least, is the basis for listening to the very important messages given within the Hip Hop community. Often I find myself coming away with newfound knowledge.

Many parts of Hip Hop's community are infused with spirituality. Dance, a great social connector in Hip Hop, can relieve stress, tell a story, detail people's struggles and open minds to new understandings of life. In the 1980s, crews would come together at community centers to battle out their differences on linoleum dance floors. Each crew member would take turns trying to show the other crew up. A winner would be determined and granted bragging rights. Rarely did the issues go beyond the dance floor. After spending three to four hours dancing, you are too tired to fight. Most members would simply go home to prepare for the next day's battle.

Many Hip Hoppers, thanks to cultural factors such as the latchkey revolution and the urban crisis generated during the Reagan presidency, come from less than ideal living situations and need a lot of support; the communities they discover in Hip Hop do that for them. For about 75 percent of my interviewees, the community they found in Hip Hop culture provided them with

- shelter from the elements of life
- companionship for life's daily struggles
- comedic relief chiefly in times of dire problems
- familial bonds, especially for those who were living without strong parental figures
- rich and deep historical context
- a social map when times got a little confusing

• sounding boards for life decisions

Interviewees who reported this type of communal support were more focused, better able to deal with life's problems, had a better ability to integrate their lives into other social situations, could better articulate their needs, and indicated that they felt connected, respected and grounded, which left them with an overall better self-esteem and self-efficacy.

The remaining 25 percent of interview subjects, who did not have strong experiences of community, displayed the following characteristics:

• were less focused

• often felt friendless, left out, forgotten by the world

• indicated feelings of hostility, anger and hatred

• could not articulate their needs as well

• were not able to deal well with sudden change

The importance of meaningful relationship is obvious. And with its emphasis on space, place and identity, Hip Hop culture has shown itself to be more relational in its theology than the conventional church. Carter Heyward suggests:

> Relational theology should be understood as a metaphysics that is built not merely on speculation but on *experiencing* one another, including the earth and other creatures in the course of our daily lives, work, and love. At the same time, relational theology must be a theo-ethics of *liberation*. It is about *noticing* the real world—our loveliness and pathos, our interconnectedness and fragmentation—and it is about *changing* this world.[31]

Heyward's observations here are central to Hip Hop's theology of community: This is where Jesus shows up. This is where growth in Christ is gained. This is where all of life intersects—the good, the bad

---

[31]Carter Heyward, *Saving Jesus from Those Who Are Right: Rethinking What It Means to Be a Christian* (Minneapolis: Fortress Press, 1999), p. 64.

and the ugly. A community of experiencing one another is a community that is not only biblical but christological.

Martin Buber asserts that true communication is "experiencing the other side."[32] We must experience someone else to truly commune. We do not experience Hip Hop in order to conquer it; we encounter Hip Hop as we enter into relationship with Hip Hop people.

In the film *8-Mile*, the main focus of community for everyone living in the cold, miserable, dejected part of inner-city Detroit was a place called the Shelter. Established in the basement of a church, the Shelter nevertheless wasn't populated by "nice," smooth and charming Christians. By the end of the film, infused with profanity and featuring gratuitous partial nudity from Eminem, we learn that in the end, you really are what you are. Eminem's self-acceptance, and the crowd's embrace of his true self, took place within the sacred place of the Shelter.

Most Christians find the authenticity so prized in the Hip Hop community hard to swallow. Many ministries doing work with Hip Hoppers thus enter into a process of "pookizing" the people they work with—telling a sanitized version of their story for an outside (and funding) audience, thus capitalizing on their identity and profiting from the caricature. Pookizing destroys authentic community, highlighting the "salvation" reel while downplaying the larger context of a life, and showcasing the ministry rather than building up the person. If we are to listen to the communal story of Hip Hop, then we must be ready to, as Buber suggests, "seek to understand what people are saying through the culture before we critique the culture."[33] Community can begin once we lay down our righteousness spears. I remember when I would go to my church youth group when I was in high school. I was always made to feel bad about the music I listened to. Rap music was seen as "worldly" and something that we all needed to "give up" for the Lord. Fast-forward years later and now I was that youth pastor, doing the same thing with the young people I was work-

---

[32]Martin Buber, *I and Thou* (New York: Scribner's, 1958).
[33]Ralph Watkins, *The Gospel Remix: Reaching the Hip Hop Generation* (Valley Forge, Penn..: Judson Press, 2007), p. 3.

ing with. I would constantly call out artists like Tupac for being "un-holy" and "lost." I would have arguments with teens about their use of "Hip Hop idols" and condemn any type of Hip Hop community. One night I looked in the mirror and had a hard reality check. I sat down with several students, and I said, "I really don't understand this, help me!" For the first time I was able to really commune with them, learn from them. But I had to get my ego out of the way for this type of community to be developed.

Fast-forward many years later. I was at the Urban Youth Workers national conference, doing my first workshop on the theology of Tu-pac Shakur. I saw one of my former students. She and I had gone back and forth about the "evil" in the music she had in her CD-player; I even questioned her salvation at one point because of the music she was listening to. This was the first time she had seen me in a teaching capacity for many years. I could tell she thought I was still "judging" artists like Pac. I told her that our conversation many years prior had sparked in me a desire to look beyond the obvious profanity of artists like Pac, and move into what Pac could actually teach us. I let her know that my workshop was actually admonishing and uplifting Pac and I was letting people know that we had to get on board with cer-tain theologies regarding Pac. The moment I told her that, it was as if her entire countenance was changed. She smiled and we began talk-ing about her life, my workshop, and just how far both of us had come since those early youth group days.

That was community. But it did not happen overnight; it was not pretty. And it involved many more arguments and frustrating mo-ments. But in that moment, she and I knew we had grown and be-cause we had the history behind us, we were able to commune to-gether, and our relationship was not only strengthened, but also deepened as a result of it.

In order to engage the Hip Hop community and really listen to it, we must first be willing to embrace the hostility that lies within that community. Jesus did. Jesus still does. More important, he does that with all of us, every day.

5

Jesuz Is Hip Hop

A THEOLOGY OF THE HIP HOP JESUZ

I can only imagine the conversation that took place among Jesus' disciples in Luke 24:13-27. They were already talking about Jesus in the past tense when we see Jesus approach and then walk with them. We are not really sure why the disciples were prevented from seeing Jesus. Maybe it was because Jesus was once again up to his unique style of teaching. Maybe it was because their faith was too weak. Maybe it was because Jesus wanted to talk with them without the "boss" being around. It is possible that this part of Jesus' life connects with other stories in which people didn't recognize Jesus. In any case, the disciples were really upset. In verse 21 we hear Cleopas (presumably) openly sharing his frustrations, doubts, questions and issues with Jesus. He had "hoped" that Jesus would redeem Israel. The root part of this word is to trust and confide in, but we clearly see that Cleopas, and the other disciples as well, are disappointed by Jesus' death; they feel "let down" by the prophecy. Cleopas, and many of the other disciples as well, had hoped that Jesus would "redeem" Israel—actually set it free, atone for it, loosen it from its bondage. Jesus allows them to continue and talk about him as if he were not there, until in verses 25-26 he breaks down his purpose for suffering and his death.

I cannot help but wonder how closely connected this story is to contemporary times. We hope that Jesus will be something that he is not, or chooses not to be. What do we do with that disappointment? What do we do when Jesus' allegedly "prophetic word" does not come true for our life? What do we do when the image of Jesus we have been shown, taught, conditioned to believe in is in fact not the Jesus of Scripture?

This story in Luke is reminiscent of today's church. We have a Jesus that does not connect to the masses. Jesus appears weak, frail or, as one young rapper put it, "too corny." We are offered five images of Jesus:[1]

- Jesus as an authoritarian Lord who reacts in authoritative ways

- Jesus as a moralist constantly judging those who do not fit that "moral" code

- Jesus as a wrathful adversary

- Jesus as an unquestioningly obedient son of his Father

- Jesus as a God who responds only to "sinful" acts

Carter Heyward observes that such theological portraits of Jesus

> no doubt have represented the real faith of countless Christians over the centuries and around the world. But they also reflect the efforts of bishops, pastors, priests, theologians, and rulers to consolidate, *in the name of* Christ, their hold over people, their authority over the church, and not infrequently their control of the larger social order.[2]

For many Hip Hoppers, such portraits of Jesus have been used as tools in the church's attempt to control and maintain status quo. So why would any true Hip Hopper want to join a religion like that? Instead, many Hip Hoppers imagine a different Jesus: not some blonde-haired, blue-eyed, White embodiment of perfection but rather a Black

---

[1]Adapted from Carter Heyward's four theological portraits of Jesus (*Saving Jesus from Those Who Are Right* [Minneapolis: Fortress Press, 1999], pp. 18-20).
[2]Ibid., p. 19.

Jesuz. Black Jesuz is multiracial. Black Jesuz understands the pain and misery of the inner city. Black Jesuz does not always answer prayers when we want him to, and yet Black Jesuz can relate to the poor, downtrodden and set-aside. Tupac developed the portrait of the Black Jesuz, and other rappers have since developed the image further. But Tupac did not create this portrait; he merely made it contextual for the Hip Hop generation.

THE BLACK JESUZ

The image of the Black Jesuz is a complex one. Tupac essentially created space for Hip Hoppers to access Jesus outside the bounds of pious conduits that did not understand or sympathize with the 'hood. The intentional misspelling of Jesus—with a *z* in the place of the final *s*—illustrates the difference and signifies the change. This was not done in blasphemy nor disrespect for Christ. The *z* represents a Jesus who is both "above," in terms of theological inquiry, but also "below," in terms of access.[3]

The Black Jesuz opposes the dogmatic Christ of early creeds and is suspicious of interpretations of Scripture that do not take context, history, and language into consideration. It reconstructs the life of Jesus from the Gospels so that the community can both participate in and find their own story in Jesus' narrative. The Black Jesuz imports sociology and psychology into the biography of Jesus, illustrating the development of Jesus to full consciousness. Consequently, it strongly criticizes traditional forms of interpretations of Christ's morality and ethics. The Black Jesuz opts for a "low Christology" (that is, a Christ who walked among the people) emphasizing his humanity, over against the "high view" that emphasizes Jesus' divinity. Prominence is given to the Gospels of Mark and John as relevant to the struggles of Hip Hoppers, and theoretical sources (such as the hypothetical Q source document for the Synoptic Gospels) are given greater credence.

---

[3]These are very similar images of Jesus that liberal Christologies and theologies have of Christ, as Veli-Matti Kärkkäinen (*Christology: A Global Introduction* [Grand Rapids: Baker Academic, 2003], pp. 95-100) would suggest.

The Black Jesuz can be traced back to James Cone, who in *God of the Oppressed* and again in *Black Theology and Black Power* argued for an image of Jesus that Blacks in America could relate to, one that was socially aware of the struggle that Blacks had to go through, and one that would have compassion on them because of their hardships.[4] Tupac took Cone's idea a step further and talked about a Christ figure for the ghetto—a Christ who smoked weed, drank liquor and had compassion for the 'hood; a human link to deity. This image was connected back to his thug life message and carried a messianic message of hope, vision and blessings for the downtrodden and hurt that dwell in inner cities. For many traditional Christians, Tupac was being irreverent and sacrilegious. Such deconsecrating of the sacred world was an act worthy of death during the Spanish Inquisition. People would hang Tupac for what he was saying—and they did, metaphorically and lyrically. But Tupac was being an irreverent natural theologian to give voice to a suffering community.[5] For Tupac, and for other Hip Hoppers who followed him, it's important to understand that Black Jesuz can handle questions, doubts, ambiguity, mystery, disorder, disarray, chaos, even madness and anger.

Theologically speaking, Tupac is "nonstandard"—neither formally trained as a theologian nor "Christian" in the traditional sense. He represents a much bigger religious debate about a God who became who we are.[6] Tupac's Black Jesuz is not the Jesus of history but a Jesuz *for* the 'hood, a Jesuz who understood the issues confronting the people of the 'hood and accepted those with such issues.

Some Hip Hoppers would say we do not want a perfect God, a God who is too "neat." The song "Black Jesuz," by Tupac and the Outlawz, addresses the contrast:

I do my shootin's on a knob, prayin to God for my squad

---

[4]James Cone, *God of the Oppressed* (New York: Seabury Press, 1975), pp. 99-105; cf. Teresa Reed, *The Holy Profane: Religion in Black Popular Music* (Lexington: University Press of Kentucky, 2003).
[5]Michael Eric Dyson, *Holler If You Hear Me: Searching for Tupac Shakur* (New York: Basic Civitas, 2001).
[6]Cf. Cone, *God of the Oppressed,* and *Black Theology and Black Power,* 5th ed. (Maryknoll, N.Y.: Orbis, 1997).

Stuck in a nightmare, hopin he might care
Though times is hard, up against all odds, I play my cards
like I'm jailin, shots hittin up my spot like midnight
    rains hailin
Got me bailin to stacks more green; God ain't tryin
    to be trapped
on no block slangin no rocks like bean pies
Brainstorm on the beginnin
Wonder how s*** like the Qu'ran and the Bible was written
What is religion?
Gods words all cursed like crack
Shai-tan's way of gettin us back
Or just another one of my Black Jesus traps[7]

Tupac and the Outlawz are here questioning what kind of God we serve. This is a fundamental theological question about the identity of God, reminiscent of questions that Thomas, Cleopas and other disciples had about Jesus after he died. Where is a Jesus that can relate to people like us?

Searchin for Black Jesus
It's hard, it's hard
We need help out here
So we searchins for Black Jesus
It's like a Saint, that we pray to in the ghetto, to get us through
Somebody that understand our pain
You know maybe not too perfect, you know
Somebody that hurt like we hurt
Somebody that smoke like we smoke
Drink like we drink
That understand where we coming from
That's who we pray to
We need help y'all[8]

---

[7]Tupac Shakur, "Black Jesus," from the album *2Pac + Outlawz—Still I Rise* (1999).
[8]Ibid.

Tupac's "Black Jesuz" thus represents a theology of liberation for ghetto peoples. Tupac imagined a heaven with a ghetto—the figurative and metaphorical image of a heaven that was made for "real" people. During some of Tupac's most difficult times, he began writing songs rooted in a Christian messianic message, fashioned from Hebrews 4:14-16:

> Therefore, since we have a great high priest who has gone through the heavens, Jesus the Son of God, let us hold firmly to the faith we profess. For we do not have a high priest who is unable to sympathize with our weaknesses, but we have one who has been tempted in every way, just as we are—yet was without sin. Let us then approach the throne of grace with confidence, so that we may receive mercy and find grace to help us in our time of need.

Jesus was a connection to a greater hope that lay in heaven. The ultimate peace and rest was with God. Passing this message to young people on the streets of America became part of Tupac's mission in the latter part of his life.[9] For subsequent rappers, this has become part of their mantra when discussing issues regarding death, afterlife, salvation, and the kingdom of God.

Tupac's life resembled his image of the Black Jesuz, an image rooted in James Cone's mandate:

> We cannot afford to do theology unrelated to human existence. Our theology must emerge consciously from an investigation of the socioreligious experience of black people, as that experience is reflected in black stories of God's dealings with black people in the struggle for freedom.[10]

One of Tupac's tattoos was Exodus 18:11. Tattooed on his back was the statement "I know now that the LORD is greater than all

---

[9]The theme of Tupac's album *Still I Rise* (1999) reinforces what I am talking about here in Tupac's mission to place peace and rest in God.

[10]Cone, *Black Theology and Black Power*, p. 15.

other gods, because his people have escaped from the proud and cruel Egyptians." The tattoo demonstrated the oppressive life he had lived in the 'hood; part of the verse speaks to the vision of hope that God can actually help in a time of need. The tattoo also, however, acknowledges the oppressive systems which Tupac, among many other Hip Hoppers, lived under. This perspective runs counter to the "peaceful" and "safe" theology of much of contemporary Christianity; political and social upheaval don't fit the Christian vision of many people—particularly White Christians. It's noteworthy that White Christians by and large find it easier to identify with Martin Luther King than Malcolm X. King protested and marched, but he advocated nonviolence and was a self-proclaimed Christian; Malcolm X advocated justice "by any means necessary," and spoke openly and critically about the White image of Jesus. While Malcolm X did believe in and follow God's Word later in life, he continued to vigorously oppose White theology and advocated for a more contextualized theology for Black and urban communities—which Tupac later sought to provide. Smith and Jackson see this effort as a helpful corrective to the traditional church's neglect of the context of Jesus' contemporary ministry. "The void of teaching that this Christ was Incarnational will continue to keep hope away from those who are seeking to understand God."[11]

HIP HOP'S LIKENESSES OF JESUZ

Hip Hop embraces many different christological paradigms. Its emphasis on social justice is reminiscent of liberal views of Jesus. At the same time, Hip Hop's emphasis on Jesus' unique nature—ambiguous, trinitarian, a mediator elected by God, an elected man—resembles Karl Barth's Christology. On still another plane, Rudolf Bultmann's view of the Christ of mythology is reflected in the postmodern hero found in Black Jesuz. For artists such as Nas, Common, Lauryn Hill and Erykah Badu, Jesuz engages the intellect, stirs the mind and

[11]Efrem Smith and Phil Jackson, *The Hip Hop Church* (Downers Grove, Ill.: InterVarsity Press, 2005), p. 124.

elicits a deep theological understanding; meanwhile, rappers such as Tupac, DMX and Mase would agree with Paul Tillich's "degree Christology"—Jesuz is different from us as a matter of degree, not of substance.[12]

The Hip Hop Jesuz is about moving people into right relation with God and acting in what Carter Heyward calls "justice-love."[13]

1. The Hip Hop Jesuz holds a moral standard but abandons moralism and the authoritarian model of relationships. The Hip Hop Jesuz allows people to grow in and through their faults, errors and sins.

2. The Hip Hop Jesuz acts redemptively to bring the spiritual power of love and cohesion to the present moment while being aware of the cost of such action, both to him and to the Hip Hop community.

3. The Hip Hop Jesuz accepts the true nature of people and encourages each person to change, intellectually, communally and spiritually, and continue the journey for consciousness and healing.

4. The Hip Hop Jesuz rejects standardized messages of salvation, church and religion while establishing new worldviews of each of these paradigms.

5. The Hip Hop Jesuz challenges the status quo and argues for equal rights, justice and cultural change in systems which oppress his people, while still allowing for the people in these oppressive social structures to change and follow him.

These five likenesses of the Hip Hop Jesuz in the justice-love concept open up powerful themes for rap:

- the end of oppression (Nas, Tupac, Odd Thomas, Common, Lauryn Hill, Eve, Ice Cube, Dead Prez)

---

[12]Paul Tillich, *Systematic Theology*, vol. 2 (Chicago, Ill: University of Chicago Press, 1957), p. 150.

[13]Carter Heyward, *Saving Jesus from Those Who Are Right: Rethinking What It Means to Be a Christian* (Minneapolis: Fortress Press, 1999), p. 123. Items (1) and (2) are adapted from Heyward.

- liberation from fear, greed, lack of confidence and low self-esteem (Tupac, Mase, BB Jay, KRS-One, Erykah Badu, Public Enemy)
- healing of personal wounds: ours, others' and the community's (Erykah Badu, KRS-One, Lecrae, Eminem)
- healing of a more global scope: peoples, nations, tribes and the earth (Jill Scott, Mary J. Blige, Mos Def)

There is, of course, a strain in Hip Hop in which Jesus is still represented by the traditional church. This Jesus is seen as authoritarian, judgmental, a moral moderator, a dogmatic deity. Hard-core gang members and other extreme participants in the street game of the 'hood tend to see Jesus and God the same way they see the streets: hierarchal, rigorous, scrupulous and rugged. Gang members who exhibit extreme behavior patterns when in the gang (e.g. down-for-life attitude; hard-core gang lifestyle) will tend to swing hard the other way when "saved":

- fundamental attitudes regarding church, Jesus, Scripture
- highly spiritualized and strongly identified with a particular church
- an adversarial relationship as regards "Christ versus culture"
- a simplistic view of faith and Jesus
- a strong emphasis on the activity of the devil
- church as the only way for salvation
- a prooftexting approach to the Scriptures

Many Holy Hip Hop rappers tend to try to scare their listeners into following Jesus through apocalyptic messages in their music. While many do so with good intentions, people who respond to their messages tend to follow Jesus out of guilt, fear, regret or shame—a marked contrast to the deep connections being made to the Hip Hop Jesuz.

One year a national urban conference featured a Holy Hip Hop group I hadn't heard before. They performed one rap during a main-stage session and were actually really good, in terms of beat and message. The evening came, and they were set to perform an outdoor night concert. I figured they would have more of the same quality at this concert so I decided to sit and listen. After performing the same song they had done for the general session, the group proceeded to get into some "new material." The first song out was a proclamation that Jesus was Lord; every other religion was destined to burn in hell. I was a little set back, but I thought maybe they just needed to get that off their chest. The next five songs were no different. Each song likened Jesus to a spoiled kid who, if not given his way, would cut you off from eternal friendship. Church was portrayed as the only means to community, learning and spiritual enlightenment. At the end of their rampage, they did an altar call, at which point people began to leave. The group yelled even louder: "If you don't accept Jesus, you're gonna burn in hell . . . and that's forever!"

Many Holy Hip Hoppers take this stance: at all times preach salvation, because Christ will hold you responsible if someone dies not hearing the message of salvation from you. By contrast, the Hip Hop Jesuz advocates and stands for a number of things:

- *True community* that not only embraces each individual but makes room for the community to learn from each other.

- *Open answers* in the spirit of Jesuz, who welcomed people's challenges, questions, even tricks and traps. Jesus knew that the truth needed no defense.

- *Rejection of the institutionalized church* while showing respect for the individual. Jesus' strongest words were reserved for "churchfolk" and religious officials. When Jesus did address "sinners," he was both respectful and enlightening. The Hip Hop Jesuz rejects the institutionalizing of his Father's house, just like he did when he beat down fools in the temple.

- *Truth as a quest,* not something to be conquered. The Hip Hop Jesuz knows all too well that truth is relative to its context. To remain transfixed by absolute-truth arguments defeats the true mission of Christ: to take his gospel to all the ethnicities and tribes (see Matthew 28:16-20).

The Hip Hop Jesuz is a *figura* of Christ in the Hip Hopper's experience, a concept from Black Christology, which borrowed it from Greek and Roman thought to express "an idea of something that both reflects something that already exists as well as projects something yet to be."[14] As James Evans states:

> Jesus Christ was a figura in the sense that he was a cosmic reflection of Adam, the firstborn, the image of God, as well as the historical reflection of Joshua, who led the Israelites into the Promised Land. Jesus Christ was also a figura in the sense that he was a cosmic projection of 'the new Adam,' the image of God restored to its original state, as well as the historical projection of liberated humanity, evident in the mystical/concrete notions of the church as the 'body of Christ' and 'the people of God'.[15]

Hip Hoppers extrapolate the *figura* of Jesus from biblical perceptions of Christ to the various heroic figures that populate the Hip Hop landscape.[16] Erykah Badu, Paris and Mase continue to have a huge effect on young audiences. Tupac embodies elements of the Jesuz *figura* in not just his music but also his life: he transcended his humble beginnings; under oppression, he spoke truth to power; his message was cut short by his premature death; he was hated by "officials." The Hip Hop Jesuz becomes an "epic hero" that takes shape in human forms many times, providing voice, shelter, identity, hope, dreams, love and passion for each new generation. Evans further states:

> It is noteworthy that continued oppression and travail did not destroy the messianic dream but intensified it. Indeed, the more evil abounded the more powerful the idea of the Messiah became. As the actual historical liberation of Israel seemed to recede into the remote provinces of probability, the Messiah be-

---

[14]Veli-Matti Kärkkäinen, *Christology: A Global Introduction* (Grand Rapids: Baker Academic, 2003), p. 206.

[15]James Evans, *We Have Been Believers: An African American Systematic Theology* (Minneapolis: Fortress Press, 1992), p. 78.

[16]Kärkkäinen, *Christology*, pp. 206-7.

came one capable not only of transforming the historical situation of the people, but of transforming history itself.[17]

The *figura* of the Hip Hop Jesuz thus better connects people with the messianic narrative. Performers such as Tupac, DMX, Mase, Lecrae, Eminem, MC Lyte, Eve and Lauryn Hill serve as *figura* images for Jesuz. Concerts—particularly the smaller venues of underground Hip Hop—become sacred spaces where people experience a communal "baptism" of sorts. Songs contain powerful messianic themes and move their listeners toward subtle and sometimes dramatic life change.

The Hip Hop Jesuz is the hostile part of Hip Hop's theology. He represents a multitude of problems, particularly for people invested in literal interpretations of the Bible. He brings with him, however, a new hope, vision and direction for Hip Hoppers.

THE MULTIETHNIC JESUZ

Hip Hop as a culture is composed of many different ethnicities. If you ask many U.S. Christians today what they think Jesus looks and talks like, they would characterize him as White, with long wavy hair and a beard, and a British accent. By contrast, the Hip Hop Jesuz is multiethnic.

Matthew 1 and Luke 3 showcase Jesus' genealogy to give witness to several key theological ideas: (1) Jesus' lineage traces back to Adam, which qualifies him to be the second Adam; (2) Jesus has a record of ancestors, situating him in a concrete history and validating his humanness; (3) Jesus is shown as not having a "perfect" lineage, making him all the more approachable, relatable and accessible.[18]

For instance, Jesus' ancestor Tamar was the daughter-in-law of Ju-

---

[17]Evans, *We Have Been Believers*, p. 79.

[18]Paul Achtemeier, Joel Green Marianne Thompson (*Introducing the New Testament: Its Literature and Theology* [Grand Rapids: Eerdmans, 2001]) assert that readers of genealogical records must typically navigate between what really happened (the facts) and the ideal in the structures of ancestral relationships. They also observe that the inclusion of these genealogies communicates something about the nature of the good news of Jesus' coming—all of which adds to the complexity and richness of Jesus (pp. 75-76).

dah. When her husband died, his brother should have fulfilled the responsibility to give her children, but "whenever he lay with his brother's wife, he spilled his semen on the ground to keep from producing offspring for his brother" (Genesis 38:9). When this brother died (apparently in judgment for his "wicked" behavior; see v. 10), Judah was hesitant to give Tamar his third son, so he sent Tamar away with a vague promise that she would marry his youngest son when the time was right. Tamar responded to Judah's failure to provide for her by disguising herself as a prostitute, catching Judah's "attention" and getting pregnant by him (Genesis 38:6-24). If that isn't baby-mama drama, I don't know what is!

Jesus was, in fact, conceived in controversy, which connects him to a larger theme that runs throughout the Bible: that of the "mess." Heroes of the faith such as Jacob, David, Ruth and Paul never really fit the mold of what a "holy person" should be. Does the fact that Jesus has this messiness around him and in his lineage make him any less divine or pious? Certainly not. Yet many pastors struggle with the notion that Jesus was anything but "perfect." Meanwhile, Hip Hoppers want a Jesuz that they can relate to, one who knows what it's like to have some "jacked up" family members—including, possibly, a drunk uncle such as the "master of the banquet" at the wedding at Cana.

This Jesuz embraces diversity, interculturalism, multiethnicity and strong race relations. Jesuz speaks up for ethnicities and engages them even when it is not popular. Just look at his interaction with a Samaritan woman in John 4:7-45. Jesus not only talks to a woman during midday, he also talks with one of the Samaritans—the "niggas" of Jesus' day—bringing love and light with him. The woman's subsequent testimony led many in the town to Jesus (John 4:39-42). This is the Hip Hop Jesuz, who not only lifts up the marginalized but allows them to carry his gospel to the people they can reach. It is hard to imagine people like DMX, Poor Righteous Teachers, Tupac and Ice Cube being "apostles" of Christ's message, but then again, look at who Jesus chose to be his disciples.

LISTENING TO THE HIP HOP JESUZ

Efrem Smith and Phil Jackson state that "the gospel according to hip-hop is a message of justice and power."[19] Part of restoring justice and power to a people is listening to the stories of injustice that the people have. When stories get overlooked and ignored, true restoration does not occur and problems continue. The Synoptic Gospels thus concentrate on narrative—Jesus' story, the disciples' story, stories of women, stories of broken people, stories of love, hate, pain and hope.

If story is central to the gospel, then part of the Christian mission is to listen. There are three key elements in the ministry of listening. First, we listen to find the aim of the story. A story's aim may be fragmented, circular or otherwise obscure, but it exists. What is the story getting at? What is the moral of the story?

Four types of narratives guide rap:

1. *The narrative of the individual.* Some rap songs tell a story about a particular individual. It can be good, bad or ugly; it can be a story of their life or their day.

2. *The narrative of a narrative.* Fictitious or factual, silly or serious, rappers write in story form about dreams or aspirations. In 1995, rapper Skee-Lo rapped about the "perfect life," in which among other things he would be a little bit. Rappers like Ice-T craft violent stories that are sometimes based in truth but more often are fictional reflections of 'hood life. Such songs are often misunderstood, by fans and critics alike: critics diminish the significance of Hip Hop by characterizing it as a celebration of violence; meanwhile, young, easily influenced fans presume that rappers such as 50 Cent really endure the challenges of 'hood life, when in reality, 50 lives comfortably in the suburbs and rolls with armed security guards.

3. *The third-person narrative.* A lot of raps are told from the perspective of an observer. Immortal Technique's hauntingly realistic song "Dance with the Devil" paints a horrific picture of a person wit-

---

[19]Smith and Jackson, *Hip Hop Church,* p. 124.

nessing the rape and murder of someone's mother. In the end, we learn that just such a horrible event has stuck with Immortal ever since he did, in fact, observe it.

4. *The triune narrative.* Some rap is crafted by joining all three of these approaches together, for example, by sharing the microphone with guest artists who bring their own perspective to the overall narrative of the album.

In each case, the aim of the story is embedded in the telling.

Second, we listen to interpret an overall point of view. The medium of rap allows the artist to break down heavy theological concepts into bite-sized pieces. Rappers like Mack10 begin to unravel the spirituality of the streets in songs like "The Testimony," offering his point of view as pertains to Jesuz. Similarly, spoken word is one of the most powerful conduits for articulating the Hip Hop Jesuz. Jesuz shows up at almost every venue. Spoken word's close cousin, Hip Hop poetry, likewise regularly gives voice to ideas about Jesuz in four-word sentences and poetic meter. And lyrical jousting such as battle raps are characterized by the attempt to connect with the audience through lyrics, space, identity, and community. Jesuz is regularly in view in such contexts. These three forms coalesce to shape the grand narrative of the Hip Hop Jesuz.

Third, we listen to allow stories to be told. Some of the greatest orators of U.S. history have been Black; rap is only the most recent incarnation of artistry in word to come out of African American culture. When I go to camp with students, one of the things I enjoy the most is listening to the stories that young people have to tell about who they are, what they fear the most, who they love, how they love, when they love, how they see Jesus, and where Jesus is at in their lives. Many times urban students will tell their story in a type of spoken word or verse style. Often it is the first time that these young people have shared their story in a safe environment without fear of rejection, laughter and cruel put-downs.

Hearing stories that have not been told is a difficult task. As religious adults, we want to "counsel" and protect our kids from harm. But often, I have found that kids just want to talk, and when allowed to talk, they are able to not just relieve stress, but connect into that narrative of Christ—with a little guidance. I have learned, over time, to only interject advice when asked, and to remain engaged merely by maintaining good eye contact and asking clarifying questions.

It's in these stories—told by kids in sacred spaces, by poets and spoken-word artists, by eager contestants in a battle rap, by recording artists, on the Internet, in film, in emerging Hip Hop churches—that Hip Hop Jesuz's story is being told. It's our task and our privilege to listen.

6

Tupac's Nit Grit 'Hood Gospel

A THEOLOGY OF
SOCIAL ACTION & JUSTICE

Being a young Blaxican (Black and Mexican) male in a small, rural, very White, racist West Texas community had many challenges. Even though my mom is full Mexican, I looked Black. I had the afro, the darker skin, bone and body structure and the nose that is typically associated with Black people. I was not a spic, wetback, or even a colored. I was a nigger.

I did not know that growing up. In fact, it was not until the second grade that I was made aware that the term *nigger* was derogatory. One day my mom asked me how my day at school went. "Do your friends have any nicknames for you?"

I responded, "I get called 'nigger.'"

My mom's face dropped, her eyes widened, and I remember her nostrils even flaring. "What did you say?" *Why would my mom be reacting so negatively to a nickname?* I said, "My friends call me nigger. They say 'nigger come here,' 'nigger go get the ball,' 'nigger go there.'" My mom stood in full distress and astonishment. After she regained her words and wit, she began to school me on the essence and nature of racism, and the power of that word. It was at that point that I knew things would never be the same. I had new knowledge.

My mom had awoken in me a new sense of justice and awareness. That is what Tupac has done for many people: awaken them to a higher sense of social awareness and made them more conscious of their context and environment, more conscious of themselves.

Tupac was in no way a perfect person. Still, there was something genuine that touched millions of people around the world in his music. Twelve years after his death, his music still lives on. When I was in Paris, France, I didn't speak French, but through just one of Tupac's songs we were able to connect on a deep level. The only way for me to communicate with Hip Hoppers in France was through Tupac.

THE GHETTO SAINT

Hip Hop culture is filled with emcees that speak openly, honestly, prophetically and passionately about social justice and social action. While Ice Cube, Mos Def, Eminem, Lauryn Hill, Eve, Dead Prez and many more talk with great passion and expertise regarding the social inequalities that exist within the 'hood, Tupac remains at the top of the social justice ladder.

Tupac embodied social justice. He was born at a time when the boroughs and ghettos of the United States were undergoing some of their strongest growing pains, and he functioned as a prophet. Prophets are divinely inspired revealers, interpreters, teachers and students—thought to have a connection with the Godhead and having divinely inspired insights into life and societal issues. Tupac was all of this, though not in the same way as Saint Jerome or Saint John. Tupac was a street prophet, one who could connect the 'hood and the thug to God through life, language, music and community. Tupac offered the 'hood a higher glimpse of the future. He functioned as a post-soul saint for those who view God from the gutter.

Of course, he was human and had his faults and sins—some might argue that Tupac was confused about or even opposed to social justice. What most people remember of Tupac was his later career, in which he was paranoid, aggressive, lost and confused about many things. In that last year of his life, he got into most of the trouble that many people now remember him for. However, this did not take away from his social justice worldview. He still embodied the mantra popular to the 1960s-era Black Panthers: community first.

Tupac was iconic in his style, life, language and messages. Michael Eric Dyson, in the documentary *Tupac vs. U.S.A.*,[1] compares Tupac's music to gospel music: his music spoke to a way of life. Tupac connected with people and gave to people out of his heart. He would frequent clubs without security and would just be "hanging out." As one young man, "Miguel," put it to me, "This was the realest nigga you could find. I mean, he was a pastor to me."[2] Michael Eric Dyson states,

> Tupac is perhaps the representative figure of his generation. In his haunting voice can be heard the buoyant hopefulness and the desperate hopelessness that mark the outer perimeters of the Hip Hop culture he eagerly embraced, as well as the lives of the millions of youth who admired and adored him.[3]

THE FORMATION OF TUPAC

Tupac bore witness to many things that a child should never witness. Drug addicts shooting up or snorting drugs, loved ones (including his mother Afeni) falling into the trap of drug abuse, friends being shot— these were just some of the experiences Tupac had during his early years. Part of a family that struggled financially, Tupac personally knew several people who lived the life described in his song "Brenda." All of this helped form part of Pac's worldview on life and the ghetto.

It was during these formative yet extremely difficult years that Tupac formed his lyrical message about social justice and social action. Using all of his past experiences, he infused his lyrics with social justice, comedy and theology. Tupac wanted a different kind of community, one that was not killing itself daily with gangs and drugs, one in

---

[1]See Ken Peters, dir., *Tupac vs. U.S.A.* (2001).
[2]Personal interview from 2003.
[3]Michael Eric Dyson, *Holler If You Hear Me: Searching for Tupac Shakur* (New York: Basic Civitas, 2001), p. 13.

which people could live peaceably together. Tupac decided young that he wanted to be committed to that change and social action.

Tupac's lyrics were beginning to take shape in early works such as "Panther Power," performed at a Blank Panther rally in East Oakland:

As real as it seems the American Dream
Ain't nothing but another calculated scheme
To get us locked up shot up back in chains
To deny us of the future rob our names
Kept my history of mystery but now I see
The American Dream wasn't meant for me
Cause lady liberty is a hypocrite she lied to me
Promised me freedom, education, equality
Never gave me nothing but slavery
And now look at how dangerous you made me
Calling me a mad man cause I'm strong and bold.[4]

All of the pent-up anger and pain was beginning to come through in his music. James Cone argues that through Black Power, a Black person is able to develop a sense of contextualized theology,[5] a theology that says that Black people have a place too at the throne of God, and that we must assert that position and fight to keep it.

Tupac knew the Bible inside out; he had grown up with it and was raised in the ways of the Lord. Dyson writes, "Tupac was obsessed with God. His lyrics drip with a sense of the divine. . . . Tupac's spiritual matters never left him, although its form and function in his later life may have become almost unrecognizable by earlier standards."[6] Esther Iverem writes:

Affinity [for Tupac] mixes what is potentially a positive attitude toward self determination with the worst definitions of that over used phrase: Keep it Real. At its most meaningful, the phrase

[4]Tupac Shakur, "Panther Power," from the album *The Lost Tapes* (1989).
[5]James Cone, *Black Theology and Black Power* (New York: Seabury Press, 1969), pp. 5-30.
[6]Dyson, *Holler If You Hear Me,* pp. 202, 207.

urges those in the hip hop nation to remain true to their beliefs and rooted in reality. At its worst, it implies that only those things ghetto centric and hard are real in black culture. It endorses the use of street ethics to settle disputes, like the willingness to bust a cap in someone, usually another African-American, if necessary.[7]

NIT GRIT 'HOOD THEOLOGY

In the context of injustice, simple answers and "simple theology" are not good enough. We need a nit grit 'hood theology.[8] Tupac knew this and rapped about it. His music raises deep questions about life, death, sin and grace, but what it does not do is give simplistic answers to such complex questions. Tupac is not trying to tell his audience that life is easy and that all we have to do is go to church. The simple answer is not always the only answer. For Tupac, there is something much deeper and more complex to life. This is where nit grit 'hood theology enters.

In nit grit 'hood theology, simplistic answers like "God wanted it this way" are not tolerated. Nit grit 'hood theology gets at the real issues that no one wants to discuss. If God really knows all our needs, for example, why would we ask him to "bless" us with a new home, car, boat, cat or dog when we know that there is someone who has none of that? More important, where do we find such individualism portrayed in the Bible as more holy? Tupac posed this question and was shunned as a heretic and blasphemer.

Nit grit 'hood theology encourages personal responsibility: sometimes the devil is not to blame, and in reality *we* are the true culprit of social injustices. Tupac would challenge pastors and theologians to

---

[7]Ester Iverem, "Tupac and the Politics of 'F*** It,'" in *Tough Love: Cultural Criticism and Familial Observations on the Life and Death of Tupac Shakur,* ed. Kwame Alexander and Michael Datcher (n.p.: BlackWords, 1997), p. 41.

[8]This is my rendition of Anthony Pinn's "nitty gritty hermeneutics" in *Why, Lord? Suffering and Evil in Black Theology* (New York: Continuum, 1995), pp. 113-38. For Pinn, simple answers like "Let's just pray about the problem" are not good enough, and what is needed is a deeper sense of action and movement during times of crisis.

think deeper about issues such as poverty, social justice and suffering. In three DVD interviews[9] Tupac asks for help from institutions such as churches, challenging the older generation to act as opposed to just "preaching" at young people. In 1992, at a Malcolm X dinner banquet in Atlanta, Tupac was invited to be a guest speaker and represent African American youth in relation to what was happening in America during that time. This was a great example of that challenge that Tupac gave to the older generation:

> It ain't time to cool out, and chill out . . . banquets all that . . . it's still on! It's still on . . . just like it was on when you was young. . . . So how come now when I'm twenty-one years old and ready to start some s*** and do some s*** everybody's tellin' me to calm down, don't curse, you know . . . go to college. . . . We had colleges for a while now, OK, and there still Brendas out there and niggas is still trapped . . . it gets me irked. . . . It's not gonna stop until we stop it and it's not just White men that's doing this . . . it's Black. We have to find the new African in all of us . . . because if we still running around saying who got the best dashiki on and best colors on, excuse my languge but we all gonna get f***ed! What I want you to take seriously is what we have to do for the youth because we comin up in a totally different world. . . . This is not the 60s, this is not that. . . . You all came up in BC—before crack; . . . right there that oughta say it all. . . . Its about you taking care of these children. . . . The pimps and the pushers are the ones who's raising our kids, cuzz you all not doing it! I'm sorry but you're not so if you gotta problem with the way we was raised it's because they was doing it. . . . I'm sorry, but you can't be no more offended of my language than what's going on out here in the 'hood. . . . If you don't put s*** into this, then don't be mad when it all just blow up![10]

[9]Ken Peters, dir., *Tupac vs. U.S.A.* (2001); Peter Spirer, dir., *Thug Angel* (2002); Lauren Lazin, dir., *Tupac Resurrection* (2003).
[10]Taken from the DVD extras on *Tupac Resurrection* (2003).

If Christians plan to "evangelize" in the twenty-first century, then we must be ready to deal with a generation that will not take "Let's just pray about it" for a final answer; we may be able to begin there, but we sure cannot end there![11] Nit grit 'hood theology engages this generation and pushes for deeper answers and solutions to complex issues—social action and social justice. The simple "sinner's prayer" is out because while I may be "saved" and feel tingly inside, if I live in the 'hood, the reality is that I still need to eat, sleep, love, and live in this place where I can grow in Christ. Nit grit 'hood theology promises that we are with you for life—through the good, the relapses, the failures, the successes, the backsliding and the getting back up. This type of theology is designed for a lifetime and not just a program. The basics of this theology as it relates to social action and social justice are as follows:

- It engages in a more complex and detailed conversation about God. This conversation is not merely discussion on the personhood of God but an active conversation about how to actually help people in their need so that they can live life better than their current situation. Social injustice is copious in the 'hood where a lot of Hip Hoppers reside. Nit grit allows for deeper probing and debate about God as relates to social justice.

- Nit grit is concerned with a person's post-salvation experience. The real excitement of faith comes in the daily life of a person—not living "for God," but simply "living." The community of God helps to address basic life needs.

- Simple answers are not tolerated. Life is complex and therefore many solutions are complex as well. The nit grit gets down into the details of events and searches out the truth and evidence to make

---

[11]Daniel Shaw and Charles Van Engen assert that "presenters of the Gospel who effectively communicate God's Word in today's world . . . are involved in the flowing development of truth through time and space" (*Comunicating God's Word in a Complex World: God's Truth or Hocus Pocus* [Lanham, Md.: Rowman & Littlefield, 2003], p. 196). To effectively communicate the gospel message, we must, as young people state, "Go there!"

sense of issues such as divorce, sex, gay marriage, immigration, and drug abuse—to name a few.

- Speaking up for those who cannot is a part of nit grit 'hood theology. The primary example of this is seen through Jesus and his voice for the voiceless. This theological paradigm challenges the status quo and urges those who are "sitting around" to take action.

- Ambiguity is a constant reality. In the search to find answers, a person will at times come up without an answer. Moreover, God works in ambiguity and at odd times. When dealing with people, some things—even extreme social inequalities—cannot be explained; they just are.

- Community is a must. Whether online or in person, evangelism needs to be performed with others around. This is what the body of Christ is about.

Nit grit 'hood theology is part of Hip Hop's social-political movement. Nit grit helps to embrace the diverse and multifaceted issues that arise within politics. Hip Hoppers are then able to become leaders in their community for social movement and social action; they can help shape identity in their community around such topics of politics and social action. The centralized leader is no longer needed; it can be done within the community of Hip Hop with many different types of leaders. Erin Trapp asserts that Hip Hop culture becomes a breeding ground for social-political movements that break the norms and traditional forms of social movements.

The threat of neoconservative ideology faced by African Americans in the Reagan era, which blamed the poor for deteriorating values and poverty, led Black artists to start a social movement through music, capitalizing on opportunities afforded by their position in the music industry. Thus, hip-hop artists adopt a critical—often hostile—stance toward the White-controlled state government, and media, often seeking to delegitimize these institutions and draw attention to racial injustices and social neglect.[12]

Tupac understood that there were always going to be gangs and drugs, but if people in the 'hood could have a peace zone, it would make things a lot better. Otherwise, as he noted in several interviews, we would kill ourselves trying to "make a buck." And yet Tupac would also argue that even with "equality" and "fair treatment," without programs to help the next generation be self-sufficient, support from the previous generation and a better relationship between the government and the 'hood, how can we truly have peace at all? The question of place was an issue for the extreme street dwellers: the pimps, the prostitutes, the drug dealers and other people who were too "ghetto" to enter into traditional forms of church. For these people Tupac began to develop the theological mantra called the thug life theos.

THUG LIFE THEOS

It is not clear whether or not Tupac would have completed a full theology of thug life if he had lived. What is clear, though, is that in order for the 'hood and hard-core Hip Hop youth to be reached, the church must be able to identify with and accept the lifestyles of individuals that are engrossed in the unacceptable living conditions of the 'hood.

While we all may live by a set moral standard, there is an entire different set of cultural rules that apply when living on the street.[13] I am not advocating violence, stealing or immoral behavior, but the 'hood evangelist must be ready to live in that environment, presenting a gospel of Christ while resisting the urge to require people to change their lifestyle, trusting instead that the Holy Spirit will do so.

Thug life theos argues that Christianity needs a facelift. If Christianity is to be the religion that helps people see Jesus better, then salva-

---

[12]Erin Trapp, "The Push and Pull of Hip-Hop: A Social Movement Analysis," *American Behavioral Scientist* 48, no. 11 (2005): 1483.

[13]Elijah Anderson, *Code of the Street: Decency, Violence, and the Moral Life of the Inner City* (New York: W. W. Norton, 1999).

tion, Bible study, evangelism and the notion of "coming to Christ" are
going to need some changing. Salvation may happen on a street corner, with a bottle of malt liquor still in the hands of the individual
being saved. Evangelism in the 'hood is often controversial, even at
times invoking the help of a Five Percenter or the Nation of Islam.

Hard-core Hip Hop youth need to know that Jesuz didn't overwork
himself: he focused on twelve individuals. And yet Jesuz stirred up a
lot of trouble in his day. Jesuz got angry and actually whipped people
as they disgraced his Father's temple. Pain, love, sorrow, anger and joy
are intertwined in the thug life theos: problems are complex and need
complex resolutions. Hard-core Hip Hop youth deserve to know the
truth that living a life for Christ is impossible without relying on Jesus
and a core community. Jesuz and Tupac alike encourage us that pain is
normal—it will come, and when it does, we are to hold our heads up.

Thug life theos involves a return to liturgy, simplicity and corporate prayer. This can be hard to believe, given the culture's general
disregard for conformity and traditionalism. However, Hip Hop concerts and spoken-word events are inherently liturgical and in many
ways prayerful, even in some ways approaching a monastic sensibility.
Hard-core Hip Hoppers want this type of discipline, and even "quiet
times" of the traditional sort are prized as a well-needed break from
the constant noise and movement in their world.

The code of the street includes principles that apply beyond street
life as well. Hustling, watching your back, standing your ground,
dealing with O.G.'s, and pimping can all come into play in "normal"
life: competing for a job, a scholarship or even a position in the academy. These doctrines of the thug life theos are imperative for the
missional advancement of the church among hard-core Hip Hop
youth—as is a connection to the narrative of Christ.

THE JESUZ OF TUPAC AND SOCIAL AWARENESS

Tupac pioneered the dialogue about theological matters in the 'hood
and Hip Hop culture, connecting the profane to the sacred. He became a lighting rod for those theological matters, both positive and

negative. But in so doing Tupac made religion, God, church and authentic community attainable for comprehension and understanding by the masses. In this respect Tupac has much in common with W. E. B. Dubois, who was fascinated with the tension in Negro spirituals between hope and despair, sorrow and joy. Likewise, as a musician Tupac inherits the tradition of blurring the sacred and profane that is found in the blues. James Cone sees the blues as depicting "the 'secular' dimension of black experience. They are the 'worldly' songs which tell us about love and sex, and about that other 'mule kickin in my stall.'"[14] The influence of the blues notwithstanding, Tupac's music was not completely "secular" in the sense of being devoid of God. Tupac blurred the lines between the sacred and the profane in search of the truth. Using his own contextual hermeneutic, Tupac interpreted the Scriptures, Jesus, salvation and heaven to craft a spiritual message that is both idealistic and realistic. Tupac connected God to man through Jesus, who himself connects humanity with God.

THE TUPAC OF JESUZ

Tupac insisted that people not reduce their hopes, dreams and vision to the level of whatever conditions they were in at the time. For some, that might be poverty or a "broken home." Hopelessness occurs when one cannot imagine a different future. Tupac encouraged his audience to keep their heads up, to keep believing for a better day. He even suggested that heaven itself might have a "ghetto." Simply put, there is a place that will accept "us" as we are.

The extraordinary hopefulness of songs like "Keep Ya Head Up" and "Dear Mama" is contrasted with songs of deep pain and suffering, reflecting the suffering he himself endured during much of his childhood. Tupac was searching for a Jesus that could deal with such pain and suffering, as seen in the song "Searching for Black Jesuz":

---

[14]James Cone, "The Blues: A Secular Spiritual," in *Sacred Music of the Secular City: From Blues to Rap*, ed. J. M. Spencer (Durham, N.C.: Duke University Press, 1992), p. 68.

Searching for Black Jesus
Oh yeah, sportin jewels and s***, yaknahmean?
Black Jesus; you can be Christian
Baptist, Jehovah Witness.
Straight tatted up, no doubt, no doubt
Islamic, won't matter to me
I'm a thug; thugs, we praise Black Jesus, all day.[15]

One thinks of Hebrews 4:15-16 (ESV):

> For we do not have a high priest who is unable to sympathize
> with our weaknesses, but one who in every respect has been
> tempted as we are, yet without sin. Let us then with confidence
> draw near to the throne of grace that we may receive mercy and
> find grace to help in time of need.

The writer of Hebrews tells us that we have a savior and deity who
can identify with us and has been through what we have been through.
Tupac made that same correlation, giving his listeners the suffering
Christ. For Tupac, Hebrews 4:14-16 demonstrated to him that Jesus
knew of the suffering of the 'hood, cared for the individuals there,
and was able to identify with people going through the 'hood's particular trials.

Suffering, as we have seen, is nothing new within Black music. However, when songs do not fall within the norms, values and morality of
the "church" advocated by church tradition, there comes a problem.
Tupac's songs came under criticism because of his "seductive" and
"profane" lyrics, yet Tupac continued to commit to rap about the un-
polished expression and lifestyle of 'hood life.[16] In his song "Hail Mary,"
Tupac wonders whether God will forgive him for all of his sins.

Bow down, pray to God hoping that he's listenin

---

[15]Tupac Shakur, "Searching for Black Jesuz," from the album *2Pac +Outlawz: Still I Rise* (1999).
[16]Anthony Pinn, *Why Lord? Suffering and Evil in Black Theology* (New York: Continuum, 1995), p. 118.

Seein niggaz comin for me, to my diamonds, when they
    glistenin
Now pay attention, rest in peace father
I'm a ghost in these killin fields[17]

According to traditional presentations of the gospel, Tupac could not expect forgiveness. In fact, he surmised, people in the 'hood are in hell already. But what if Jesus really did die so that everyone could be saved? This was one of the fundamental and foundational elements of Tupac's spiritual message within his lyrics and music: a new ideology for salvation and a new definition for sin.

Makaveli in this . . . Killuminati, all through your body
The blow's like a twelve gauge shotty
Uhh, feel me!
And God said he should send his one begotten son
to lead the wild into the ways of the man
Follow me; eat my flesh, flesh and my flesh[18]

Tupac's ultimate criticism was not of Jesus but of the organized church. None of his lyrics ever blasphemed the name of Jesus. Tupac would have his listeners connect to Jesus through different stories and allegories—theological reference points for people who otherwise never set foot in a church. Tupac contextualized the gospel message and made it "digestible" for those who were otherwise shunned by the church (the pimps, prostitutes, gang members, street thugs).

LISTENING TO TUPAC'S MESSAGE

Listening to Tupac's message is not for the faint of spiritual hearts. Tupac presents a very realistic, unadulterated, pure and fresh message about any number of subjects: 'hood life, God, Jesuz, sexuality, social inequalities, and so on. The delicacy of such subjects makes many

[17]Shakur, "Searching for Black Jesuz."
[18]Tupac Shakur, "Hail Mary," from the album *Makaveli—The Don Killuminati: The 7 Day Theory* (1996).

Christians uncomfortable. Facing truths is never easy for many people because it means that in some sense, possibly some of our theologies and notions about God just might be wrong. Tupac was not afraid to learn from his mistakes and admit when he was wrong—although not always right away.

Tupac's theology is not something to be taken lightly nor without careful study of his life. Many Christians would rather disregard people like Tupac because they are too difficult to deal with. The Tupacs of the world question too much, appear as "trouble makers," have deep theological questions of God that cannot be answered in three point sermons, live in a constant state of ambiguity, accept and sometimes embrace their sin-life, appear arrogant and do not fit any type of "normal" Christian faith. On one hand you have Tupac's illicit language, debaucherous mannerisms, profuse use of marijuana and alleged violations of Jesus' commandments. Flip the script and you have Tupac empowering communities, admitting to all of his shortcomings and failures, attempting to make a direct link between God and man, asking for a location in heaven, and declaring a love of Jesuz, lifting him up so that nonchurchgoers can connect to him. What does one do with that?

Contemporary evangelical Christian theology would not embrace such a paradoxical, "liberal" pedagogy of Jesus. Moreover, those within the Black and urban church would reject the mere thought of having an "unsaved" Tupac in their midst. But the Tupacs of the world need to be listened to—and not listened to merely as a pretext for converting them to a more traditional approach to life and faith. These are some of the listening roadblocks that do not yield good results with the Tupacs of the world:

- Listening to offer advice. Probably the most common style of listening, this approach does not really take the other person's narrative into consideration.

- Listening to hold someone "accountable." People are going to do what they want to do. Many experience accountability as a renewed assertion of power and control over a person, particularly those who are going through adversity. I have seen the greatest and most lasting change come when someone feels the freedom to share about their life, even when they've "messed up."

- Listening for control. Many who feel insecure in their own life want to control and declare power over the person they are listening to. This damages the relationship and does not promote authentic community for Hip Hoppers or for people in general. The Tupacs of the world hate it when people try to control their lives. They despise anyone trying to manipulate them. Moreover, this is not the way of Jesus.

- Listening to shame. Shame is never God's intent. However, many pastors use shame as a form of theological authority over their parishioners. It only pushes the Tupacs of the world further away from the church.

- Listening to later rehash. This style of listening is done in order to gain a type of "ammunition" to use in later conversations. The Tupacs of the world will not deal with this style very well and tend to "sniff" out this style of listening very quickly. It does not serve any other purpose other than to put down the person.

- Listening to correct. It is sometimes hard to distinguish between a person listening to correct out of pure intentions, and a person merely asserting their own agenda. In any case, listening to correct makes the listener feel superior to the person they are listening to. The Tupacs of the world will only heed this style of listening for a moment and then find other paths or people to engage with.

I remember one time a young man entered my office in great angst. He seemed troubled but did not know exactly how to articulate his trouble. We jostled around a couple of "how's the weather" remarks, spoke on some trivial sporting events, but I could tell there was something really troubling this young man. So, I just asked, "What seems to be the problem?"

Initially, he did not know what to say and simply replied, "Nothing, nothing at all . . . why do you ask?"

I returned, "Well, it just seems as though you had something on your mind and it seems like you're really in deep thought about something."

"Well, not really . . . I mean, I'm cool . . . Well, there is sorta an issue I've been dealing with. . . . I've been really struggling with . . . well . . . naw, you wouldn't understand."

He began sharing with me how he had been struggling with his sexuality for quite some time. As I sat there only asking clarifying questions, this young man opened up how he had been struggling with women and sexual images. I understood his hesitation. I would not be that eager to share much about my own struggles in the environment we were in: conservative, structured, traditional, very bibliocentric in an unhelpful way. But after almost an hour discussing his struggles and concerns, it seemed as though a weight had been lifted off his chest and his countenance was lifted. I asked him if he had spoken with anyone else about these struggles; he told me that he had, he had spoken with his pastor. "I told him I was struggling with women, and without even listening to the rest of what I had to say, he told me to read the Bible. So I says, 'where?' And he was like, 'Just read anything, it's all good.' So the last four nights I've been reading Jeremiah . . . but I'm still horny!"

We spent the next hour or so talking about practical ways to deal with his sexuality struggles. This young man was going to be all right, but what he needed was that nit grit 'hood theology—someone to listen without casting judgment. Tupac yearned for relationships like this. Tupac wanted conversations where he could just tell his story openly and without the judgment of others. Songs like "Only God Can Judge Me" and "So Many Tears" talk about open and honest conversations about real deep down struggles which, in effect, we all have—whether or not we care to admit it. There is a lot of Tupac in all of us.

Finding Jesus in the Shadows

A THEOLOGY OF THE PROFANE

Growing up I quickly realized that the world was not exactly black and white; there was a lot of gray. My mom, for example, was a proud woman. She raised me to speak up for myself and to be community minded. She did the best she could to give me all that she could during my childhood. She was, however, the "other woman."

I was raised in a fairly conservative Seventh Day Adventist home. I grew up not eating pork, keeping the Saturday sabbath and memorizing Bible verses from the King James Version. The preacher would preach that adultery was a sin and debauchery would land you in hell. The deacons and elders would warn us youth that the path to hell was laid out in sexuality. So for many years I worried about my mom's salvation and her mortal soul. I would pray for her. I would ask God to change her. I would ask that God intervene in her life so that she would make it to heaven. I did all of the things a young boy was taught to do, and I did them methodically.

Yet my mom continued to live this secret life. I saw her belittled, mistreated and scorned by the men in her life. I made up in my mind that I would never treat a woman the way my mom was treated. I decided early on that "cheating" and infidelity were nothing that I wanted to be a part of.

One Saturday, after Sabbath School, I witnessed one of the elders in the church talking to my mom. This particular elder was outspoken against "immorality." Every time he got up to preach, he would talk about adultery being the sin that God hated the most. I believed him, being the impressionable young man that I was, so I thought nothing of this day's interaction between him and my mom. For many years I did not catch any of the subtle nuances between them.

Several years later, when this elder had moved on to another church, my mom and I were talking about life in general and I asked if she had ever heard from this elder. She told me that on several occasions he had returned just to see her. I thought, *Wow, that's cool. Why didn't he get hold of me—and did he bring his wife?* My mom cautiously and openly revealed to me that she had been having an affair with this man for quite some time. Moreover, he had been having affairs with several women in the church and the community.

How could this be? How could the deacon that always preached about sexual immorality be committing the same sin?

I was confused. I was perplexed. I was disappointed in many ways. However, most of my disappointment did not reside with my mom but with my religious beliefs. I was told I served a God that could do anything. I was taught that God struck down sinners and punished them. I was shown, through sermons and lesson plans, that God did not allow sin into his presence; we had to be clean in order to even talk to God. So what did all of this mean now? How could I compute all of this new data in my preadolescent brain? And, was God really angry at my mom and this deacon?

My mom loved Jesus. I am sure this deacon loved God too; he would go on crusades where many were brought into the community of God. My mom witnessed to a lot of her friends and coworkers, and gave me my first theological training, raising me to believe in the Ten Commandments and the Trinity, and to have a personal relationship with Jesus Christ. So were all of these people going to hell for the "sins" they committed? Was God really not hearing their prayers? Moreover, how could God use such murky people to do his work?

And what about all of the confusing and mixed messages that not only I received, but also the hundreds of other people that came in contact with this elder?

Many years later, after I was able to gain some context and perspective on the situation, I was able to see that all of us possess these profane areas in our lives. Some of us just know how to cover it up better.

THE INTERSECTING POINTS OF THE
SACRED AND THE PROFANE

Hip Hop was a great beacon of light for me in those years for me. I was able to accept myself for who I was as well, and I was able to see my mom and this deacon as just human—imperfect and flawed just like all humans. Jesuz resides not just in the hallowed, sacred, holy and "nice" places in life, but also in the reprehensible, despicable, contemptible and profane places too. God communicates with not just seemingly perfect people but also with the people who need him the most: the "wicked," the lost, the marginalized, the "given up on," the iniquitous, the people who have gone astray.

Hip Hoppers "tell it like it is," calling out the truth in a way many are not able to digest well. Hip Hoppers call out deacons, pastors and other "officials" that pretend to be "perfect," all the while accepting the frailty of the human condition—breathing it, indulging it, putting it on display for further consideration.

The profane is nothing nice. We have been socialized to stay away from the profane, and avoid it at all costs. Yet it represents all of us collectively. So for Hip Hop, the profane is just another dimension to life. Early on, I could not realize or comprehend this last statement. I was raised to believe that God did not have anything to do with sinners, but, as I would later find out, what is the purpose of Christ's mission? What is the meaning and point to John 3:16: "God so loved the world that he gave his one and only son"?

Before we move any further we must first define the sacred and the profane as they relate to Hip Hop.

From a sociological perspective, the profane are social realities in life that occur every day, are ordinary, common, general. They have no real mystery to them. The profane also include the contours of life that are deemed evil, wicked, immoral and corrupt. This type of profanity is typically deemed as "sin" and avoided at all costs. Yet for the Hip Hop community, it is the reality of life, especially in the projects.

From a sociological perspective, the sacred areas of life are typically deemed "special" and/or hallowed; they are the areas that are meant to be taken with great care in a mindful manner. The sacred typically involve an authority figure performing a ritual. Typically associated with religion, the sacred can involve intimate moments with God through prayer or meditation. For the Hip Hop community, this is also a regular part of life—though not typically every day.

Mircea Eliade contends that the sacred manifests itself differently in us than the profane.[1] The sacred engages the individual with a deeper sense of spirituality.[2] Hip Hoppers, however, encounter far more spiritual experiences in the profane.

When Eddy Murphy was on *Saturday Night Live*, he played a character named Mr. Robinson, a parody of Mr. Rogers. Murphy took the same everyday life situations that Mr. Rogers went through—coming in to a warm home, taking off his coat and talking with his television neighbors—but placed them in the context of the 'hood. Mr. Robinson was much more attractive to the Hip Hop community than Mr. Rogers because he represented the profane—a social reality that is commonplace for those living in the 'hood—while indicting the idealized "sacredness" of upper class White society and Reaganesque meritocracy. The group Living Color would further articulate this disparity in their song "Which Way to America?" from the 1988 album *Vivid*.

I look at the T.V. Your America's doing well.

I look out the window; my America's catching hell.

---

[1]Mircea Eliade, *The Sacred and the Profane: The Nature of Religion,* trans. Willard R. Trask (New York: Harcourt, Brace & World, 1959), pp. 10-11.
[2]Ibid., pp. 26-29.

I just want to know which way do I go to get to your America?

In the face of such disparity, Hip Hoppers seek outlets for rage, outlets that account for the the deep reality of nihilism and disillusionment with the appeal to "focus on the things that are sacred." Sociologist Daniel Bell suggests that postmodernism "rages against order."[3] As a postmodern phenomenon, Hip Hop likewise "rages" against the order of life it encounters,[4] remixing social realities to make its own. Comedian Dave Chappell has many characters similar to Murphy's Mr. Robinson. But Chappell went further, transposing the presumed social norm into a social realist meal that one could digest in a comedic way. Chappell embraces both the sacred and the profane in his comedy, expertly remixing what mainstream America has deemed "good living" for an urban, Hip Hop context.

Hip Hop's problem with Christianity has nothing to do with Jesus, God or even the Bible. It has everything to do with the perceived superiority that many Christians revel in. Hip Hop says, "You ain't any better than us just cuzz you look good. You ain't all that, I know what's in your dark closet!"[5] Hip Hop calls out the profane in all of us, echoing (and affirming) Romans 3:22-27:

> There is no difference, for all have sinned and fall short of the glory of God, and are justified freely by his grace through the redemption that came by Christ Jesus. . . .
>
> Where, then, is boasting? It is excluded. On what principle? On that of observing the law? No, but on that of faith.

In Hip Hop's eyes all are equal at the foot of the cross; none have transcended the profane element of life. Life has its profane moments, and when they come we just have to live in them. What my mom and

---

[3]Daniel Bell, *The Coming of a Post-Industrial Society: A Venture in Social Forecasting* (New York: Basic Books, 1973).

[4]Scott Lash, "Postmodernism as Humanism? Urban Space and Social Theory," in *Theories of Modernity and Postmodernity*, ed. B. S. Turner (Thousand Oaks, Calif.: Sage, 1990), pp. 130-34.

[5]Personal interview, July 2008.

that deacon did was wrong. Yet God still loved them and still loves them today. God used them both, if for nothing else, then to challenge me to go deeper into a relationship with Christ. And, whether we like it or not, God allowed those actions to happen. So what do we do with God now? How do we contend with a God that allows such sinful people to propagate his message? These are deep and perplexing questions that the Hip Hop community contends with on many occasions.

Dealing with the profane is difficult because it involves distinguishing what is moral from what is simply trash. I am not suggesting that anything goes with God or that God allows transgressions to go unchecked. However, if we are going to live an authentic life, then we must be open to having discussions that do not always "feel good" or end "good." We must unfasten the belief that says life is "all good" once you follow Christ and abandon the worldview that curse words will land you in hell.

The theology of the profane for Hip Hop takes on five key elements that help shape its entire ethos:

1. It calls out the double standards and hypocrisies. For Hip Hop, authenticity is the fountain of life. When one leaves that fountain and begins "frontin'," they enter into hypocrisy. Hip Hop calls this out. Television commentator Bill O'Reilly argued that Ludacris's lyrics were immoral and misogynistic, indirectly causing Pepsi to drop Ludacris as a spokesman. One year later O'Reilly himself was sued for sexual harassment. Rappers like David Banner called out O'Reilly's hypocrisy in 2005's "Letter to the President": "Bill trying to get some p**** like the rappers! Come on now!"

2. "Four letter" words are at the disposal for Hip Hoppers not, generally, to tear people down but to make a larger point. Language is seen as being socially constituted, rooted in social relationships and produced in the conduct of social life. Thus, rappers like Tupac ask the question, "How can I be an Angel when I'm surrounded by Devils?"[6]

---

[6]More commercial rap, divorced from the social consciousness of the broader Hip Hop movement, may use language to demean and even verbally abuse its listeners,

3. Wry humor is a coping mechanism for Hip Hop. One of the things that made Dave Chappell's "Crack Muppets" so uproarious is that it is tinged with reality. A strung-out Muppet makes jokes as he searches for crack. While many would find such humor repulsive, ask any war veteran: irreverent humor helps people to cope with untenable situations—otherwise, "You'd just go crazy and blow your head off, man!"[7]

4. Hip Hop does not settle for the imposed perfection of mainstream society. When First Lady Nancy Reagan first announced the "Just Say No" anti-drug campaign, all within the 'hood knew that was a joke. Simply saying that would get you killed in the 'hood. It is easy to forecast idealism and perfection on another environment, but Hip Hop resists such imposition. There are degrees of "the good life" for Hip Hoppers, but perfection is only something you reach when you leave this life.

5. Institutions by and large are not trusted by Hip Hop. Tom Beaudoin sees Generation X as opposed to "domesticated churches and Jesus";[8] as a parallel generation, Hip Hoppers are no less tolerant of those forms. Institutions represent a power structure that hinders diversity and multiethnicity, the stale Mcdonaldization of Christ and the modernistic depiction of religion. Ice Cube's song "Go to Church"[9] on first glance appears blasphemous, but in fact he is lamenting the church's "sissifying" of Jesus.

The struggles of Hip Hop's heroes are in view among the Hip Hop community. Some of those heroes are even found in the pages of the Bible, where we find the transcendent, the spiritual, in some very profane contexts.

---

but such misuses of language are recognized in the Hip Hop community as departures from acceptable use.

[7]Taken from a 2006 interview.

[8]Tom Beaudoin, *Virtual Faith: The Irreverent Spiritual Quest of Generation X* (San Francisco: Jossey-Bass, 1998).

[9]Ice Cube, "Go to Church," from the album *Laugh Now, Cry Later* (2006).

KEEPIN' IT REAL: PROFANITY THROUGH THE BIBLE

The use of profane people throughout the Bible is amazing. God used "ordinary" people to do his work. God used "profane sinners" to proclaim his message. This type of mission could be considered *missio Hominum*—human instrumentality in God's mission. Many Hip Hop artists bear remarkable similarities to characters in the Bible. Place Lauryn Hill in Esther. Put Big Syke as Joshua. Cast Lil' Kim as Tamar. You have a band of Bible heroes that are nowhere near "perfect" yet embody God's missional plan. Let us start in Genesis, where we will find profane acts beginning.

Genesis 27–28. Genesis 27 commences with Isaac wanting to bless his older son, Esau. Deathbed blessings (and curses) were important in the life and literature of ancient peoples. It was believed that such blessings irrevocably determined the character and destiny of the recipient. Chapter 26 makes clear that this is Isaac's transfer of a divine blessing first given to Abraham (Genesis 12:1-3).[10] Chapter 27, however, is replete with deception and drama. Younger brother Jacob was aided by his mother in perpetrating an act of dishonesty worth its weight in a Hollywood blockbuster. Rebekah waited for Esau to leave, then set Jacob up to scam his father and receive the blessing meant for Esau, who had not done anything wrong. The only "blessing" left for him was the prediction that he would serve his younger brother (27:39-40).

Now, you cannot imagine the son of Billy Graham stealing his father's name, swindling money and property, and still being blessed by God. It would be inconceivable; Billy's son would be shunned by the Christian community. But God gives Jacob a dream and promises him land and the assurance of his presence until God's purpose is fulfilled through Jacob (Genesis 28:12-16). A preposterous and curious thing for God to do indeed, but God did it anyway. Israel, the twelve tribes of which came from Jacob's offspring, would be the cen-

---

[10]Michael Coogan et al., eds., *New Oxford Annotated Bible: New Revised Standard Version* (New York: Oxford University Press, 2001), p. 48.

terpiece people that God used in the Old Testament. But their very beginnings were formed from lying and cheating. "Indeed Israel herself was a standing witness to the power and reality of who Yahweh was and what he had done in their history."[11]

From Jacob's "mess" we can learn three missional issues:

1. God can use profane activity. Jacob's role in God's mission despite his dubious morality sends a strong missional message to those that feel they "mess up" all the time with God. God doesn't honor Jacob's schemes, but God honors Jacob's sincerity toward him, and uses it so that many others might come to him. God uses Jacob's imperfections to reach a world through a nation.[12]

2. God is not afraid of a little mess. Jacob wrested with God's angel all night long. He knew that he needed God, even though he was not the "model" follower. He was renamed "The one who strives with God (Israel)" as a result of this engagement (Genesis 32:28). God was not afraid to deal with Jacob's shortcomings and readily accepted him with open arms—a missional message to the people the church perceives as "unwanted."

3. God sets a nonstandard for people who "don't fit" to come to him. God demonstrated through Jacob that anyone could come to him, even when they have done great harm and damage. Jacob broke several traditions and customs, not to mention he lied. Still, God used him as an example to people that have fallen away from the church and or God.

Jacob can therefore be seen as a model that breaks typical church stereotypes of what a Christian has to be.

Psalms 141–142. Helen Montgomery, arguably one of the greatest women missionaries, sees poets as "the ever 'makers,' the 'see-ers'

---

[11]Walter Kaiser, *Mission in the Old Testament: Israel as a Light to the Nations* (Grand Rapids: Baker Books, 2000), p. 54.

[12]This is an example of *missio Hominum*—human instrumentality in God's mission. They are both simultaneously "just" and "sinful" yet God uses them for a bigger plan.

who lead the advance of human thought, and so it is not strange that some of the clearest missionary passages of the Old Testament should be found in the Psalms."[13] The Psalms flirt with the profanity of life, while giving homage to the sacred and reverent power of God. Tupac often used the Psalms as a "template" for his outcry for the inner city. Tracks like "Keep Your Head Up," "Dear Momma" and "How Long Will They Mourn Me?" all draw from Psalms 140–145.

Many in the ghetto have echoed David's lament to God about how rough and dire a situation is: "I call upon you, O Lord; come quickly to me; give ear to my voice when I call to you" (Psalm 141:1 NRSV). One of the greatest pleas of Gen Xers, of whom the Hip Hop community are peers, is that they be given a voice in the public sphere.[14] Many in the inner city have the same cry: "Help me, O Lord, cause I ain't got nobody else!" Often times though, the Black church will say that suffering is a direct result of a lack of faith, and if the person had more faith or gave larger tithing, they would be blessed and not be going through such ills.

What do we do when our enemies keep coming toward us with increasing anger and hatred in their eyes? David asks God to "cover his lips" and "set guard" over his mouth. If we look into the passage a little more clearly, we might see that David needed God's help to not cuss his adversaries out and thus make a fool of himself in public.

David was considered a "man after God's own heart," but he was far from perfect. David set his own boy up so that he could get at his wife. Not only that, David loved some women. In the church we would have this brother in a twelve-step program on sex and lust. The elders would be giving David a Bible study on how we should not look at women in lust. Yet, David is in the Bible. The Psalms is one of the most used books for the inner city. Could it be that David, in spite of his shortcomings and failings, just might have been considered "right-

---

[13]Helen Montgomery, *The Bible and Missions* (Brattleboro, Vt.: Central Committee on the United Study of Foreign Mission, 1920), p. 26.

[14]Craig Detweiler and Barry Taylor, *A Matrix of Meanings: Finding God in Pop Culture* (Grand Rapids: Baker Academic, 2003), p. 30.

eous" because of his honest and open heart to God?

David holds nothing back. He begs of God to not let his heart turn to evil so that he would not be preoccupied with wicked deeds (Psalm 141:4). However, at the end of Psalm 142 David brings it all back and asks God to help him and forgive him for the other sins he had done (v. 7). David was honest and transparent before the Lord, something that many Christians cannot be. Psalm 142 is filled with laments to God; still God listened and honored David even in his time of doubt and anger.

Missionally, God was trying to use David's doubt, anger, frustration, and lack of faith to demonstrate that we are all human before him, so that others could be encouraged of his love for them. Further, we can all lament to God, without worry that we would be chastened by God.

Sometimes we forget that David was human. Walter Kaiser writes:

> Over and over again the psalmists called on all the peoples of all the lands and nations to praise the Lord (Pss. 47:1; 67:3,5; 100:1; 117:1). Even more directly, these ancient singers of Israel urged their people to tell, proclaim, and make known the mighty deeds of Yahweh (Pss. 9:11; 105:1) and to join in singing praises to God from all the nations (Pss. 18:49; 96:2-3). The psalmists themselves offer to sing God's praises among the nations (Pss. 57:9; 108:3). The expected result would be that all the ends of the earth would turn to the Lord and all the families on earth would bow down in worship to him (Pss. 22:27; 66:4; 86:9).[15]

This is a great message for Hip Hop. God allowed these laments by David to show that some of the same problems existed then as they do now. However, David does not stay in his lament or anger; he asks God to help him "move on." What an encouragement for people who are facing eviction because of an unfair landlord, financial troubles, teen pregnancy, homosexuality and many other issues that the Black

---

[15]Kaiser, *Mission in the Old Testament*, p. 37.

church is not ready to deal with. God used David in many ways, in all his "ugliness" and "profane" language. Prophetic voices in Hip Hop should be given the same consideration as well.

Daniel 3–4. God wanted to bring all people to him—not just a few. God used people outside the people of God (Gentiles) to proclaim his message.[16] In Daniel 3–4, for example, we find king Nebuchadnezzar filled with his own pride and lust of his own kingdom. And yet God used Nebuchadnezzar in several ways.

God allowed Nebuchadnezzar to accumulate many riches and fame. God allowed him to be filled with pride as he built a monument to himself. After God gave him a conscious vision of who God is (Daniel 3:28) Nebuchadnezzar lost the vision, only to regain it again and proclaim God's glory in his kingdom (Daniel 4:37).

Nebuchadnezzar was used in his pride. If Nebuchadnezzar had never had such arrogance, he never would have built the statute to himself, the three Hebrew boys never would have demonstrated God's power, and the people of Babylon would not have been given such exposure to God. It was law that the people of a kingdom follow the king's religion. God knew this. Nebuchadnezzar's pride made him build such a monument and God allowed that. We can almost see the arrogant statements that Nebuchadnezzar made: "I'm tha man! No one can stop me!" "You'd better serve me, fool; don't you know who I am? You'd better recognize!"

God uses Nebuchadnezzar's kingdom to proclaim his word through the miraculous events that happened with Shadrach, Meshach and Abednego. Nebuchadnezzar was amazed at how much power God had; he was probably in awe for the first time. Nebuchadnezzar's pride just didn't go away after seeing the power of God, however; he had to witness it once again. The church might say that Nebuchadnezzar "lost his salvation" or needed a "mentor" to walk with him, but something else is happening here. After the *experience* in the fields of eating like an animal (Daniel 4:30-33), Nebuchadnez-

---

[16]Cf. ibid., pp. 40-44.

zar truly understood the power of God. He stood up, praised God and extolled God's power (Daniel 4:36-37); one can imagine that his kingdom looked a lot differently after the second time he had witnessed God's power.

God's mission was not just for the nation of Israel. We overlook that God wanted the people in Nebuchadnezzar's kingdom to be saved too—not just Shadrach, Meshach, and Abednego. God wanted all the people to not only know his power but his love for them. God worked through the king to reach the people in the streets.[17] Even though most Christians see Nebuchadnezzar as proud, arrogant, overconfident and a luster of riches, God used him anyway.

What a powerful message for the hustlers, pimps, prostitutes, gang members and drug lords: despite their obvious issues and character flaws, they can be used by God. More important, God wants them in his kingdom.

The Old Testament is filled with God's missional plan. We must simply get past the "simple" and "easy" Scriptures and look for what God is doing through all people.[18] For Hip Hoppers, this could not be any truer. From the Old Testament passages, we see three things that stand out:

1. *God is not afraid of questions and complaints.* God is a big boy. He can handle a little criticism and questioning. Jacob wrestled not only physically with God, but spiritually. He wanted God's blessing, but surely felt guilt for what he had done. Yet God used him to build a great nation. David asked God why he had left him and why he was allowing his enemies to gain ground on his life. Once again, God used David and had him proclaim his word to many. God can handle things the church seems to think he cannot.

---

[17]Arthur Glasser, *Announcing the Kingdom: The Story of God's Mission in the Bible* (Grand Rapids: Baker Academic, 2003), pp. 118-19.

[18]Richard Ridder, "The Old Testament Roots of Mission," in *Exploring Church Growth*, ed. W. Shenk (Grand Rapids: Eerdmans, 1983), p. 184. Here Ridder discusses how many have used the simple and easy way of reading the Bible to set up any program they have in their church. The Bible then becomes a tool for "proof" rather than it being a light unto the world.

2. *God uses dysfunction as an example of his love.* Time after time humans mess up. But God uses these dysfunctions to demonstrate that ordinary people lived in Old Testament times—shepherds, cattle herders and simple farmers. We make these biblical characters bigger than life, but Jacob was a simple street hustler who hustled his way toward God. Nebuchadnezzar was a proud and arrogant king whose kingdom was used to build *God's* kingdom.

3. *God wants all people to know him.* God will go to the ends of the earth so that people will know his love for them. Jacob had to have his hip broken before he realized that God wanted to use him. Nebuchadnezzar had to eat and live like an animal before he knew how God really loved him. David was in the wilderness for a long time questioning God, but then brings his issues back before God for his blessing. God goes to the furthest extent for his missional plan to unfold, and we see his love for all people, not just the ones who "do right."

We can begin to see that God uses the profane activity of people to glorify the sacredness of his love and grace on our lives. Moreover, we can see that people who would have been criticized, corrected and humiliated by the church were the very ones God used to fulfill his plans to reach *all* people. Once again, if we are open enough, we can see God reaching out to Hip Hoppers just like he did for people in the Old Testament.

NEW TESTAMENT OFFENSES

The New Testament brings about much controversy for many outside the Christian canopy. The selection of books, the accuracy of translation, the perplexity of authorship on certain books and the person of Jesus are all subject to debate. Newer religions have attempted to broaden the New Testament canon. For Hip Hoppers—particularly Five Percenters—the New Testament is a vast field for interpretation; one should never think that they have "figured it out" completely.

Just a few New Testament offenses will illustrate the theology of the profane. For many Hip Hoppers (and others as well), these offenses are the untold story of the New Testament.

Matthew 9:9-26. Jesus did not flinch when it came to living among known sinners. Jesus was motivated to deal with the profanity and unsightliness that life often brings.[19] "According to Matthew, mission is also motivated in Jesus' compassion. From the beginning Matthew underscores the real nature of Jesus' Messiahship."[20] Jesus was not concerned with what people thought; rather his vision was that he might help "sinners" know his love better.

The religious people of Jesus' day looked down on tax collectors. Most Pharisees would not be caught with any known sinners for fear of shunning. Jesus, however, overlooked the obvious mess and engaged right where people were at: in their homes.

Matthew was a tax collector, one of the most hated groups of people of that time—much like drug dealers, pimps, and hustlers are in the 'hood today. They were seen as evildoers and "cheats"—and in many respects, they were. But, Jesus engaged Matthew by breaking bread with him.[21]

At dinner, the food one ate, and one's table companions, were important aspects of defining one's group membership.[22] Jesus wanted to be identified with sinners. He wanted to know these people not as "sinners" but as people. Jesus knew that he needed to get out of the church in order to do this. He shows excellent communal traits here, which the Hip Hop community is extremely fond of. Dining with someone is one of the most important and influential things a person could do; for many in the ghetto it still is.

As Jesus was eating and dining with the known "sinners," there came one of his accusers from the synagogue, who asked humbly for

---

[19]See Detweiler and Taylor, *Matrix of Meanings,* esp. chap. 3 , "Future Saints."
[20]Johannes Nissen, *New Testament and Mission: Historical and Hermeneutical Perspectives* (New York: Lang, 1999), p. 24.
[21]The translation for "dinner" is "reclining" or "at ease," according to the NRSV. That means Jesus was at ease and reclining with known sinners in their house, tolerating their language and culture for the bettering of the kingdom.
[22]Adapted from Coogan et al., eds. *New Oxford Annotated Bible,* p. 20.

172 THE SOUL OF HIP HOP

Jesus to raise his daughter from the dead (Matthew 9:18). Jesus could have either said, "Aha! I knew you fools would need me. Well, you can beat it now, punk." I would have done this, unfortunately. Jesus' other choice was to raise this girl from the dead, and love on this person as a grand example of his universal love for all people despite their short-comings. That is what Jesus did, and many in the town believed (Matthew 9:26) and came to know who Jesus was.

Jesus knew his mission, and in spite of all their profane culture, language and thoughts, he still loved people and engaged them where they were.[23] This is a true Hip Hop principle, and Jesus' example can be our example in the church as well. We can look to Jesus' example of showing patience when dealing with human flaws.

John 4:7-42. Arguably one of the strongest missional passages in the New Testament is Jesus' engagement with the woman at the well. We see several strong missional aspects occurring here:

1. Jesus was engaging with a Samaritan[24] woman. Jesus had to have heard all the negative comments that were said about Samaritans, but he still overlooked those and connected with the woman in her environment. Jesus knew very well what this could mean for his reputation, yet once again he ignored the social pressure to conform to tradition. Jesus knew the woman needed his love.

2. Jesus entered into the life of a sinner. He knew that the woman had many issues; she even argued with him about some of them. Jesus was not offended; he stayed right in there and dealt with the problems at hand. Jesus sat and asked the woman questions about her life, even though he knew her whole story. He opened up a dialogue with her, and she felt better connected. Jesus did not start off with a verse or a "salvation" message. He was asking for help and service. He came humbly before her, not arrogant and self-

---

[23]Nissen, *New Testament and Mission,* pp. 80-81.
[24]Samaria, between Judea and Galilee, was inhabited by remnants of the northern tribes of ancient Israel who worshiped the Lord God and used the Pentateuch. Jews did not acknowledge the authenticity of the Samaritan observances; see John 4:9 (Coogan et al., eds., *New Oxford Annotated Bible,* p. 153).

aggrandizing (John 4:7-8). Jesus helped the woman find her story in him so that she could see the bigger picture (John 4:11-13). Jesus sat at the well and began to open up his love for her by narrative.

3. Jesus knew very well that this woman was involved in a difficult lifestyle that did not honor him. Yet it was not until verse 16 that Jesus engaged the woman about her issues. He even allowed her to question his authority (John 4:12) and did not miss a beat. Jesus wanted all people to know that no matter what the issue, the sin or the problem, he is there.

4. Jesus used a Samaritan to serve others. Jesus used a person that the "church" of his day would not consider "normal" or righteous. Through all her mess and setbacks, the Samaritan woman was able to evangelize many (John 4:39-42). For many in the church, the pastor is the one who does the evangelizing and the "saving." That is just not so in these particular passages (and not many other places in the New Testament either). A sinful, guilty, proud, strong-willed Samaritan woman was used to better God's kingdom and demonstrate, once again, God's love for all people despite their religious training or prominence.

Jesus knew that the prophets of his time would come from "popular culture."[25] More importantly, because Jesus was noticeably a Jew, she was probably able to speak into more Samaritan lives than he could, working with different families to proclaim the love and mission of Jesus. David Bosch writes that the resurrected Lord announces that, after Jerusalem and Judea, Samaria will be the recipient of the gospel (Acts 1:8); the Samaritan mission suggests a fundamental break with traditional Jewish attitudes.[26] Jesus broke tradition while engaging with the perceived vulgarity of life.

Jesus focused on a centrifugal mindset rather than a centripetal

[25]David Dark, *Everyday Apocalypse: The Sacred Revealed in Radiohead, the Simpsons, and Other Pop Culture Icons* (Grand Rapids: Brazos, 2002), pp. 13-15.
[26]David Bosch, *Transforming Mission: Paradigm Shifts in Theology of Mission*, American Society of Missiology 16 (Maryknoll, N.Y.: Orbis Books, 1991), p. 91.

one. Even though he could have commanded people with one word to come to him, he knew that the best way for his love to be shown was to go out among them. The New Testament is filled with God using the profane to benefit his outward, centrifugal mission. As such, the New Testament is a connecting point for Hip Hoppers to better understand the richness and love of Jesus. Jesus ignored the traditions of the day and gives us a great example of how we should ignore the minor areas of a "sinner's" lifestyle and focus in on the major parts— why they are hurting and how to overcome that hurt. All the cursing and foul way of living will change over time—Jesus knew this and was patient. He did not try to rush anything, and people like Matthew (a former tax collector), the Samaritan woman (a former "ho"), and a religious leader (a former criticizer of Jesus) were all used to glorify him and demonstrate God's universal love for all people. Sounds kind of Hip Hop to me.

JESUS' USE OF PROFANE LANGUAGE

Most find it hard to believe that Jesus said anything that did not ring true to conservative, fundamental, evangelical Christianity. Moreover, most would find it hard that Jesus used strong illicit language to make his points. But in fact, Jesus did, using language which most in his day would consider to be profane. In reality, Jesus was a profane prophet. He consistently did things that most Christians would consider to be rude, mean, condescending or discourteous. Jack Miles[27] records several instances in Jesus' life that make him "The Lord of Blasphemy":

- In John 5:1-18 and 7:19-24, Jesus flagrantly violates the law of Sabbath rest by healing an invalid.

- Jesus argues with the religious officials of his day and attempts to shame his opponents.

- In John 8:2-11 Jesus refuses to condemn an adulteress, which, in

---

[27]Jack Miles, *Christ: A Crisis in the Life of God* (New York: Alfred A. Knopf, 2001), chap. 3.

his day, men were able to do—especially religious officials.

- Jesus issues a new commandment to be kind to strangers and makes new commandments about the old commandments.

- In Matthew 25:31-36 Jesus states that there will be victory over death and insists that he is the path to God's kingdom.

- Jesus constantly uses the phrase "I am," which inflames the hostility and tensions with the church of his day.

All of these instances were extremely controversial for Jesus' day. Jesus had several death plots against him for "blasphemous" acts. In today's Westernized, dampened Christianity, by contrast, we do not take into consideration the amount of trouble that he stirred up. We have made Jesus into this submissive, passive, goatee-wearing, guitar-playing runt!

Jesus uses strong language when he deals with his enemies, words that if used today would discredit him as a foul-mouthed "hoodlum" for many Christians. In Matthew 3:7, we see Jesus calling the Pharisees "vipers." This word today is very soft contextually; it does not connote much irreverence in our context. However, "viper" in Jesus' day was the equivalent of the F-word today. For Jesus to use this word—especially given the hostility with which we are led to believe it is used in Matthew—was considered a profane act. Other translations have Jesus saying "You spawn of Satan" or "You imposters! Damn You!"[28] We cannot fathom a Jesus that talks this way, yet in several other occurrences, he did. In Matthew 23:13-15, for example, Jesus is seen using the word *hypocrite* to call out the Pharisees. This particular word was never used to describe a high-ranking teacher in Jesus' day. The word *hupokrinomai* can mean an actor under an assumed character (stage-player), a dissembler ("hypocrite") or the type of person we identify today as a "hypocrite."

Similarly, Jesus' use of "flesh," "eat" and "drink blood" would

---

[28]Robert Funk and Roy Hoover, *The Five Gospels: The Search for the Authentic Words of Jesus: New Translation and Commentary* (San Francisco: HarperCollins, 1993), pp. 241-44.

have been considered profane in traditional Jewish culture. One was never to touch, much less "eat" the flesh of another human.[29] Yet Jesus requests as much of his followers in John 6:52-58. Many of his disciples turn away in disgust and shock that Jesus would even use this type of language (John 6:60-67). Jack Miles observes that "the notion that God Incarnate should propose even the symbolic drinking of his own blood is so obscene as to seem almost deranged—a charge that has been made against Jesus already."[30]

Charles Kraft states regarding language and communication, "Contexts/settings, like other vehicles, and the words, gestures, and so forth that flow though them, mean something because they are interpreted to mean something."[31] We assign meaning to words. Words do not contain meanings; people do.[32] Hence, when we condemn young people for using vulgarities we essentially condemn that story.

If a young person walks up to you and says, "Man, can we talk? My f***ing grandmother just died and I'm all f***ed up about it!" And your first response is, "Hey, that's messed up, but can you watch your language?" You have in essence belittled that person's dead grandmother and destroyed that young person's narrative of life struggles. If I were that young person, I would not be inclined to share any part of my life with you.[33] Language is an arbitrary system of assigning meaning to life, culture, and context.[34]

Now, this does not mean that "anything goes" and anyone can use any word any old way. No, that is not right either. Then again, after

[29]Miles, *Christ: A Crisis.*

[30]Ibid. p. 140.

[31]Charles Kraft, *Communication Theory for Christian Witness* (Maryknoll, N.Y.: Orbis Books, 1991), p. 131.

[32]Ibid.

[33]Every one hundred to one hundred and twenty years, we—as a collective society—reshape and redefine what "curse" words are. Language is redefined and we assign meaning to words, not the reverse. For example, the word *gyp*, which we now use to refer to someone who has cheated us, was a derogatory word toward gypsies.

[34]See Stella Ting-Toomey and Leeva C. Chung, *Understanding Intercultural Communication* (Los Angeles: Roxbury, 2005) for an in-depth look at the intricacies within communication, language and vernacular studies.

having been in ministerial work for the last fifteen years, I have seen plenty of times when pastors, priests, lay workers and prophets alike have destroyed, humiliated, debased, degraded and verbally abused people never once using a four letter word. Language is what we make it to be. So when young people come up and begin dropping F-bombs and "curse" words, I do not flinch until the moment those words turn toward someone or something and begin to belittle, demean, or verbally abuse another person.

THE HOLY PROFANE WITHIN BLACK TRADITIONS

Hip Hop did not create profanity. Those elements of life and society existed long before Hip Hop arrived into our culture. America has some vicious roots and has been sexist since its inception. Hip Hop merely picked up where others left off and speaks to a lot of the truth. Hip Hop is sort of like the 'hood's social commentary on life and social events.[35]

The "Holy Profane," as Teresa Reed puts it, is a deep part of the rich religious tradition in Black popular music. Reed states that, "The relationship between sacred and secular has been a source of controversy in both the African-American and the West-European musical traditions."[36] This controversy has roots that go back into the early nineteenth century when Blacks were developing their brand of musical genres. Most Whites considered "Black gospel" an abomination in

---

[35]This particular study of profane music within Black traditions is nothing new. There are many scholars that discuss this issue at length. The parameters of this book limit the scope of this section to paragraphs, but that in no way diminishes the work that has gone before me. For an in-depth study I recommend Jon Michael Spencer, ed., *Sacred Music of the Secular City: From Blues to Rap* (Durham, N.C.: Duke University Press, 1992); Cheryl L. Keyes, *Rap Music and Street Consciousness* (Chicago: University of Illinois Press, 2002), particularly chaps. 1-4; Eileen Southern, *The Music of Black Americans*, 2nd ed. (New York: W. W. Norton, 1983); Christa K. Dixon, *Negro Spirituals: From Bible to Folk Song* (Philadelphia: Fortress Press, 1976); Howard Thurman, *The Negro Spirituals Speak of Life and Death* (Richmond, Va.: Friends United Press, 1975); and Jon Michael Spencer, *Blues in Evil* (Knoxville: University of Tennessee Press, 1993).

[36]Teresa Reed, *The Holy Profane: Religion in Black Popular Music* (Lexington: University Press of Kentucky, 2003), p. 1.

the eyes of God; they did not see Black gospel music as a valid form or source of spirituality.[37] Slaves embraced late-night worship, concealing their narratives and music to avoid punishment by the slave owners.[38] Fast-forward into the twentieth century and you have the emergence of blues and jazz as music forms. The blues speak to a style of "living," according to Anthony Pinn. The blues, like Hip Hop, move the individual to ponder deeply the issues of life.

> The blues, then, is a recognition of the value of African Americans through their ability to shape and control language and thus a world—a world full of sarcasm and tenacious black bodies. This has been a mature depiction of life that recognizes the often absurd nature of encounter in a way that avoids nihilism and calls into question the nature of social crisis. This music teaches that life can be harsh, but these crises are not always 'unto death,' and in some cases are quite laughable.... It teaches that life is survivable and more.[39]

The blues musical tradition runs in the veins of many soul, R & B and rap artists that top today's music charts.[40] Like blues and jazz, Hip Hop continues the "experimentation with black orality . . . taking the themes and sensibilities housed in musical expression for centuries and giving them a postindustrial twist."[41]

But in the development of the Black church there is a distinction between music that is morally "right" or "wrong." Reed further asserts, "The emergence of the blues against the backdrop of the burgeoning black church at the end of the nineteenth century further ensured the recognition of two distinct categories of music: one that

---

[37]See Donald Paul Hustad, *Jubilate: Church Music in the Evangelical Tradition* (Carol Stream, Ill.: Hope Publishing, 1981); Eileen Southern, *The Music of Black Americans*, 2nd ed. (New York: W. W. Norton, 1983).

[38]Reed, *Holy Profane*, pp. 17-21.

[39]Anthony Pinn, ed., *Noise and Spirit: The Religious and Spiritual Sensibilites of Rap Music* (New York: New York University Press, 2003), pp. 6-7.

[40]Ibid.

[41]Ibid., p. 14.

was appropriate for church use and one that was not."[42]

One of the great scenes in Taylor Hackford's 2004 film *Ray* was when Ray Charles was playing in a scanty night club. Charles had combined Black gospel music with his own style of contemporary blues, infused with an early rendition of soul. Church members burst through the doors calling out Charles for the blasphemous act he had done in combining "God's music" with the "devil's music." Some of the attendees felt guilty and left with the avid church evangelists, including Charles's own band members. But, assured of his relationship with God, Charles continued playing to the crowd's delight. Forty-five years later, Ray Charles's music is, ironically, played at different church events.

So, for quite some time, there has been a tension between "sacred" music and "profane" music within most Christian traditions. For Blacks however, this sacred and profane element of music really gathered steam during the early twentieth century. Blacks were now more fragmented.[43] Cornel West states that "Afro-American music is first and foremost, though not exclusively or universally a countercultural practice with deep roots in modes of religious transcendence and political opposition."[44] Jazz, blues, funk and soul music are all a part of this "Holy Profane." Rod Gruver even calls blues as a "secular religion" that many find transcendence in.[45] This is no different than

---

[42]Ibid., p. 9.

[43]For an in-depth study of Black vernacular, its traditions and connections to Hip Hop, see Cheryl Keyes, *Rap Music and Street Consciousness* (Chicago: University of Illinois Press, 2002), chap. 2; Geneva Smitherman (*Talkin and Testifyin: The Language of Black America* [Boston: Houghton Mifflin, 1977]; *Black Talk: Words and Phrases from the Hood to the Amen Corner* [Boston: Houghton Mifflin, 1994]; *Talkin That Talk: Language, Culture, and Education in African America* [New York: Routledge, 2000]) discusses street vernacular and the infamous A.A.E.V. (African American English Vernacular). All of these have a direct connection with rap music and street consciousness.

[44]Cornel West, "On Afro-American Popular Music: From Bebop to Rap," in *Sacred Music of the Secular City: From Blues to Rap*, ed. J. M. Spencer (Durham, N.C.: Duke University Press, 1992), p. 282.

[45]Rod Gruver, "The Blues as a Secular Religion," in *Sacred Music of the Secular City: From Blues to Rap*, ed. J. M. Spencer (Durham, N.C.: Duke University Press, 1992).

what James Cone talks about in his book *The Spirituals & The Blues*. "By taking seriously Afro-American . . . music, one can dip into the multileveled life-worlds of black people."[46]

Contradictions arise when Black Christian performers like Kirk Franklin release music that creates a strong debate about what is "holy" music and what is not. Franklin's 1997 gospel rap song "Stomp" was being played right alongside Cisco's "Thong Song" and other sexually explicit songs. Some tried to argue that Franklin was merely "reaching out" to people; others tried to say Franklin had "sold out" and was too "worldly." Zanfagna states, "But in the face of current popular culture, where aesthetics often exist for their own sake, Franklin and other holy hip-hop artists are making noble attempts to align popular black aesthetics with relevant spiritual messages."[47] Franklin, in essence, created a new path to God, thereby widening the discussion of the profane and the sacred. Moreover, Dyson states that "it is a central moral contention of Christianity that God may be disguised in the clothing—and maybe even the rap—of society's most despised members."[48]

THE NEO-SECULAR SACRED WITHIN HIP HOP

Within the gray and blurred areas between the sacred and the profane lies what I call the "neo-secular sacred" within Hip Hop. This concept is directly derived from my doctoral research on Tupac's gospel message. It is a concept that has loosely and indirectly been discussed by authors and scholars such as Craig Detweiler and Barry Taylor, Tom Beaudoin, David Dark and John Drane.

I do not intend to make God into something ugly or blasphemous. Nor do I contend that God loves the "sinful" nature of humanity. Yet, it is a part of all of our lives. None of us is without "sin" and none of

---

[46]James Cone, *The Spirituals and the Blues: An Interpretation* (Maryknoll, N.Y.: Orbis Books, 1991), p. 282.

[47]Christina Zanfagna, "Under the Blasphemous (W)rap: Locating the 'Spirit' in Hip-Hop," *Pacific Review of Ethnomusicology* 12 (2006): 4.

[48]Michael Eric Dyson, *Holler If You Hear Me: Searching for Tupac Shakur* (New York: Basic Civitas, 2001), p. 209.

us is "all good" all of the time. There are moments in our lives, that we, whether indirectly or by choice, engage and embrace the profane element to our lives. Some of us just seem to do a better job of hiding the profane than others do.

If you have ever served in any form of professional ministerial work, then you know all too well the pressures which exist in that line of work to maintain the "pristine" outward appearance that decorates church hallways. It is that pristine look, after all, that gets us the promotion, the plaque on the church walls, the medals of honor and the ever-esteemed "you changed my life" statements. The neo-secular sacred, by contrast, in its search for deeper meaning to life, embraces the not-so-perfect aspects to life that often seem to come up when we least expect them to. The neo-secular sacred is the fine line that exists within most people that forms the quirks, idiosyncrasies, peculiarities, oddities, "bad sides," and sinful natures which, as my good friend Ron Hammer would say, make us all lovable by God.

To put it another way, without those things—quirky, idiosyncratic, peculiar, even "sinful" elements—that manifest uniquely to us, we are unable to approach God uniquely, distinctly. God didn't make a race of automatons; he made a human race to "seek him and perhaps reach out for him and find him, though he is not far off from each one of us" (Acts 17:27). Within this theological paradigm, there is the opportunity to finally be human and, after all the makeup has been taken off and the "show" of church is over, be authentic with yourself and God.

The neo-secular sacred within Hip Hop has existed from its inception as both a culture and musical genre. Hip Hop, as we have seen, has its roots in the controversial holy profane, so it should be no surprise when Hip Hoppers embrace this element of God. For Hip Hop, the neo-secular sacred begins to answer some of the questions they have regarding sin and salvation. It also allows for certain contradictions many of us possess within our own lives to flourish while we "work out" the details with Christ. Christina Zanfagna states that "Hip-hop's spirituality—its mystical allusions, contradictory images, and profaned exterior—can be 'tricky' and elusive to the average out-sider not borne or 'baptized' in the streets."[49] The neo-secular sacred within Hip Hop is difficult to comprehend much less clinch. Hip Hop percolates with a plurality of religious traditions—which make it dif-ficult for many Christians to even connect with—and many of its per-formers do not settle down with one religion, or God for that matter. Zanfagna further states:

> It follows that rap music embodies the pluralism of current reli-gious energies as well as the spiritual touchstones of hip-hop's exalted predecessors, such as James Brown's wails for black power, the 'sexual healing' of Marvin Gaye, Stevie Wonder's prophetic preaching, the meditative bedroom lamentations of Al Green and Prince's lyrics of erotic deliverance.[50]

Still, the neo-secular sacred within Hip Hop is, overall, about a transcendent experience in the most obscure places of life. Therefore, the neo-secular sacred concept has three major elements to it that help it to take shape within Hip Hop.

First, it has a panentheistic manner. The term *panentheism* (Grk. *pan*, "all," *en*, "in," and *theos*, "God") was first coined by K. C. F. Krause (1781-1832) for the view that God is in all things, which must include the secular—or that which is supposedly "devoid" of God, even the things that are not so pretty. This fits nicely into an omnipresent theo-logical paradigm and sees God as present to everything, including that which most people care not to talk about. This particular element of the neo-secular sacred often sees the world and God as mutually dependent for their fulfillment—in other words, God needs just like we need him, to fulfill his ultimate *missio Dei*. God acknowledges the "profane" within our lives, yet uses us for his ultimate purpose, because God can use anything he so chooses to broaden his kingdom.

Second, Hip Hop sees life as having both good and bad elements to it. The neo-secular sacred theological concept argues that there is

[49]Zanfagna, "Under the Blasphemous (W)rap," p. 3.
[50]Ibid., pp. 3-4.

both good and evil present in our lives. When one begins to deny the presence of one or the other, one essentially denies the self, because like the sacred, the secular is a constant within all of us. The neo-secular sacred is just that: embracing the two conflicting, at times opposing, forces within life that make us all "tick."

Finally, Hip Hop rejects religionism as the only form of reaching God. Religionism is the belief and ritualistic practice of dogmatic, rigorous, religious traditions. Religionism believes that within those rituals God is found at a higher level. Religionism is either-or, never in between or maybe. While not discounting its occasional usefulness, the neo-secular sacred rejects religionism as the only way of attaining a "direct line" with God. Within religionism, rational answers are preferred over the ambiguous and indefinite conclusions that the neo-secular sacred concept brings. For Hip Hop, religionism explains away life, making God into an idol which no one can reach. Paul Tillich comments on religion and both its glory and perils:

> Religion opens up the depth of man's spiritual life which is usu-
> ally covered by the dust of our daily life and the noise of our
> secular work. It gives us the experience of the Holy, of the some-
> thing which is untouchable, awe-inspiring, an ultimate mean-
> ing, the source of ultimate courage. This is the glory of what we
> call religion. But beside the glory lies its shame. It makes itself
> the ultimate and despises the secular realm. It makes its myths
> and doctrines, its rites and laws into ultimates and persecutes
> those who do not subject themselves to it. It forgets that its own
> existence is a result of man's tragic estrangement from his true
> being. It forgets its own emergency character.[51]

The neo-secular sacred ultimately remembers its "emergency character" while also making room for Tillich's glory of the Holy. These two worlds coexist within us, causing confusion for many, denial for

---

[51]Paul Tillich, *Theology of Culture* (New York: Oxford University Press, 1959), p. 9.

still others, and for the very few acceptance of who we, as humans, truly are: both fallen and risen when in Christ.

LISTENING TO THE JESUS OF THE PROFANE: MISSIONAL CONCERNS

Missionally embracing Hip Hop will not be easy, even for those who consider themselves "liberal" or "open minded." Aside from a few off-track outposts, there is yet to exist a true Hip Hop church movement. As Hip Hop enters its late thirties, I find this extremely disconcerting and troubling. Will Hip Hop ever be truly embraced without totally looking, acting, and talking like a Christian?

I am not sure. Some Holy Hip Hoppers only pretend to be "down" when in reality; they resemble a religious fanatic that sags their pants. Some Holy Hip Hoppers are no different from a fanatic fundamental pastor—they just look Hip Hop, but in reality they are still the same old machine. Some Holy Hip Hoppers identify so strongly with their religion and ultimately their rendition of Christ that they are unable to break away from those social constructs and hold—even for a second—a newer notion of finding Christ. Still other Holy Hip Hoppers place all their self-worth within their *religion* so when it is criticized or even challenged, it is as if their very souls are being placed on trial. So I am both apprehensive and pessimistic about a complete embrace of Hip Hop among Christian churches.[52]

One of the religions that has not been mentioned much in this book is the Nation of Islam, one of the more favored religions within Hip Hop. This makes Hip Hop an even larger target within the church. The Nation of Islam has embraced the Hip Hop culture and has provided the needed room for it to grow in its religions traditions.[53] For many Christians the mere thought of partnering with the Nation of

---

[52]It is interesting to note the stalling of "new Christians" in the U.S. by the mid-1990s; many report that Christians are simply being "moved around" to new churches.

[53]See Felicia M Miyakawa, *Five Percenter Rap: God Hop's Music, Message, and Black Muslim Mission* (Bloomington: Indiana University Press, 2005), for an in-depth look into the Five Percenter ideology and the Nation of Islam.

Islam spells syncretism and smells of sin. The few that do venture out into the waters of pluralistic street evangelism are quickly scorned and marked with the all too common phrase "back sliders."

The sexual innuendoes, the misogyny, the lyrics defaming women and the flagrant arrogance it flaunts in videos make Hip Hop an easy target for its critics. Moreover, Hip Hop tends to favor the showmanship of its rappers rather than consciously lifting up its community. So, it is no wonder that Hip Hop falls under the tight scrutiny of those within the church.

Still, in Matthew 28:16-20 Jesus commands us to commune with, learn from, and teach the ethnos for his kingdom. Jesus never once said to hand out tracts, clobber people over the head with Bible verses or guilt people into following Him, yet somehow this is the message that many Christians have received in regards to "evangelism." What is even worse, some Christians have never even entertained the thought of "local missions." Missions have always been seen as "far off," never local. So the mere thought of Hip Hop missions is absurd for some Christians. So what do we make of the Great Commission then?

As we conclude this session and enter into our last session, we are confronted with conflicting issues of spirituality. How do we confront a hostile message of Christ? How do we contend with sexuality that appears, and at times is, out of control? What is the Christian church's response to a culture that appears to be overcommercialized and too proud for God? How do we become a community with those we do not always see eye to eye with?

Herbert Edwards laid out the path for a new theology to emerge. Discussing Black theology in contrast to White theology, his approach is useful for Hip Hop theology because it (1) proves the inadequacy of the preceding theology, (2) demonstrates its own adequacy for the present moment and (3) establishes itself among the continuity of expressions of faith. Let us, then, enter into the much-needed dialogue of missionally embracing Hip Hop culture and seeing where Christ is moving for the next generation.

SESSION THREE

Missionally Engaging Hip Hop's Theology

The Christian church, largely, has misunderstood the culture of Hip Hop. The church has also set up unreasonable goals in attaining "true spirituality" for young people. Many rap theologians discuss the issue of forgiveness from a "broken-vessel" perspective; rap artists know their limitations as humans and as sinners, yet still wonder if Christ will forgive all of their sins, based on the message that they, and so many other youth, have received in church. Other Hip Hop artists such as Ice Cube and Lauryn Hill[1] contend that there is a God who forgives all sin and that all are equal at the cross. These artists have also spoken of Jesus talking directly to them to help reach this generation of young people.

The difficult part for most urban churches to take from these artists is their irreverent spirituality.[2] Hip Hop culture minces no words, mixing the sacred and the profane in almost all of its music and lifestyle. The urban church has seen Hip Hop culture as a "secular" entity that is devoid of God and any kind of spirituality. And yet a certain level of spirituality is reached when one is able to be open and

---

[1]See John Teter and Alex Gee, *Jesus and the Hip-Hop Prophets* (Downers Grove, Ill.: InterVarsity Press, 2003).

[2]Tom Beaudoin, *Virtual Faith: The Irreverent Spiritual Quest of Generation X* (San Francisco: Jossey-Bass 1998).

honest with how they feel regarding life, love, culture and Jesus. The central spiritual message of Hip Hop—God loves you no matter what—empowers Hip Hoppers to feel that they can help transform the world.[3]

Hip Hop culture is, as a community, not the evil, violent, and hedonistic culture that the church has often made it out to be. This misunderstanding of a culture has created a large portion of urban youth that attend church every Sunday morning simply to appease grandmothers and parents. If we are to missionally engage culture, then we must begin to embrace Hip Hop's good, bad and ugly sides.

---

[3]Michael Eric Dyson, *Holler If You Hear Me* (New York: Basic Civitas, 2001), p. 205.

8

The Scandal of Loving the Ethnos

BEGINNING THE DIALOGUE
OF HIP HOP MISSIONS

I had just moved to Southern California for grad school and I was on the hunt for work. I had found a job on an online forum that listed ministerial jobs. It was a youth pastor position, about twenty minutes from where I was going to live. The location of the church was directly in the neighborhood I wanted to be in, and the pay was exactly what I was looking for. Only a week before, a friend of mine had a "vision" that I was to be working as a youth pastor in the Southern California area. So it was a shoo-in for us. *What a find,* I thought. All I needed to do was "ace" the interview, right?

My wife and I walked into the interview and noticed that all of the interviewers were much older than we had anticipated. We also noticed, via church group photos, that the church was predominantly White in a predominantly Black and Latino neighborhood. But we waited to get to know the people before we cast any type of judgment.

They started with the basic questions—how long had I been doing youth work, how long had I known Christ, what were some of my passions. Then they asked if I played basketball. Then they asked if I played the guitar. A few questions later, I was asked if I was a fan of Black gospel music. Not very sure where those random questions came from, I felt, overall, that the interview was going well. I patiently answered all of their questions until it came time for me to ask them some questions. Then the senior pastor walked in.

He was a younger pastor, so I thought that he would better understand the plight of a youth pastor. He was adorned with a very large crucifix that hung down to the middle of his chest. I thought it odd for such bling, but hey, to each their own, right? He started a short and very weird conversation with me about the Cowboys versus the Eagles—very strange for a job interview.

I was a little put off by this awkward interaction. He finally seemed to pull himself together long enough for me to ask a few questions. So I started in with my questions; I wanted to confirm the pay range, the hours, what they expected of me as a youth pastor. All was good—except the last question. With that last question, the entire committee told me that they expected me to work primarily and exclusively with only their youth.

I was a little thrown off. They had told me that most of their youth had grown up in the church and came from Christian homes. A large portion of their youth had familial roots in the church tracing back a hundred years. I asked, "What about the community around you guys here? Are you all willing to work with any of their kids?"

The entire committee looked at me with a puzzled glare. "What do you mean?" asked the senior pastor.

"Well," I said, "It seems to me that if a church that has mostly Christian youth, is in a neighborhood that is predominately Black and Latino and from lower economic brackets, one might be thinking of doing some missional work and growing the church group using the established youth to lead the way."

One committee member responded by insisting that their youth needed the most attention. So I persisted. "I'm just saying that this church is in a great location, the youth appear to be on the right track, and the church can be grown from the youth department."

Then the senior pastor chimed in, "What kids are you talking about? Are you talking about the ones with tattoos around their necks and the ones with sagging pants down to their ankles?"

I then said, "That's exactly who I'm talking about!" At this point the entire committee in one glance looked toward the senior pastor as if to say, "What you gonna say now?"

The pastor, in complete seriousness, said, "No, we're not interested in those kids. They are the scary kids; they'd scare away our older churchgoers, especially the ones who tithe well."

I turned to my wife, looked her in the eye, turned back to the committee and said, "Thanks for your time, it's been educational," and proceeded to walk out. One day later I got a call telling me that I did not get the job. Thank God!

There is a scandalous element to the Great Commission that many, not just this particular church, do not fully understand nor weigh when contemplating missions. The "stranger" for many Christians is someone who is scary, different, someone with problems and nothing of themselves to offer, estranged from God and to be avoided until they become more like us. It is with many of these preset ideas that a lot of Christians venture out into communities in an attempt to "evangelize." The stranger, then, becomes someone who only needs salvation and once that is attained they receive the ever-desired "You have arrived" button. Once the stranger becomes familiarized with the Christian cultural norms, language, symbols, customs and code, they are domesticated and mounted in a church pew. They are no longer the stranger but indeed "one of us." They no longer need attention, because they are "saved" and no longer sin. If they show any signs of their former lifestyle, they are quickly reminded that hell is hot and that salvation can be lost. If they insist on being different, then they run the risk of being sanctioned; if the insistence continues, they will return to the labeled "stranger" and only be "prayed for"—never engaged with.[1]

---

[1]The parameters of this book limit me to briefly cover the topic of missiology. However, there is a rich body of literature that exists on the topic. I suggest beginning with Wilbert R Shenk, *The Transfiguration of Mission: Biblical, Theological & Historical Foundations*, Missionary Studies 12 (Scottdale, Penn.: Herald Press, 1993); *Write the Vision: The Church Renewed* (Valley Forge, Penn.: Trinity Press International, 1995); *Changing Frontiers of Mission*, American Society of Missiology Series 28 (Mary-

Missiologist and cultural theorist Wilbert Shenk states that "Western theology has weakened the force of the gospel message," and that Jesus' Sermon on the Mount "cannot possibly have been intended as the basis for ethical guidance."[2] This particularly becomes an issue when questions of oppression, unjust actions, oppressive systems, racism, classism and warfare are raised—for many evangelicals these are moot points and have no real connection to the gospel of Christ,[3] yet they are key and tantamount issues for Hip Hop.

Shenk defines the goal of missions as

the establishment of God's new order in which righteousness, justice, and peace dwell. The gospel of peace is nothing less than the vision of shalom into which God invites all people. The gospel is not first of all a program but an invitation to new relationship within a new order of reality. Evangel and ethnics are not opposites or even separable parts but an identity which is the basis of both missionary witness and discipleship.[4]

So if we are to truly embrace missions, let alone Hip Hop, then we must first deconstruct many of our Christian theological models of evangelism, salvation, church, culture and the person of God. It is through this deconstructive process that we are able to begin the missional dialogue with Hip Hop culture.

Still, missionally embracing the Hip Hop ethnos is scary. It is dangerous. It is culturally challenging. Because if we are truly able to let the Holy Spirit work, then we run the serious risk of yielding up our control and dominance and handing it over to God. If we are truly to engage the ethnos, then we must allow them to grow at their

---

knoll, N.Y.: Orbis Books, 1999); *Enlarging the Story: Perspectives on Writing World Christian History* (Maryknoll, N.Y.: Orbis Books, 2002); and David Jacobus Bosch, *Transforming Mission: Paradigm Shifts in Theology of Mission*, American Society of Missiology Series 16 (Maryknoll, N.Y.: Orbis Books, 1991).

[2]Shenk, *Transfiguration of Mission*, p. 11.

[3]As seen in interviews by many conservative evangelical Christians including John McArthur, James Dobson, Pat Robertson, and political figures like Rudy Giuliani.

[4]Shenk, *Transfiguration of Mission*, pp. 11-12.

own rate and speed. But that would mean we do not get to tell their salvation story in the local church newsletter by Christmas so that donors will give for the next year. It also means that the ethnos find God in their own context and do not show up to church wearing preassigned clothing and talking preassigned lingo that makes them blend in even more. No, engaging the ethnos is provocative. It can be offensive to some.

Who or what is the ethnos? In Matthew 28:16-20 we have Jesus issuing what is now termed "The Great Commission": "Therefore go and make disciples of all nations . . ." That word *nations* in the Greek is called *ethnos*, which is where we get the word *ethnicity* from. It primarily deals with ethnic "cultural" aspects and is concerned particularly with different "tribes." Jesus uses it here to illustrate his point that his message was to be taken to people who were specifically "foreign"—meaning non-Jewish, pagan, Gentile, heathen, diverse nations and different people groups. This is a powerful statement from Jesus not just to his disciples, but to us as well.

The ethnos is not an inviting bunch. They are strangers to many of us. Many find it difficult to even entertain the thought of "missions" to "other" people. For still others, missions take place in foreign lands among people who are "savages." Many Black churches see no need for missions, particularly to people groups that are different from them, because their approach to church and their own cultural history makes them already "missional." Thus, the Great Commission is stifled and usually only carried out with people who think, act, talk, look, feel, love, eat, sleep and worship like us.

Hip Hop missions is not something that is taught in seminaries—in fact, courses in urban studies typically mention Hip Hop only as a footnote. Meanwhile, I am regularly bombarded with pastors and laypeople alike who are puzzled, even scared, about Hip Hoppers. Many feel ill prepared to even have a conversation with Hip Hoppers, much less entertain them in their homes or churches.

This chapter is built around beginning the dialogue about Hip Hop missions. There are some hard-core facts regarding the Hip Hop generation:[5]

- 95 percent of all Hip Hoppers have some understanding of who Jesus is.

- Of that 95 percent, three-fourths have roots in the Christian church.

- 98 percent of Hip Hoppers report that they desire spiritually centered conversations.

- 95.5 percent of Hip Hop Christians want more Hip Hop in the church.

- 56.6 percent of Hip Hoppers agree that the Hip Hop community is a "spiritual" place for them.

- 53.5 percent of Hip Hoppers see church as a spiritual community for them too.

With this chapter we begin the journey of Hip Hop missions. This chapter will lay some groundwork for engaging culture and for better understanding how to get our hands around Hip Hop's multi-theological philosophy and lifestyle.

REINHOLD NIEBUHR'S PARADIGM

Over fifty years ago, Reinhold Niebuhr inadvertently laid down foundational work in his *Christ and Culture* that is extremely valuable in missionally engaging with the Hip Hop generation. He observes several postures toward culture that Christians have taken over the centuries:

- Avoidance: Christ versus culture; culture is bad, so leave it alone.

- Caution: Christ and culture in paradox; be careful, the "world" might influence you.

- Dialogue: Christ transforms culture; let's talk about the issues at

---

[5]Facts, percentages and numbers are all taken from a national survey, administered between July 2008 and December 2008, of 212 random respondents who considered themselves to be "Hip Hop Heads."

hand and maybe we will get somewhere, but we must still use caution, because the "world" can influence you to do evil.

- Appropriation: Christ of culture; Jesus is in every part of culture. We can see him in the good, the bad and the ugly.

- Divine encounter: Christ above culture and the transformer of it; Jesus governs this world, both the sacred and profane.

Most Christians find Niebuhr's concept of "divine encounter" conflicting. The notion that Christ shows up in strip clubs and foul-mouthed battle raps is disconcerting. By contrast, avoidance and caution each bring with them two key elements in each of them that make them appealing.

Caution, for example, allows the Christian to "venture" out a bit. And it provides the needed "See, I told you I could hang" effect; people appear to give off the "I'm down" vibe, despite being uncomfortable, even scared, and often annoyed at the need to be "contextual." Caution does not really believe that God is in control and is based on fright.

Consequently, caution as a posture toward culture promotes, breeds and incubates trepidation and anxiety within its users. We hear it all the time from the pulpit: Do not do this, avoid that, get out of this, vote against that, defend this, otherwise it will overtake our nation. Such sermon themes prevail in many churches.

Trepidation gets reinforced when Christians decide to isolate themselves from culture—having only Christian friends, listening only to Christian radio, watching only Christian films and television. We form what is called the sacred canopy:[6] we can see out, but unless outsiders know the code, they can never come in. Contemporary Christianity that adheres to this "caution" has thus halted its missiological influence on culture.

I grew up with the theology that said our guardian angel cannot follow us everywhere, so we must exercise caution when entering worldly

---

[6]A term first used by Peter Berger in *The Sacred Canopy: Elements of a Sociological Theory of Religion* (Garden City, N.Y.: Doubleday, 1967).

events. As a kid, this is truly frightening and it keeps children on spiritual lockdown, controlled by religious fear. But anxiety is not only in church, it is within the family structure as well. Having taught in Christian higher education for the last seven years, I have seen far too often students that enter my classroom paralyzed with fear that a "Negro" is teaching their class. I cannot tell you the number of times that students have told me they have never had a male professor of color teach them. I teach the most difficult classes in Christian higher education—intercultural communication—and I can maybe mention Malcolm X in class, but if I continue down that rhetoric, I will not be rehired. I even had a coworker question me one time: "What are you teaching in there? As long as you're not teaching them Black power, its OK!"

When I sit down and talk with my students, who fall into the generational category of "Gen Y," I find that their family structure has insulated them with overly cautious Christian propaganda. Gen Yers' parents are often called "helicopter parents"; anytime a student comes home with new ideas, something that is too "out of the box," a phone call is placed to the dean and president.

Besides "caution," the posture toward culture that produces the most damage is "avoidance." Avoidance produces excuses for the Great Commission:

- If someone won't change, they must be lost and we can't reach them.
- I don't want my children being influenced by people outside the faith.
- God is not honored when we dine with sinners.
- My family is not a worldly family.
- We would be allowing too much iniquity to enter into our lives if we entertained people outside the faith.
- Going to people outside the faith is just too dangerous.[7]

Avoidance gets justified by way of Scripture proofing and religious

---

[7]Believe it or not, these are all excuses I have personally heard over the last decade.

rationalization. I am not contending that all Christians are called to gay and lesbian strip clubs. Nor am I suggesting that you disregard good discernment in being led by the Holy Spirit. If someone came up to me asking that I participate with them in a human sacrifice, I am going to say no. So don't get it twisted. Yet, oftentimes avoidance is used as an excuse to disregard people who are different. Avoidance does not produce true community; it only reinforces the us-versus-them concept.

Avoidance is not a friend to open and honest relationships. It only crushes them because it says, "We really can't be friends unless we both think, act and talk alike." Avoidance is not in the language of the Great Commission, nor is it part of the gospel. Rather, we find avoidance when we misuse and misinterpret Scripture. We find a God who seemingly hates anything that is not Christian.

But, if we can somehow begin to move into a dialogue (a Christ as the transformer of culture) about theology and culture, then we stand a chance of embracing the ethnos and beginning a new narrative. Dialogue produces

- healthy discussions that do not always end in consensus
- open minds that are challenged by new ideas and philosophies
- authenticity in relationships without agenda
- the dismantling of the us-versus-them concept

Through dialogue the church is able to see Hip Hop's multifaceted and pluralistic theologies and not judge it or criticize it, but work with it. A dialogue produces new critical thought and allows the "other side" a chance to state where they are coming from. Dialogue, for example, allows the Tupacs of the world to be heard, not disregarded prematurely based on their use of "foul language."

The conversionists' understanding of the relations of Christ and culture is most closely akin to dualism, but it also has affinities with the other great Christian attitudes. That it represents a distinct motif, however, becomes apparent when one moves from the Gospel of Matthew and the Letter of James through Paul's epistles to the Fourth Gospel, or proceeds from Tertullian, the Gnostics, and Clement to Augustine, or from Tolstoy, Ritschl, and Kierkegaard to F. D. Maurice. The men who offer what we are calling the conversionist answer to the problem of Christ and culture evidently belong to the radical distinction between God's work in Christ and man's work in culture, they do not take the road of exclusive Christianity into isolation from civilization, or reject its institutions with Tolstoyan bitterness.[8]

Dialogue produces the ability to move on to the next area, which is appropriation. Appropriation is a new frontier for much of Christianity, in which we venture out of our sacred canopies and into the unknown and uncharted waters of popular culture. Hip Hop is a foreign land for the church, with many cultural idiosyncrasies. But appropriation means that we are to be fluid in our theological foundation, knowing that God is in control of all things. We should not have to worry about "worldy influence" because God has already taken care of that element with the cross of Christ. A Christ of culture means that we are able to see that Christ can actually make it his own, in due time.

Appropriation understands that there is no five-step process to salvation; in reality, people are on a journey. Appropriation thus allows Hip Hoppers the freedom to find God through art, dance, television, concerts, spoken word venues and other creative outlets not traditionally used by many mainline Christian churches. A Christ of culture means that we can watch a film like *Scarface* and find, for example, that Tony is a communal person, wanting to be in community. We can observe that Tony reflects our own sinful condition, our own need to fit in. We can acknowledge that Jesus would have loved on Tony, understanding that Tony had no discipleship, love or connection to a Christian community. We would remember that Jesus shows us the final effects of sin for us all, not just people that look and act

[8]Richard Niebuhr, *Christ and Culture* (San Francisco: HarperCollins, 1951), p. 190.

like Tony. We would wrestle with the uncomfortable truth that there is much grace where sin abounds. We would accept that Tony is a product of his context and society; as ministers of the gospel, we would recognize that the Tonys of the urban world are abundant, and some of us are called by God to that environment.

Or we can watch a film like *Hustle & Flow* and appreciate how the film recognizes that sexuality is a part of life, although in the 'hood often sex and relationships are viewed through a distorted lens. We can be alert to the spiritual connections between the "Dirty South" rap music and the blues that predated it. We can recognize that pimps, prostitutes and hustling are realities for many in poverty-stricken Southern states and in fact bear similarities to the marginalization Zacchaeus experienced in New Testament culture (Luke 19). We can acknowledge the realism of Key's character, with one foot in the church and the other on the streets. We can consider the spiritual significance of the "making it" syndrome affecting many young people in inner cities. We can take strip-club culture seriously enough to ask how it will intersect with Jesus, and how we might be better agents of change. We can wrestle with the notion that Jesus would have been in the club, cheering on Djay, loving on the women and helping them day by day to find another mode of life. We can even consider that Jesus would have identified with the themes in the music; he would have considered himself a part of the community there.

Missiologist and cultural theorist Wilbert Shenk makes the distinction that "mission is prior to church. The church can only be called into being by the preaching of the gospel of the kingdom."[9] Therefore, how can Hip Hop become a church without missions to it first? Seeing Christ as above culture and the transformer of it means that we recognize the many avenues to salvation available to God. In contrast, many Christian churches illuminate only two or three avenues for salvation, typically involving church, church and more church. A Christ throughout culture is not the conventional theologi-

---

[9]Shenk, *Changing Frontiers of Mission*, p. 15.

cal paradigm that many churches teach and preach on.

Having a divine encounter in culture means looking again at issues of sexuality, film, music, language, relationships, and then merging those ideas with a biblical hermeneutic to discover new ways to understand evangelism, salvation, church, culture and even God. We move from being consumers of God's love to participants in God's loving kingdom. To do so we must first examine our own lives and investigate the nuances that make us who we are.

THE JUNCTURES OF LIFE AND SPIRITUALITY

Most of us go through six junctures in our lives.

1. Chaos

2. Awakened/Churched

3. Traditioned/Institutional

4. Doubt

5. Mystery

6. Enlightenment[10]

Often churchgoers insist on remaining in one stage, defining any move into another stage as "sin." Add in religionism and you have junctures that can remain stagnant and sluggish with people on their journey or the person never moves through them at all. And yet these six stages are foundational in better understanding our own lives, let alone our part to play in the mission of God.

Chaos. Chaos represents the unconscious state for most people before they have a spiritual awakening; in our case, an encounter with God, or a "road to Damascus" event that awakens the spiritual side and makes the person aware of the chaos. Everyone has some sort of chaos in their life. Everyone has gone through a certain amount of

---

[10]These six stages are based on Scott Peck's four stages: chaos, churched, doubt and mystery (*The Different Drum: Community-Making and Peace* [New York: Simon & Schuster, 1988]). I add the extra two and broaden the description to fit the Hip Hop context.

drama. Living in the 'hood is almost synonymous with chaos and drama. There is chaos from the police, parents, friends, enemies, opposing sets, and even church. This can cause confusion and disorder within a person's life. Chaos can cause fear and anxiety, which can make the person feel hopeless and discouraged.

Chaos can bring about much worry and stress. It is not something most people would verbalize that they want. Chaos is, however, something that the unconscious self often desires, because it gives us attention and makes us noticeable among our peers. Many are addicted to chaos, in fact, and thus chaos continues to prevail in their lives. While we can all be very quick to find people in our own circle who emulate this characteristic, let us not be too hasty in our judgment. Many within professional Christian service are addicted to chaos. We thrive off eighty-hour weeks. We are encouraged by the "drama" of our lives, and chaos becomes a part of our identity.

This is the unconscious mind, as KRS-One would say—the mind that has yet to be opened and challenged. It is in this stage that a person does not truly know their self. Chaos can thus also represent the "lost" person, who has not realized a Jesuz in their life and does not know what it means to be "spirit-filled." Once this person is made aware of a "better life," they are then moved into a conscious state and begin to understand who God is in their life.

Awakened/Churched. The eager pupil waiting to hear a message from God about their life has been awakened. It is in this stage that the newly conscious Hip Hopper is ready to grow and ready to move out on the new lessons in life.

This is the period we often call "young in Christ." Many who come off the streets enter this stage becoming zealous for God. The person is made aware of salvation, basic concepts of theology, church traditions and norms, a foundational understanding of the Bible, and the nature of the church's "mission."

The awakened person is typically happy and full of joy. I remember when I made a serious decision to follow Christ. I was walking on top of the world. I wanted to let everyone know. I wanted everyone to know this feeling, at any cost and using any method. Church, then, became a natural thing—the same way it does for people in this stage. It is just part of life. Church is something that you just do, and do a lot of.

This is good, most of the time; people coming out of chaos need the break. Chaos is a harsh mistress and demands a lot on the person. Church is a haven and a place of spiritual rest. Moreover, the person is, most of the time, eager to learn more about who God is and learn more about God's Word. Awakening is a time of learning who God is and how he works in the life of a person. It is the period that the author of the book of Hebrews calls the "milk" period (Hebrews 5:11-14).

Yet many scholars such as George Barna argue that if a "new believer" is not put to work within a year and a half of conversion, their entire world will become "Christianized" and therefore make the Great Commission null and void. Within two years, this person will no longer have "worldly" friends; their circle will consist of only Christians who tend to agree with what they believe.

Traditioned/Institutional. It is within this stage that the person, who was once vibrant and "on fire" becomes domesticated and traditioned. This period typically happens after about two years from a "Jesus conversion."[11] This period comes on very subtly and does not appear, at first glance, as being traditionalized.

Hip Hoppers resist institutionalization on almost every level. They see it as being confined in one area. This is why graffiti artists love to climb highway bridges and make their mark on dangerous overpasses—even though they are free to tag the local youth center with their art. Such impulses to reject confinement is a resistance to the traditional.[12]

However, this period has become a staple for many Christians and

---

[11]In my 2004-2005 research on evangelism in the twenty-first century, I followed the Billy Graham crusade around, studied several churches and analyzed data on salvation numbers to find that within two years of conversion, people become traditioned and stale in their Christian walk.

[12]Graffiti artists have shared this with me often.

a landmark for "growth" and accomplishment. People in the traditioned/institutional stage are given awards for their "faithfulness," even as complacency takes over, the status quo reigns, church norms become law, and Christ becomes domesticated and tamed in their life. Their "fire" turns into a smoldering ash pile; it looks good on the outside, yet it fulfills nothing of the mission of God.

Being in this stage has its advantages. When done right, it gives you clout in church organizations. It shows "stability" and the infamous and adorned title "being seasoned." It shows that a person can "walk the talk" with Christ by demonstrating the person's ability to do the same thing repeatedly. It also brings with it a sense of accomplishment and success. If you "look good" on the outside, you typically get a lot of accolades that mount up to "jewels on your crown." So there is a lot at stake for traditionalism. To question traditions and customs means that quite possibly there might be something different out there, and the "rules" might have to change.

One of the most debilitating things this stage does to people is that it keeps them in the "milk" stage of their spiritual life. This stage insists on the person remaining in a pre-adolescent stage of spirituality, for to move would mean its demise. The stage fights to keep itself alive in people through comparision: "Look how it worked for this person," and "If you go too far, this is what will happen." The traditioned/institutional stage can limit people's ability to fully embrace a missional attitude.

Yet, every now and then, we as humans have what I call a "Job moment." This is a time in a believer's life when we did all the seemingly "right" things yet yielded horrible results. It is not the chaos stage where we had no consciousness of Christ, but what we've become accustomed to is not working, and even after we have done all the rituals that were prescribed to us by our pastor, life seems "unfair" and very difficult. The next stage begins to bark at the front door of our life.

Doubt. To doubt is to not trust. To not trust is to not have faith, and if you do not have faith, then alas, you have sinned. Or so we are told.

Doubt has a funny way of creeping up on a person. It typically illuminates the holes in many of the theologies we are taught in church. Doubt rises up when God does not act the same way as in prior events. When God's "action" does not work, doubt arises and causes stress. God appears to be unavailable. God's image does not look familiar anymore, and three-point sermons do not seem to console the soul.

Doubt tends to send people back toward the traditioned/institutional stage—because its gravitational pull is powerful, in part because those who are uncomfortable with doubt push people in that direction—and can at times send people back into chaos. But often doubt begins a time of deep pondering and profound thought.

For Hip Hoppers, doubt is life. Doubt is just expected. Will you live or will you die? Will you get food tomorrow or will you have to steal for it? These types of doubts are just a normal part of life. So to tell a Hip Hopper not to doubt is roughly equivalent to telling them not to think. Rather, Hip Hoppers must be encouraged to move through doubt with a view toward the new understandings that lie on the other side of its uncharted territory. The mystery stage is the first step into a new world.

Mystery. While systematic approaches and methods to understanding God have their place and pedagogical value, we are foolish to think we can boil God down. Such methods and processes are often not helpful within difficult situations and only add more stress and chaos to a person's life when what they really need is time to sit in the mystery of God.

God is mysterious to many true Hip Hoppers. Interview after interview revealed that the Hip Hopper actually wants a mysterious God, a God who does not always do what we expect.

The narratives in the Bible strongly suggest that God does not "show up" the same way twice. Mystery surrounds God. We are not sure what God is. God is multifaceted. God is diverse. God is multifarious. God is a complex being that human minds cannot begin to understand.

Mystery is the beginning of a new consciousness and awareness of our Lord. Mystery elucidates the areas of our life that are not so "neat" and prepackaged. Mystery asks a host of questions like "Where did

God come from? Why did God create evil? Where is heaven? Why has God not blessed me?" Mystery is scary to the traditioned/institutional. Instability, loss of faith, backsliding, and a wavering lifestyle are all labels assigned to those in the mystery stage because in mystery, people are finding their own story in Christ.

Mystery eventually gives way to a sixth stage, which can be the most difficult place to be for anyone who wants to remain being called a Christian.

Enlightenment. Enlightenment is a new awakening to God. Enlightenment opens up an entire new worldview and sees the Bible for what it is: a narrative about the life of God and the people who have followed thereafter. Enlightenment consents to questions and doubt along the journey of faith. Enlightenment does not care if you have all the answers or only have one. In fact, enlightenment says that answers are not always the end to the drama, and in fact can at times be the beginning: once you know something, then you are responsible for it.

Enlightenment makes room at the table for the narrative of the 'hood. Enlightenment begins a new journey in search of answers, yet realizing that answers may never come. The enlightenment stage challenges people to press on in the midst of doubt and uncertainty, while encouraging them that doubt and uncertainty are not a sin but in fact a part of the human experience—we all doubt at some point in our journey. God is filled with joy at a person's journey into enlightenment, which prepares them for the "sold food" that Hebrews 5:14 is talking about.

These stages are not static but extremely fluid. Yet it is important to engage in these six stages as we look into a missiology for Hip Hop culture. Because without true introspection, we are leaving ourselves open to the domestication of Christ.

ABANDONING RELIGIONISM AND EMBRACING THA JESUZ OF HIP HOP

At first glance it would appear that I am arguing for a complete doing away with of liturgy, tradition and church values. But the Hip Hop community loves liturgy, Eucharistic traditions, church and Jesuz; they just do not want religionism.

Plenty of pastors around the country have shared with me their deep hesitation with contextualization and "seeker friendly" theologies. Much Christian doctrine revolves around an us-versus-them paradigm. A relic of the Enlightenment era, these type of theologies put people into fixed categories of "moral" and "immoral." How can you be friends with someone you have labeled "immoral"? How can you embrace someone you are "against"? You cannot. So we are left at an impasse; Hip Hoppers are labeled quite quickly.

Abandonment of religionism begins with moving away from theologies that alienate people from the rest of society and toward theologies that bring members of a church society into community with the people around their neighborhood. It's a move from what I call "confined set" theology, which necessarily dampens missiological efforts.[13]

Confined set theology has strong set borders; moving from the periphery to the center requires special "entry pass codes." God is static; access to God from the outside is impossible without the help of someone from the "inside."

Now, flip the script and we have another theology that allows room and time to grow, flourish and develop in Christ. "Fluid centered theology" acknowledges a center, Jesuz. Within fluid centered theology there are clear divisions between people moving in and moving out, but the center, not the boundary, is emphasized. A diversity of perspectives and even ambiguity are acknowledged and accommodated within the paradigm, since in dynamic sets something is always happening to an object[14]—a person may be growing, not growing, growing slowly or rapidly. Fluid centered theology allows people to be in

---

[13]This theological framework relies heavily on Paul Heibert's bounded and centered set theories. In his article "Conversion, Culture, and Cognitive Categories (*Gospel in Context* 1, no. 4 [1978]: 24-29), he discusses a theoretical model that is extensive in the many Christian churches: bounded set theory, which suggests that things or objects are "bound" to certain structural characteristics—that is, they force us to look at things in a certain way, such as who is in and who is out (p. 26).

[14]Ibid., pp. 27-28.

different locations in relation to Jesuz; no special "pass code" is required to enter into a relationship with Jesuz.

If a church says that to be considered "saved" and thus eligible for membership, one must perform certain rituals or ceremonies, Jesuz and his message is effectively confined by the church. There is not much room for disagreement or movement. Challenges to a pastor, for example, often lead to automatic punishment; the challenger is banished to the outside until they "learned their lesson." For fluid centered theologies, things are a little different. Some people's understanding of Jesuz and his message might be extremely "out there," while others might be closer to the center, but what's importance is the direction. As Hiebert observes, "Some things may be far from the center, but moving *towards* the center, therefore, they are part of the centered set. On the other hand, some objects may be near the center

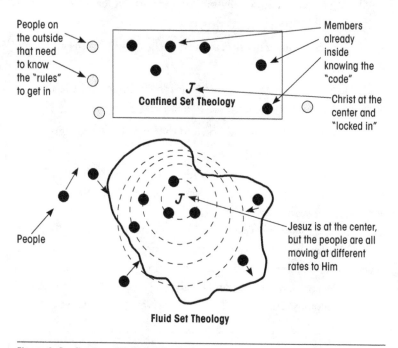

Figure 6. Confined- and fluid-set theologies

but are moving away from it, so they are not a part of the set."[15]

Fluid set theologies are more open and receptive to people who question theology and think differently—like Hip Hoppers (see figure 6). The center is around Jesuz, but people move closer to or farther from him depending on what is happening in their lives. Fluid set theology allows the Hip Hopper to grow in their spirituality rather than have it all figured out after they are baptized. With fluid sets there are still personal and cultural limitations, but there is less stress on maintaining the boundary in order to preserve the existence and purity of the body of believers.[16]

The dismantling of religionism in Hip Hop church models would look more like a community. Several key items from Hip Hop culture would facilitate the growth of community:

- Spoken word: language that speaks to the group

- The DJ: a voice making powerful points without fear of strong language

- The emcee: someone who can lead the group in discussions and events

- A decentralized leadership team: leaders who attend the church and help run it but de-emphasize hierarchy

- Emphasis on knowledge of God and the knowledge and consciousness of the self

These parameters are just a few ideas that might be helpful in beginning a Hip Hop church. The "come to us, we have all the knowledge" form of evangelism needs to give way to a more communal sense of "let's learn together." The temptation will be to develop a plan that results in salvation, but true salvation is more of a journey than an event. When we are able to abandon religionism and allow for the Holy Sprit to lead, we then open ourselves to an entire new dimension of both theology and missiology. As Harvey Cox observes, "The

---

[15]Ibid., pp. 28-29.
[16]Ibid., p. 29.

church is not in the first instance an institution. It is a people. The Bible calls it the *laos theou*, the 'people of God.'"[17] His words will carry us into our final chapter.

---

[17]Harvey Cox, *The Secular City: A Celebration of Its Liberties and an Invitation to Its Discipline* (New York: Macmillan, 1965), p. 125.

See You at the Crossroads

JESUZ, HIP HOP & MISSIONS IN POST-9/11 AMERICA

It was the third time I would speak during a weekend youth camp—typically the talk that "brings home" the gospel and includes an "altar call" for lost teens. However, I had decided early on that I was going to take a different approach.

I had been told ahead of time that, despite their coming from a relatively suburban context, this was to be an "urban" group coming to camp. In my mental tapes, I pictured Black, Latino and ghetto White youth rolling in Friday night listening to rap. I got the rap part right, but these youth were a hybrid mix. Most of the crowd were affluent Whites, along with some Latinos and sprinklings of Blacks and Asians. Most of these teens were churchgoers and knew who Jesus was. About 80 percent of them considered themselves to be "saved." The leaders were, with a couple of exceptions, older, predominantly White, upper-middle to upper class.

So I felt no need to beat these teens over the head with an altar call. I decided that I was going to talk instead about their hurts, needs, wants, desires and ultimately where they stood with Christ as a personal friend.

During the late 90s in cities like Los Angeles, the 'hood started to move from the cities out to the suburbs. City centers, or central business districts, were now becoming less "centrally" located and more fragmented. Orbiting communities like Hollywood now had their own "downtown" and were more self-sufficient; someone living in a suburb like Burbank no longer had to travel into the city for groceries, living materials, or even social events. Edward Soja describes this as "exopolis," or "the restructuring of urban form."[1] While this type of urban restructuring had been occurring for twenty five years,[2] during the 1990s it became more acute.

Los Angeles is a good example of the postmodern fragmented city. Most urban researchers and scholars have replaced Chicago with Los Angeles as a case study for city development.[3] Fractal and fragmented,[4] in Los Angeles you can go from 'hood to luxury in a matter of blocks, all the while being surrounded by the surreal beauty and fantasy of Hollywood. Los Angeles, then, as LeGates and Stout put it, "is often held as the quintessential postmodern city."[5]

The 'hood can thus creep up on a community. During the 1960s, South Central Los Angeles was a prosperous community, Blacks started to move in to work in the factories, and many Whites did not like their new neighbors, packed up, and within a matter of five years, left the area. Factories themselves were moving overseas. The community was left with an extreme high class and an extreme low class—the rest is history.[6] Suburban parents now wonder why their twelve-year-old children listen to rap, why they want to be in a gang, or why they're being beaten up every day. This is where we find ourselves regarding missions to Hip Hop.

Many churches, unaware of the social changes occurring within

---

[1]Edward Soja, *Postmetropolis* (New York: Wiley-Blackwell, 2000).

[2]J. John Palen, *The Urban World*, 2nd ed. (New York: McGraw-Hill, 1981).

[3]Soja, *Postmetropolis*; Richard LeGates and Frederic Stout, eds., *The City Reader,* 2nd ed. (New York: Routledge, 2000).

[4]Soja, *Postmetropolis*.

[5]LeGates and Stout, *City Reader,* p. 180.

[6]This is taken from my own research on Los Angeles county for courses I teach on urban studies and urban youth ministry.

inner cities, march out like military personnel ready to assail the streets with the gospel of Christ. But they find themselves in a sea of plural religious options, for which their methodology no longer applies. The poor, urban youth, and the city all get lumped into one stereotype that they are all "lost," "sinners," "bad," "scary" or "evil" and must be "evangelized." David Bosch has observed of the erosion of mission that "the adjective 'poor' was increasingly used to qualify the noun 'heathen.'. . . The patent needs of the 'poor heathen' became one of the strongest arguments in favor of mission. . . . God's love had deteriorated into patronizing charity."[7]

Those kids I spoke with that weekend loved what I had to say to them. Because I did not follow the traditional form of camp speaking, I was able to dial into some felt needs that they were experiencing. Some of the leaders did not agree with my direction; they felt I didn't use "Jesus" enough in my prayers. I was OK with that.

Defenders of the old approach to mission in the Hip Hop community often appeal to John 15 (NIV), in which Jesus tells his disciples:

> If the world hates you, keep in mind that it hated me first. If you belonged to the world, it would love you as its own. As it is, you do not belong to the world, but I have chosen you out of the world. That is why the world hates you.

Many young people hear this passage out of context and come to see Jesus as authoritarian, hostile and reactionary.[8] They move away from, not toward, a Jesus like that. A new kind of mission attempts to reverse the hermeneutical flow.

REVERSING THE HERMENEUTICAL FLOW

Larry Kreitzer uses film to interpret different biblical messages from

---

[7]David Bosch, *Transforming Mission: Paradigm Shifts in Theology of Mission*, American Society of Missiology Series 16 (Maryknoll, N.Y.: Orbis Books, 1992), p. 290.

[8]Still, that is not to say we excuse every lifestyle and make "everything" acceptable unto God. That is not what I am suggesting. I am suggesting that we seriously consider the power of community that each person comes in with.

the Old and New Testaments.[9] This reversing of the hermeneutical flow can also be applied in the culture of Hip Hop, using Hip Hop's many stories to reveal new insights into Jesus.[10] For example, many of Tupac's songs—including "Young Black Male," "Brenda's Got a Baby," "How Long Will They Mourn Me?" "Cradle to the Grave," "I Ain't Mad at Ya," "Hail Mary" and "Black Jesuz"—deal with such theologically significant issues as death, social justice, poverty, life after death, and the connection between man and God. These songs acknowledge that such issues require a different lens for the ghetto than would be useful for mainstream America. Tupac's theological understanding of Christ is in contrast to the muddied and marred "White" theology that suggests you have to be "perfect" in order to enter heaven.

Daniel Shaw and Charles Van Engen observe that "the spiraling process of missiological hermeneutics begins with missional intention."[11] In their "hermeneutical spiral," the divine and human levels meet through a spiraling process over time, yielding new missiological perspectives and a converging praxis.[12] "The purpose," they suggest, "is Gospel proclamation through crossing barriers."[13] Kreitzer's position is similar in that he suggests that we find God in culturally contextual ways.[14]

REVERSING THE HERMENEUTIC WITH THE FILM *8-MILE*

I reference Curtis Hanson's 2002 film *8-Mile* in almost every class I teach. It continues to resonate with students, especially those entering

---

[9]Larry Kreitzer, *The New Testament in Fiction and Film: On Reversing the Hermeneutical Flow* (Sheffield, U.K.: JSOT Press, 1993); *The Old Testament in Fiction and Film: On Reversing the Hermeneutical Flow* (Sheffield, U.K.: Sheffield Academic Press, 1994); *The Dreaming Spires Version of Paul's Letters* (Oxford: Alden, 2002).

[10]Along with Kreitzer, I contend that in doing this we maintain a Christlike feel by continuing to use the Bible as a reference point.

[11]Daniel Shaw and Charles Van Engen, *Comunicating God's Word in a Complex World: God's Truth or Hocus Pocus* (Lanham, Md.: Rowman & Littlefield, 2003), p. 80.

[12]Ibid., pp. 80-81.

[13]Ibid., p. 80.

[14]Kreitzer, *New Testament in Fiction and Film*, p. 11.

urban youth ministry. Not primarily about Black youth, 8-Mile flips the script by focusing on the life of Hip Hop culture mogul Eminem. Theologically, 8-Mile demonstrates to the church a clear view of what happens when all of your inadequacies, fears, insecurities and drama are placed into the public eye. Eminem elevates his personal life's problems in the final scene, where he displays all his drama in a battle rap, leaving nothing for his opponent to use against him, a posture reminiscent of Jesus' invitation to bring all of our burdens to him (Matthew 11:28-30). So many times we take such burdens to people who cannot help or who make the matter worse for us, or we act as if there is nothing wrong. But in 8-Mile, Eminem demonstrates that we are set free when we quit trying to act as if things are good.

Connections to Christianity run throughout the film, an indication that in 8-Mile the hermeneutic is being reversed. First, there are names that connect with the gospel. The messianic figure within the film, played by Mekhi Phifer, is named Future and displays Christlike characteristics such as forgiveness, leadership and peacemaking. He embodies several of Jesus' qualities yet is still seen as human, or fallen. The Shelter—the place where the battle raps take place—is in the basement of a church doing outreach to Hip Hoppers. Watch the scene closely when Jimmy is walking up to the church, prior to his last battle rap; the doors of the church are opened to young people, offering a safe place to do their raps—four letter words, weed smoking and all.

Authenticity in relationships and experiencing freedom in the mess of life are key themes in 8-Mile. Eminem was already rich and famous when he began work on 8-Mile, but with his character, Jimmy, he opted for a more grassroots depiction of himself and where he came from—a move reminiscent of Luke 14:11, where Luke discusses those who humble themselves being exalted. Similarly, Christ's mission of setting people free from bondage (e.g., Luke 4:18; John 8:36) is reflected in the freedom Jimmy experienced as he accepted his reality. In fact, at the end of the film, instead of picking fame and glory, Jimmy simply goes back to work. In 8-Mile we find Jesuz in the mundane, dirty parts of inner-city Detroit, embracing the Jimmys of the world with people like Future and churchlike places such as The Shelter. When we reverse the hermeneutic between culture and the Bible, we find that movies, television and music not only entertain us but help us make sense of life, shaping our perceptions, understanding and ways of thinking.[15]

THE PARADOX OF CRAIG G. LEWIS

The reverse hermeneutic is not without controversy, thanks in large part to the suspicion so often applied to Hip Hop. I was first made aware of a DVD collection produced by Craig Lewis when a friend of mine recommended it to me as a message "everyone who listens to rap needs to hear." To boil his message down, Lewis argues that Hip Hop culture is evil and must not be accepted by Christians. He calls it a "Trojan Horse" that has infiltrated Christian theology. Even Holy Hip Hop is dismissed as evil. Now, almost every time I speak, I get asked the question, Is Lewis right?

Lewis makes some convincing arguments in favor of moving away from commercial rap and Hip Hop. I would agree that we need to listen critically and that not all parts of Hip Hop are good.[16] However, I hold that there is no one culture that is either completely evil or completely holy.

During my time in the music industry I happened to work on several of the albums that Lewis references (Bone Thugs-N-Harmony and DoggyStyle). Lewis argues that there is a "curse" derived from black magic and sorcery on the back of a Bone Thugs-N-Harmony record (*E 1999 Eternal*), printed in reverse so that it would have to be held up to a mirror; reading the curse activated it.[17] This is not accurate. Bone Thugs wanted to have original cover art on the album that

---

[15]William Romanowski, *Pop Culture Wars: Religion and the Role of Entertainment in American Life* (Downers Grove, Ill.: InterVarsity Press, 1996), p. 312.

[16]If you have not heard of Craig G. Lewis, go to <www.exministries.com> for an overview of what he is talking about.

[17]See Perry M. Rodgers, *Aspects of Western Civilization: Problems & Sources in History*, vol. 1, *The Medieval World* (Upper Saddle River, N.J.: Prentice-Hall, 1997), pp. 281-371.

represented life and death—the theme of the album. The "curse" on the back of the album is actually a blessing meant to encourage young people living a life on the streets, to present a hope and a message of optimism where there is little.

Lewis claims that all of Hip Hop culture is derived from satanic worship and musical trances that originated with the founding fathers of Hip Hop: Africa Bambatta and Cool Herc. Here Lewis has fallen into the "Christ against culture" trap. If we apply his line of reasoning to every aspect of culture, we must dismiss almost 95 percent of the classic "gospel spirituals," derived largely from bar room songs.[18] Steeples on churches are considered sacrilegious by some religions.[19] And an honest study of history reveals that even Christianity itself has been used for evil.[20]

Lewis uses "God" as the stamp of his approval. Anytime you begin saying "God told me this" and/or "God gave me that in a dream," you automatically place yourself in the no-contest category. After all, who wants to challenge God? Moreover, many who want an easy answer find such assurances comforting and therefore feel as though Lewis is "speaking truth."[21] I would in fact assert that Lewis is a product of the traditioned/institutional stage of religious life. Although "seasoned" in his faith, he still views life and God in rigid way and serves as an example of what the soul community still believes about culture in general, seeing things generally in "absolute" terms with very little gray areas.

---

[18]See Mellone V. Burnim, "Religious Music," and "Dena J. Epstein, "Secular Folk Music," in *African American Music: An Introduction*, ed. M. V. Burnim and P. K. Maultsby (New York: Routledge, 2006); Alan P. Merriam, *The Antrhopology of Music* (Chicago: Northwestern University Press, 1964).

[19]See Walter Martin and Hank Hanegraaff, *The Kingdom of the Cults,* rev. ed. (Minneapolis: Bethany House, 1997), pp. 517-608.

[20]See W. H. C. Frend, *The Rise of Christianity* (Philadelphia: Fortress Press, 1984), pp. 869-83; cf. Charles Kimball, *When Religion Becomes Evil* (San Francisco: HarperCollins, 2002).

[21]I and others have tried on several occasions to get ahold of Craig Lewis to have him defend his position on the radio or a public forum; on all attempts he refused and offered instead a recording of his position.

But Lewis has not, to my knowledge, revealed his sources and methods of evaluation. While I agree that we must protect our minds and think on those things that are of God, this is subjective; what I consider "godly" is likely very different from what my neighbor considers "godly." Hip Hop does not meet Lewis's closed-set criteria for what it means to be a Christian. This puts Hip Hop in the us-versus-them category and paralyzes any type of Hip Hop missions.

I mention Lewis in part because many older adults who already have biases against Hip Hop are convinced by him. Moreover, with his critique Lewis injects fear into people that paralyzes his audience when it comes to engaging the influential Hip Hop cultural movement. I hope that we as a Christian family can begin to see beyond such fear tactics and move toward an embrace of the "strangers" amidst our communities, but sadly, many churches are rooted in fear: fear of the unknown, fear of "losing salvation," fear of not living up to the life in Christ, thereby incurring punishment. There is a fear of God that is not good—not reverence and respect but a fear of hell and other "bad things" associated with God. In the shadow of fear, missions becomes out of the question.

Moving beyond fear and into a missional mindset will take more than a good sermon, or even a good book! It will take critically engaged study of culture, God, Jesuz, Scripture and society.

THE PIG WITH LIPSTICK SYNDROME

A professor of mine in grad school by the name of Eddie Gibbs used to tell us a metaphoric story about the pig with lipstick. Gibbs would go into detail about how certain pigs would be dressed up, cleaned up, and made to smell good in order to be paraded down the aisles at the county fair. However, as Gibbs would put it, in the end, they were still pigs, and they would instinctively go back to the mud and mire. It would take several handlers just to keep them from eating the lipstick off of each other.

A pig will only do what a pig knows how to do because it's what a pig has always done.

Gibbs would then talk on how many churches today feel as if they can add just one more candle and one more couch, and somehow they will be "emergent" or "postmodern." But in the end, postmodern people who encounter these churches still receive the same old message. Adam Hayden (MC Till) makes a similar observation of churches that superficially employ Hip Hop: "They are simply trying to prostitute Hip-hop in attempt to get more people to their 'church.'"[22] Once people have taken the "bait" of Hip Hop features at the church, they are given the same evangelical message that has rung false with so many Hip Hoppers.

In order to begin missions to Hip Hoppers, I suggest six urgent missiological directions that the urban church needs to address. These suggestions emerge from the significance and analysis of my research over the last five years, as well as fifteen years of urban ministry experience. They will enable the church to be missional in the 'hood.

PREPARING THE WAY

The first and fundamental missiological essential is that the urban church must *prepare the way*. Recall that David Bosch noted that missions to the poor and the city were always equating "heathen" and "evil" with "poor."[23] Cities were looked upon with "pity" and "shame." Missions to the inner cities have thus been distorted by guilt, pity and a sense of shame.[24] In my tenure as a minister in the inner city, I have seen this to be shockingly true. The outlook the church holds about culture, and people in general, needs to shift if the church is to "prepare the way."[25] A spring cleaning of sorts is in order.

"Preparing the way" is not a one-size-fits-all approach, but for too long the church has been a symbol of distrust, corruption, lies, sexual misconduct and the misappropriation of Christ. A solid missional church opens up its doors and helps the people they are working with;

---

[22]Email interview, 2008
[23]Bosch, *Transforming Mission*, pp. 290-91.
[24]Ibid., p. 290.
[25]Ibid., p. 299.

it does not decide for them or act in the place of God for their lives but allows them to think for themselves.

Wilbert Shenk states:

> The power of the church's witness depends on the extent to which God's kingdom defines and shapes that witness. When the church attempts to make its ministry relevant by rendering "respectable" service, it has adopted an alien criterion and it becomes merely mundane.[26]

In this perspective, the church has become irrelevant and the message of God is "watered down" so much that the people do not have a clear perspective of God. Part of preparing the way means that we must keep God in the forefront of the message, while remaining contextual, never sacrificing "program" for true relationships.[27] Nevertheless, for a church to open its doors and actually prepare the way, it must engage culture in all its profanity and sacredness.

In the context of the Hip Hop community, the church opens its doors and prepares the way by becoming a place of sanctuary, rest and refuge. For the 'hood, a break from the madness of life—a Sabbath place—would be an oasis within a barren land.

ANNOUNCING GOOD NEWS

The second missiological essential is to *announce good news.* The good news of Jesuz, that he loves you no matter what and will forgive you, is what people in the 'hood need to hear—and see. Announcing good news within a postmodern context is not so much about speaking as it is about living a lifestyle that reflects that good news.

Urban churches are great at making sermons that make you feel the very flames of hell. But people in the 'hood do not need to hear that. Within the 'hood many people are already living in hell. What they need to hear is that Jesus still cares for them.

Good news for Hip Hoppers goes beyond the "health and wealth"

---

[26]Shenk, *Changing Frontiers of Mission,* p. 16.
[27]Ibid., p. 189.

good news. Many pastors who run inner-city churches are living lives of luxury while their church members suffer. What kind of "good news" is that? Hip Hoppers have seen far too many pastors asking their church members for Bentleys while nothing changes in the church family and/or community. The heart of Jesuz' message, may simply be that someone is listening, someone cares, someone is there during a time of crisis. The good news of Jesuz is not simplistic advice in the face of complex and despairing problems, such as "It was all in God's plan; they're in heaven now" at a memorial service. What Hip Hoppers, along with urbanites in general, need is more "good news" about life—vision about their family, hope for tomorrow, reassurance that in the midst of life's trouble, God is still present. In the 'hood, even acknowledgment of life's ambiguity can be "good news."

IDENTIFYING WITH SINNERS

The third missiological essential is being able to *identify with sinners.* The church is typically concerned with appearing good and often loses that connection with the reality that we are all still sinners in process. Everyone makes mistakes; that this applies to people in the church needs to be transparent to the people in the community.

Christians grow when they have nonbelieving friends outside the church family. We are stretched in different areas when we have friends that do not always think and act the way we do. Too many times such people get labeled as "sinners," while simultaneously Christians fail to acknowledge their own "sin" and shortcomings. "Sin" gets pushed under the church rug until it is a large lump that blocks entry.

Now, this does not mean we allow anything to go unchallenged. Jesus knew how to engage and identify with sinners without legitimizing sin. In John 4, Jesus is seen in the middle of the day talking with a Samaritan woman known to have had many husbands—all cultural "no-nos" of his day. Still, Jesus engaged and identified with her, and she was used to save many in her village (John 4:39-42).

CONFRONTING SOCIAL INJUSTICE

The fourth missiological essential is *confront social injustice.* For too long churches have ignored the problems of the inner city.[28] If we are to move forward, the church must be a leading authority in confronting social injustice within the 'hood, even if this comes at the cost of losing donors that do not agree with this policy. Jesus continually confronted the injustices of His day and made it a point to help individuals see their own justice issues. This is seen in his dealing with the rich young ruler (Mark 10:17-26).

For many urban churches, social justice means feeding the homeless one night a week or protesting the latest homosexual member of city council. But if you live anywhere near a 'hood, you know that social injustice is a reality and a constant. How can a church identify with the Hip Hop generation if it does not have a grasp on social justice issues in its own neighborhood?

Jesus knew how to do this and was not worried about saving face. John 6:66 records that many disciples left him because what he had told them was too hard to hear. Jesus doesn't miss a beat, turning to the Twelve and asking if they would leave him too (John 6:67). We must be ready for people to hate us, disagree with us, quite possibly try to kill us; but we must stand our ground and confront the opposition where we see it—even among other Christians. This is part of the calling of Hip Hop mission.

POWER OF THE HOLY SPIRIT

The fifth missiological essential is *operate in the power of the Holy Spirit.* This is a simplistic sounding missiological essential, however: far too often churches move out in mission without ever truly listening to the voice of the Holy Spirit. Moreover, the church must be will-

---

[28]See Michael Eric Dyson, *Between God and Gangsta Rap: Bearing Witness to Black Culture* (New York: Oxford University Press, 1996); *Holler If You Hear Me: Searching for Tupac Shakur* (New York: Basic Civitas, 2001); Harvey Cox, *The Secular City: A Celebration of Its Liberties and an Invitation to Its Discipline* (New York: Macmillan, 1965).

ing to hear that voice in unfamiliar people. The church must be willing to embrace new avenues to the mystery of God.

One of the most important aspects of living in the 'hood is knowing when to move on certain issues and when to wait. Far too many times ministers, especially in the urban context, take on unnecessary work because it makes for great newsletter copy. What many urban pastors do not realize is that Jesus himself did not take on the world. He was focused on a small geographical location with an even smaller group of people. If we are to move forward in the urban church, then we must be focused by the Holy Sprit and not led by the "holy ego." We must regularly ask why we are here and listen for the answer from the Holy Spirit.

We listen through the music and poetry of our context. Hip Hop clutches its spiritual world tightly. We also listen through understanding and interpreting God's Word for our own lives. When this can take place, we are able to minister more effectively with less.

ACCEPTING AND DEALING WITH THE NATURE OF THE 'HOOD

The sixth and final missiological essential is *adequately accept and deal with the true nature of the 'hood.* Elijah Anderson argues that the 'hood lives by a different set of rules, or "codes," than the rest of society.[29] These codes are from and about the streets. They are a part of everyday life and they govern the daily life of many.

If the church is to be a missionary figure, then understanding, accepting and then dealing with that code is essential. This does not mean that the church accepts a five-year-old girl being shot and does not move beyond their fear of the shooters toward calling the 'hood to justice for the victims. Absolutely not. It does mean, however, that Christians seek to understand the elements behind such a horrific event. In relationships, you can only begin with where the relation-

---

[29]Elijah Anderson, *Code of the Street: Decency, Violence, and the Moral Life of the Inner City* (New York: W. W. Norton, 1999).

ship is. That is all you have, nothing more. When we try to impose our own expectations and requirements, the relationship fails and we are both disappointed and dismayed by the relationship.

This does not mean we overlook having vision for people or installing hope and dreams into people that do not have visualization for their own life. It simply means we come to the table and accept the stage both the environment (the 'hood) and people (Hip Hoppers) are in. Growth begins there and, with hope, moves forward.

This is a radical shift away from the unrealistic expectations placed on people by closed-set theology. Often when a pastor looks at the city, the goal becomes to "change those sinners." Barbarically, they enter into neighborhoods and mow down and destroy any cultural artifact that may exist as "forms of the old life." But there is a certain culture that comes with living in a city. And we must let people express that culture and their way of living without imposing our belief system. If a young person is "saved" and yet listens to "secular rap," it's more constructive to ask them what message they hear in the music, how they are interpreting the songs, what need is being met in their enjoyment of the music, than to tell them to turn it off.

Acceptance is difficult and comes with many hard bumps in the road. Yet, that is what community, relationships, and loving each other is all about: the good, the bad and the ugly. When we enter into a relationship, we essentially take the same vows a married couple takes: "For better or for worse." That is the way Jesuz approaches us; why can't we do the same with both ourselves and the people we minister to?

I realize that these six concepts may appear to be "simplistic" and "idealistic." But, in reality, I have been practicing them for quite some time now. I know of several other close friends, peers, and colleagues that do the same with great success. They are the basic ingredients to Hip Hop missions and the beginnings of an evangelistic strategy for the urban and multicultural church. One church cannot solve all the issues facing the inner city, and so the church must look for opportunities to cooperate with the other organizations in its neighborhood, rejecting jealousy over numbers or presumptions that only Christian organizations help people. Hip Hop strongly criticizes Christians that refuse to live in a "new day," and such criticism should not be taken lightly.

REIMAGINING MENTORING AND DISCIPLESHIP FOR THE HIP HOP GENERATION

Missionally engaging Hip Hop will mean that eventually, there will be a group of people ready to move beyond the "milk" of the gospel and into the meat. Hip Hoppers need strong mentoring/coaching as life throws them curve balls, as they rediscover Christ and new theological foundations for their own lives.

Programs do not make disciples, nor does teaching equal training; only hard-core relationships with individuals in a small group can facilitate good discipleship. Greg Ogden's discipling through triads[30]—that is, groups of no more than three to produce intimacy, a safe place, and an open space to share and grow in a spiritual relationship—is a very good start to discipleship and mentoring. Ogden's method is good for four reasons.

- There is a natural shift from the unnatural pressure to natural participation, from the hierarchal to the relational. This is much needed in the urban church; people come into the church ready to get involved, but they learn that they must reach "high" status in the church first. Through Ogden's triads, this pressure becomes less and less, and people concentrate on growing.

- There is a shift from dissemination to dynamic interchange. One of the most harmful things to happen with any young person is to sit them down in a room, have them be as quiet as possible out of "respect," and then speak at them for an hour. By contrast, the three individuals involved in a discipleship triad learn from each other and grow as a group, not from information being dissemi-

---

[30]Adapted from Greg Ogden, *Transforming Discipleship: Making Disciples a Few at a Time* (Downers Grove, Ill.: InterVarsity Press, 2003), chap. 8.

nated from above. Everyone is encouraged to share, and mutual respect and trust is built.

- There is a shift from limited input to wisdom in numbers. In the 'hood, many men do not have the capacity or maturity to share openly in a large setting. Nor would they want their information shared with a pastor so that it can be prayed over. Sitting face to face in a small group allows them to share openly and honestly.

- There is a shift from addition to multiplication. One of the largest ways for pastors to boast about the churches they run is to talk numbers. Through triads the emphasis remains on value and quality, not quantity.

Ogden describes a "hot-house" effect in his triads, where the Holy Spirit enters and brings about rapid growth toward Christlikeness when we (1) open our hearts in transparent trust to each other (2) around the truth of God's Word and (3) in the spirit of mutual accountability.[31]

1. *Transparent trust.* In the 'hood and in Hip Hop culture as a whole, nothing is regarded more sacred than trust. If your business is all over the streets, then you are vulnerable, and that is not good. Many adults in the church cannot keep their mouths closed when it comes to private matters, but in a discipleship triad, there is a sense of openness because of the trust being built together. Bible study alone doesn't generate transparent trust. Walking with one another through difficult times helps people become better reflective listeners who assist one another in confessing sin and hearing God's guidance.[32]

2. *The truth of God's Word.* Bruce Demarest says that Christian spirituality concerns the shaping of our inner beings into the likeness of Jesus Christ.[33] In the 'hood, there are many theories about who Jesus is. So many young people have a distorted view of God and

---

[31]Ibid., pp. 153-54.
[32]Ibid., pp. 155-56.
[33]Bruce Demarest, *Satisfy Your Soul* (Colorado Springs: NavPress, 1999), p. 70.

salvation. In a large group setting, those theories can't be tested. In a triad, however, people are able to ask their questions and learn at their own pace. By studying Scripture firsthand in a place of mutual trust, they are able to rely on God's Word and not simply the church, which they often view with suspicion.

3. *Mutual accountability.* I used to take hundreds of students to camp every summer, where without fail a handful would make a commitment to Christ. We would be excited and genuinely happy for them. But then they would return to hell in their home, stop coming to church, lose their connection with our group and return to the gangs. They would feel guilty and cut off contact with us. And often we would sit in judgment of those young people, because as is often the case in the traditional church, we were concerned with the "decision" more so than the "process" of salvation. Triads, being voluntary and personal, entail a commitment to certain standards and a voluntary submission to review by others.[34] Everyone, without regard to hierarchy, is held accountable to the set standards.

Disciples are made through life investments. Our godsons have a great home, a loving mother and a great community in Minnesota. But every summer they come to see my wife and me in California. We're invested in their lives for the long haul, even though we live halfway across the country from them. It takes a community to raise a child; churches need to get back to thinking that way.

Open and honest discipleship through life investments can help in the deconstruction of religionism, the pig-with-lipstick syndrome and overspiritualization. When we approach people as they are, not for

---

[34]Ogden, *Transforming Discipleship,* p. 168. It should be noted here that there must be a mutual agreement with the person. What happens so many times is that people are forced into discipleship programs that they never really wanted to be a part of in the first place. Ogden (pp. 179-80) argues that if this is apparent—that the person really does not want to be in the group and is "flaking"—then it is time to ask that person to leave and come back when he or she is ready. In the 'hood, this will happen often; not everyone is ready for discipleship, even those that appear to have made a sold decision for Christ.

what we want them to become, we stop being evangelistic mechanics and start being missionally minded, caring people.

In general, in the urban church, disciple making looks something like figure 7. Missing from this approach is the priority of relationships and authentic input from the community. Sure, there is the *possibility* that some may come to know Christ better, but by far there is no real commitment to *grow* in him. We have failed to appreciate the power of being with others on an intimate level over time. Instead, small groups organize events that have very little relevance for the context and people they are meant to help. People end up thinking *We've seen this before*. Relationships in a post-soul era are formed and grow beyond the four walls of a church (see figure 8).

Figure 8 differs from figure 7 in that instead of signing up, attending and doing assignments for a program or class, people are invited into relationships of mutual love, transparency and accountability.[35] People's needs are taken into account, and the community benefits as a result of it.

This type of framework moves away from the pastor-centered church to a balance of power. It is post-soul because it rejects the notion that a traditional leader speaks for "all" the people. It embraces the reality of the streets, and it allows for Christ to emerge from the morally ambiguous ideologies that arise in a post-soul context. This type of discipleship allows for people to move at their pace and not the pace of the pastor. It respects the past but is not enslaved to it. It allows for fluid-set theology to have its place. People are able to doubt, question, even shout at God in a small group that does not simplify, modify, marginalize or patronize their issues away. God is not let off the hook in times of trouble. Fluid-centered theology, when combined with a basic post-soul mentoring paradigm, can guide us past our ideas about God into communion with God.

This takes time, of course, and time is the hardest thing to do. We wait as people figure out their life and ask how Jesuz fits into it.

---

[35]Ibid., p. 124.

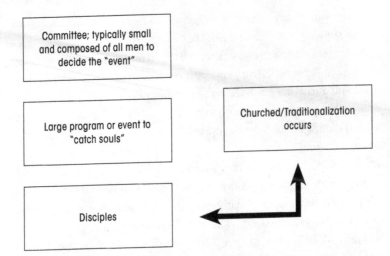

Figure 7. Traditionalized discipleship in the urban church (adapted from Greg Ogden, *Discipleship Essentials* [Downers Grove, Ill.: InterVarsity Press, 2003], p. 123)

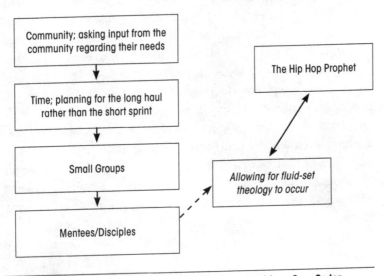

Figure 8. Post-soul Hip Hop mentoring/discipleship (adapted from Greg Ogden, *Discipleship Essentials* [Downers Grove, Ill.: InterVarsity Press, 2003], p. 124)

FROM STREET SAINTHOOD TO JESUZ

Moving and growing in a relationship with Christ should produce a heart for missions, of some type. Hip Hop mission begins when people in the Hip Hop generation who are growing in a relationship with Christ (moving toward the center) reach toward the outer boundaries using the language and idioms of their culture. As missiologists Dan Shaw and Charles Van Engen state:

> We are increasingly convinced that even in revelation the primary focus goes beyond communication to relationship. If that is the case, then Gospel communication becomes an introduction of the text in a new context from which, because of different assumptions, new understanding emerges. Communicators introduce God to receptors who in turn gain a new understanding of God via the presentation. People build a new relationship with God because of how they perceive the text vis-à-vis their context. And relationships are dynamic. If knowing God is the objective, then the focus must be on communication of a relationship rather than simply the transfer of information.[36]

Shaw and Van Engen have it correct. Hip Hoppers do not need more information about God; they need relationships and the freedom to contextualize the gospel into their own terms without strings attached. Hip Hop's theological message can be taken as an evangelistic conversation that begins on the street. Sexuality, death, love, drugs and life itself are all categories rap discusses in its music. However, to help the listener move from that pre-evangelistic conversation to one that is deeper in Christ and missionally minded will require a critical eye and mind. To begin this process entails four important principles.

- *Engage culture.* If Hip Hop culture is not understood, connected with and critically engaged, then relationships with people are in jeopardy. One of the most essential skills that any Christian must learn is suspending judgment while studying culture. Jesus went

---

[36]Shaw and Van Engen, *Comunicating God's Word in a Complex World*, p. 122.

where the people were and dealt with them on their level to bring salt and light to their lives.

- *Emphasize relationships over programs.* In this postmodern world, community and personal touch is a high priority. One of the things that Tupac understood well was that relationships are sacred. Jesus knew this too. Jesus lived, breathed, ate and worked with twelve individuals who did not really comprehend his message until he was gone. Still, Jesus "stuck it out" because he understood the power of relationships. Our commitment to the success of our programs can cause us to resent and even reject the people who complicate them. Failure and disappointment is inevitable when dealing with people, but true relationships can do what no program can: absorb and deal with letdowns and frustrations.

- *Get past pants on the ground and the F-word.* Far too many times the "symptoms" of people get dealt with rather than the real problem. There are greater issues in the 'hood that need to be addressed than a young person's pants that are riding below their knees. Saggin' pants are a type of fashion statement; "Pick up your pants" doesn't address a person's felt needs. Similarly, the F-word generates much discussion, but the most constructive discussion involves asking how and why the word is being used. When the church can begin with a question rather than immediate judgment and sentencing, the real issues below the surface can be identified with and contended with.

- *Listen to the story of people.* This book project has ultimately been concerned with telling a story about a culture. In order to move from street sainthood and closer to Jesuz, the story of individuals in the 'hood are important. It is simple to merely judge a person by how they appear. But every human in this world was carried and given birth by a woman; each person comes with a story. While not all stories are neat and end well, Jesus has created each of us and has placed us here on this planet to fulfill his mission: calling people to his kingdom.

A sea of opportunity awaits us if we are bold enough to venture into a relationship with the Hip Hop community. These suggestions may not be immediately relevant in every context. But Hip Hop is the voice and pastoral guide for many youth today. We are implored by Christ in the Great Commission to listen to such outcries and embrace the pain in them. If we are open to it, and just bold enough, we might actually see God use the Hip Hop generation to inaugurate an amazing "revival" of sorts. I hope that is the case!

Epilogue

REFLECTIONS FROM A HIP HOPPER

Hip Hop has far outlasted early predictions that it would fade and die out. Hip Hop continues to be at the forefront of popular culture not just in the United States but around the world. The other day I was watching an episode of *Sesame Street* for the fiftieth time with my daughter Mahalia. It was one of "Elmo's greatest moments," showcasing Elmo over fifteen or so years. One of the things that stuck out to me the most was the fact that Elmo used rap in many of his songs. Moreover, Elmo befriended rappers and also became one at several points. This is amazing, a children's learning video that uses Hip Hop in a positive way. This is just one of many examples on how Hip Hop has been used for good.

Hip Hop is here to stay. If you think it is going away, or that your kid is eventually going to stop listening to rap, think again. The phenomenon that started in the gutters of the 'hood now wines and dines with some of the richest people in the world. When my wife, Emily, completed the Nike 10K Human Race in the fall of 2008, Kanye West performed afterward for the eclectic bunch of ethnicities and cultures. The people who stayed and watched Kanye (his set started way too late in the evening for us) seemed to know almost every Kanye song on every album.

We have a historical movement on our hands. If Christians are not able to even begin the dialogue with Hip Hoppers, then we will have failed at the Great Commission. This dialogue will not be easy, especially for those who have not been exposed to racial and economic inequalities. Some will find the conversation too distressful and "angry" for them to engage with. Hip Hop is in your face and loud. It can be difficult for White people, for example, to listen to rappers contend that their ethnicity has been the oppressor for centuries. Particularly young Whites sometimes struggle to understand why race is still an issue. Also confusing is the current state of commercialization in Hip Hop. The commercialism that has replaced the social consciousness that once made Hip Hop into a real force is a matter of real confusion. When rappers are paid bonuses of over a million dollars all for rapping misogynist lyrics, there is a problem. When record companies ignore the needs of lower-income communities and market entirely to suburban and upper-middle-class communities, there is a problem. So, Hip Hop is filled with its own contradictions and hypocrisies. When rap artists move out of their communities and forget their roots, there is a problem. Most rappers in the public eye are disconnected from their 'hood roots. Hip Hop icon 50 Cent may be originally from the 'hood and have ghetto roots, but he no longer lives in that 'hood; he lives in a gated community far from the clutches of the 'hood, constantly surrounded by ten bodyguards. How can Hip Hop be a significant cultural movement when its most visible artists live lives so dissonant from the culture's image?

I am not ignorant of the issues that weigh Hip Hop down and make it difficult for many people—especially Christians—to embrace. What this study has done, in essence, is open up the door for more research to be done on the religion of Hip Hop, the intricacies of each theology of Hip Hop and how each of them interrelate with each other. Research is needed in the areas of other religious groups such as the Nation of Islam and Five Percenters (not to mention a growing number of Kabbalah and Jehovah's Witness worshipers). I completely understand that this book will cause debate. But Hip Hop culture simply cannot continue to be dismissed just because it does not fit into any preset mold. I wrote this book in order to help educate those who wish to engage in Christian mission and ministry to the Hip Hop culture. I wait to see what comes next and who will build, critique and challenge this body of work. But what I most look forward to is the missional engagement of Hip Hop culture by a church that is not threatened by questions, ambiguity, mystery or doubt, but rather is moved by the Ethnos and is the *laos theou*. I look forward to Hip Hop's coming role in the mighty force called the body of Christ.

References Cited

Achtemeier, Paul J., Joel B. Green and Marianne Meye Thompson. 2001. *Introducing the New Testament: Its Literature and Theology*. Grand Rapids: Eerdmans.

Allman, Mark. 2000. Eucharist, Ritual & Narrative: Formation of Individual and Communal Moral Character. *Journal of Ritual Studies* 14 (1):60.

Alper, Garth. 2000. Making Sense out of Postmodern Music? *Popular Music and Society* 24 (4):1.

Anderson, Elijah. 1999. *Code of the Street: Decency, Violence, and the Moral Life of the Inner City*. New York: W. W. Norton.

Anderson, Raymond D. S. 2003. Black Beats for One People: Causes and Effects of Identification with Hip-Hop Culture. Ph.D. dissertation, Communications, Regent University, Virginia Beach, Virginia.

Aries, Philippe. 1974. *Western Attitudes toward Death: From the Middle Ages to the Present*, translated by P. M. Ranum. New York: Knopf.

August, Melissa, Leslie E. Brice, Laird Harrison, Todd Murphy and David Thigpen. 2001. Hip-Hop Nation: There's More to Rap Than Just Rhythms & Rhymes. In *Common Culture: Reading & Writing About American Popular Culture*, edited by M. Petracca and M. Sorapure. Upper Saddle River, N.J.: Prentice-Hall.

Bakke, Ray. 1987. *The Urban Christian*. Downers Grove, Ill.: InterVarsity Press.

Baldwin, Davarian L. 2004. Black Empires, White Desires: The Spatial Politics of Identity in the Age of Hip-Hop. In *That's the Joint! The Hip-Hop Studies Reader*, edited by M. Forman and M. A. Neal. New York: Routledge.

Bauman, Zygmunt. 2000. *Liquid Modernity*. Malden, Mass.: Polity Press.

———. 2003. *Liquid Love*. Malden, Mass.: Polity.

Beaudoin, Tom. 1998. *Virtual Faith: The Irreverent Spiritual Quest of Generation X*. San Francisco: Jossey-Bass.

Bell, Daniel. 1973. *The Coming of a Post-Industrial Society: A Venture in Social Forecasting*. New York: Basic Books.

Berger, Peter L. 1967. *The Sacred Canopy; Elements of a Sociological Theory of Religion*. [1st] ed. Garden City, N.Y.: Doubleday.

Berger, Peter L., and Luckmann Thomas. 1966. *The Social Construction of Reality: A Treatise in the Sociology of Knowledge*. Garden City, N.Y.: Doubleday.

Blackwell, Albert L. 1999. *The Sacred in Music*. Louisville, Ky.: Westminster John Knox Press.

Blair, M. Elizabeth. 1993. Commercialization of the Rap Music Youth Subculture. *Journal of Popular Culture* 27 (3):21-46.

Blake, Andrew. 1997. Making Noise: Notes from the 1980s. *Popular Music and Society* 21 (3):19-51.

Bloch, Maurice. 1996. Religion & Ritual. In *The Social Science Encyclopedia*, edited by A. Kuper and J. Kuper. New York: Routledge.

Bosch, David Jacobus. 1991. *Transforming Mission: Paradigm Shifts in Theology of Mission*. American Society of Missiology Series; No. 16. Maryknoll, N.Y.: Orbis Books.

Bourdieu, Pierre. 1986. The Forms of Capital. In *Handbook of Theory and Research for the Sociology of Education*, edited by J. G. Richardson. Westport, Conn.: Greenwood.

Boyd, Todd. 2002. *The H.N.I.C.: The Death of Civil Rights and the Reign of Hip Hop*. New York: New York University Press.

Buber, Martin. 1958. *I and Thou*. New York: Scribner's.

Burnim, Mellone V. 2006. Religious Music. In *African American Music: An Introduction*, edited by M. V. Burnim and P. K. Maultsby. New York: Routledge.

Chang, Jeff. 2005. *Can't Stop Won't Stop: A History of the Hip Hop Generation*. New York: St. Martin's Press.

Chidester, David. 1990. *Patterns of Transcendence: Religion, Death, and Dying*. Belmont, Calif.: Wadsworth.

Clay, Andreana. 2003. Keepin' It Real: Black Youth, Hip-Hop Culture, and Black Identity. *American Behavioral Scientist* 46 (10):1346-58.

Cone, James. 1992. The Blues: A Secular Spiritual. In *Sacred Music of the Secular City: From Blues to Rap*, edited by J. M. Spencer. Durham, N.C.: Duke University Press.

Cone, James H. 1969. *Black Theology and Black Power*. New York: Seabury Press.

———. 1975. *God of the Oppressed*. New York: Seabury Press.

———. 1984. *For My People: Black Theology and the Black Church*. Maryknoll, N.Y.: Orbis Books.

———. 1991. *The Spirituals and the Blues: An Interpretation*. Maryknoll, N.Y.: Orbis Books.

———. 1997. *Black Theology and Black Power*. 5th ed. Maryknoll N.Y.: Orbis Books.

Cox, Harvey. 1965. *The Secular City: A Celebration of Its Liberties and an Invitation to Its Discipline*. New York: Macmillan.

———. 1984. *Religion in the Secular City: Toward a Postmodern Theology*. New York: Simon & Schuster.

Dark, David. 2002. *Everyday Apocalypse: The Sacred Revealed in Radiohead, the Simpsons, and Other Pop Culture Icons*. Grand Rapids: Brazos Press.

Datcher, Michael, Kwame Alexander and Mutulu Shakur. 1997. *Tough Love: The Life and Death of Tupac Shakur, Cultural Criticism and Familial Observations*. Alexandria, Va.: Alexander.

Denzin, Norman K. 1991. *Images of Postmodern Society: Social Theory and Contemporary Cinema*. Thousand Oaks, Calif.: Sage Publications.

Detweiler, Craig, and Barry Taylor. 2003. *A Matrix of Meanings: Finding God in Pop Culture*. Grand Rapids: Baker Academic.

Deuze, Mark. 2006. Ethnic Media, Community Media and Participatory Culture. *Journalism* 7 (3):262-80.

Donalson, Melvin. 2003. *Black Directors in Hollywood*. Austin: University of Texas Press.

Drane, John William. 2000. *The Mcdonaldization of the Church: Spirituality, Creativity, and the Future of the Church*. London: Darton, Longman & Todd.

Dyson, Michael Eric. 1995. *Making Malcolm: The Myth and Meaning of Malcolm X*. New York: Oxford University Press.

———. 2000. *I May Not Get There with You: The True Martin Luther King Jr*. New York: Free Press.

———. 2001. *Holler If You Hear Me: Searching for Tupac Shakur*. New York: Basic Civitas.

———. 2003. *Open Mic: Reflections on Philosophy, Race, Sex, Culture and Religion*. New York: Basic Civitas.

————. 2004. *The Michael Eric Dyson Reader.* New York: Basic Civitas.

————. 2005. *Is Bill Cosby Right? Or Has the Black Middle Class Lost Its Mind?* New York: Basic Civitas.

————. 2006. *Come Hell or High Water: Hurricane Katrina and the Color of Disaster.* New York: Basic Civitas.

Early, Gerald Lyn. 1997. Dreaming of a Black Christmas. *Harper's*, January, 55-61.

Edwards, Herbert O. 1975. Black Theology: Retrospect and Prospect. *Journal of Religious Thought* (32):46-59.

Eliade, Mircea. 1959. *The Sacred and the Profane: The Nature of Religion.* New York: Harcourt, Brace & World.

Erskine, Noel Leo. 2003. Rap, Reggae, and Religion. In *Noise and Spirit: The Religious and Spiritual Sensibilities of Rap Music*, edited by A. Pinn. New York: New York University Press.

Evans, James E. 1992. *We Have Been Believers: An African American Systematic Theology.* Minneapolis: Fortress Press.

Evelyn, Jamilah. 2000. Cover Story: The Miseducation of Hip-Hop. *Black Issues in Higher Education* 17 (21):24.

Floyd, Samuel A. 1995. *The Power of Black Music: Interpreting Its History from Africa to the United States.* New York: Oxford University Press.

Forman, Murray. 2002. *The 'Hood Comes First: Race, Space, and Place in Rap and Hip-Hop.* Middletown, Conn.: Wesleyan University Press.

Funk, Robert Walter, and Roy W. Hoover. 1993. *The Five Gospels: The Search for the Authentic Words of Jesus: New Translation and Commentary.* San Francisco: HarperCollins.

Geerlings, Jacob, and Kenneth W. Ogden, eds. 1968. *Family E and Its Allies in Luke.* Studies and Documents 35. Salt Lake City: University of Utah Press.

George, Nelson. 1999. *Hip Hop America.* New York: Penguin Books.

Gibbs, Eddie. 2000. *Churchnext: Quantum Changes in How We Do Ministry.* Downers Grove, Ill.: InterVarsity Press.

————. 2000. *In Name Only: Tackling the Problem of Nominal Christianity.* Wheaton, Ill.: BridgePoint.

Glasser, Arthur F. 2003. *Announcing the Kingdom: The Story of God's Mission in the Bible.* Grand Rapids: Baker Academic.

Gottdiener, Mark. 1985. Hegemony and Mass Culture: A Semiotic Approach. *American Journal of Sociology* 90 (5):979-1001.

Grenz, Stanley J. 2001. *The Social God and the Relational Self: A Trinitarian Theology of the Imago Dei*. Louisville, Ky.: Westminster John Knox Press.

Gruver, Rod. 1992. The Blues as a Secular Religion. In *Sacred Music of the Secular City: From Blues to Rap*, edited by J. M. Spencer. Durham, N.C.: Duke University Press.

Guevara, Nancy. 1996. Women Writin' Rappin' Breakin'. In *Dropping Science: Critical Essays on Rap Music and Hip Hop Culture*, edited by W. E. Perkins. Philadelphia: Temple University Press.

Gutiérrez, Gustavo. 1987. *On Job: God-Talk and the Suffering of the Innocent*. Maryknoll, N.Y.: Orbis Books.

Harvey, David. 1993. From Space to Place and Back Again: Reflections on the Condition of Postmodernity. In *Mapping the Futures: Local Cultures, Global Change*, edited by J. Bird, B. Curtis, T. Putnam, G. Robertson and L. Tickner. New York: Routledge.

Hebdige, Dick. 1998. Postmodernism and 'the Other Side'. In J. Storey, *Cultural Theory and Popular Culture: A Reader*. London: Prentice-Hall.

Heyward, Carter. 1999. *Saving Jesus from Those Who Are Right: Rethinking What It Means to Be a Christian*. Minneapolis: Fortress Press.

Hiebert, Paul G. 1978. Conversion, Culture, and Cognitive Categories. *Gospel in Context* 1 (4):24-29.

Hodge, Daniel. 2003. Can You Hear Me Calling: Hip Hop/Gangster Culture & the Future Urban Church. Thesis, Fuller Theological Seminary's School of Intercultural Studies, Fuller Theological Seminary School of Intercultural Studies, Pasadena.

hooks, bell. 1990. *Yearning: Race, Gender, and Cultural Politics*. Toronto: Between the Lines.

Hustad, Donald Paul. 1981. *Jubilate: Church Music in the Evangelical Tradition*. Carol Stream, Ill.: Hope Publishing.

Jacobs, Alan. 2003. What Narrative Theology Forgot. *First Things* (135):25.

Kaiser, Walter C. 2000. *Mission in the Old Testament: Israel as a Light to the Nations*. Grand Rapids: Baker Books.

Kärkkäinen, Veli-Matti. 2003. *Christology: A Global Introduction*. Grand Rapids: Baker Academic.

Kauffman, Richard A. 2007. Suffering God. *Christianity Today* 51 (3):71.

Kelley, Robin D. G. 1994. *Race Rebels: Culture, Politics, and the Black Working Class*. New York: Free Press.

Keyes, Cheryl L. 2002. *Rap Music and Street Consciousness*. Chicago: University of Illinois Press.

Kingsbury, Jack Dean. 1995. The Gospel of John. *Interpretation* 49 (4):341.

Kirk, J. Andrew. 2000. Following Modernity and Postmodernity: A Missio-logical Investigation. *Mission Studies* 17 (1):217-39.

Kitwana, Bakari. 2003. *The Hip Hop Generation: Young Blacks and the Crisis in African-American Culture*. New York: Basic Civitas.

———. 2004a. The Challenge of Rap Music from Cultural Movement to Political Power. In *That's the Joint! The Hip-Hop Studies Reader*, edited by M. Forman and M. A. Neal. New York: Routledge.

———. 2004b. The State of the Hip-Hop Generation: How Hip-Hop's Cul-tural Movement Is Evolving into Political Power. *Diogenes (International Council for Philosophy and Humanistic Studies)* 51 (3):115-20.

———. 2005. *Why White Kids Love Hip-Hop: Wankstas, Wiggers, Wan-nabes, and the New Reality of Race in America*. New York: Basic Civitas.

Kraft, Charles H. 1991. *Communication Theory for Christian Witness*. Mary-knoll, N.Y.: Orbis Books.

Kreitzer, Larry J. 1993. *The New Testament in Fiction and Film: On Reversing the Hermeneutical Flow*. Variation: The Biblical Seminar 17. Sheffield, U.K.: JSOT Press.

———. 1994. *The Old Testament in Fiction and Film: On Reversing the Hermeneutical Flow*, The Biblical Seminar 24. Sheffield: Sheffield Aca-demic Press.

———. 2002. *The Dreaming Spires Version of Paul's Letters (the Codex Ox-oniensis)*. Oxford: Alden.

KRS-One. 2003. *Ruminations*. New York: Welcome Rain Publishers.

Kübler-Ross, Elisabeth, ed. 1975. *Death: The Final Stage*. Englewood Cliffs, N.J.: Prentice-Hall.

Kuçuradi, Ioanna. 2004. Rationality and Rationalities within the Framework of the Modernism-Postmodernism Debate. *Diogenes* 51 (2):11-17.

Lash, Scott. 1990. Postmodernism as Humanism? Urban Space and Social Theory. In *Theories of Modernity and Postmodernity*, edited by B. S. Turner. Thousand Oaks, Calif.: Sage Publications.

Lefebvre, Henri. 1991. *The Production of Space*. Oxford: Basil Blackwell.

LeGates, Richard, and Frederic T. Stout, eds. 2000. *The City Reader*. 2nd ed. New York: Routledge.

Long, Eugene Thomas. 2006. Suffering and Transcendence. *International Journal for Philosophy of Religion* 60 (1-3):139.

Lynch, Gordon. 2005. *Understanding Theology and Popular Culture.* Malden, Mass.: Blackwell Publishing.

Lyotard, Jean-Francois. 1984. *The Postmodern Condition: A Report on Knowledge.* Minneapolis: University of Minnesota Press.

Maher, George Ciccariello. 2005. Brechtian Hip-Hop: Didactics and Self-Production in Post-Gangsta Political Mixtapes. *Journal of Black Studies* 36 (1):129-60.

Miles, Jack. 2001. *Christ: A Crisis in the Life of God.* New York: Alfred A. Knopf.

Miyakawa, Felicia M. 2005. *Five Percenter Rap: God Hop's Music, Message, and Black Muslim Mission.* Bloomington: Indiana University Press.

Moltmann, Jürgen. 1990. *The Way of Jesus Christ: Christology in Messianic Dimensions.* San Francisco: HarperSanFrancisco.

Montgomery, Helen B. 1920. *The Bible and Missions.* Brattleboro, Vt.: The Central Committee on the United Study of Foreign Mission.

Morgado, Marcia A. 2007. The Semiotics of Extraordinary Dress: A Structural Analysis and Interpretation of Hip-Hop Style. *Clothing and Textiles Research Journal* 25 (2):131-55.

Moss, Otis. 2007. Real Big: The Hip Hop Pastor as Postmodern Prophet. In *The Gospel Remix: Reaching the Hip Hop Generation,* edited by R. Watkins. Valley Forge, Penn.: Judson Press.

Neal, Mark Anthony. 1997. Sold out on Soul: The Corporate Annexation of Black Popular Music. *Popular Music and Society* 21 (3):117.

———. 2002. *Soul Babies: Black Popular Culture and the Post-Soul Aesthetic.* New York: Routledge.

Nelson, Angela S. 1991. Theology in the Hip-Hop of Public Enemy and Kool Moe Dee. In *The Emergency of Black and the Emergence of Rap,* edited by J. M. Spencer. Durham, N.C.: Duke University Press.

Niebuhr, Richard H. 1951. *Christ and Culture.* San Francisco: HarperCollins.

Nissen, Johannes. 1999. *New Testament and Mission: Historical and Hermeneutical Perspectives.* New York: Peter Lang.

Nuland, Sherwin. 1993. *How We Die: Reflections on Life's Final Chapter.* New York: Vintage Books.

O'Connor, Kathleen M. 2008. Lamenting Back to Life. *Interpretation* 62 (1):34.

Odum, Howard W. 1968. *The Negro and His Songs: A Study of Typical Negro*

Songs in the South. 36 vols. Westport, Conn.: Negro Universities Press.

Ogden, Greg. 1990. *The New Reformation: Returning the Ministry to the People of God*. Grand Rapids: Zondervan.

———. 1998. *Discipleship Essentials: A Guide to Building Your Life in Christ*. Downers Grove, Ill.: InterVarsity Press.

———. 2003a. *Transforming Discipleship: Making Disciples a Few at a Time*. Downers Grove, Ill.: InterVarsity Press.

———. 2003b. *Unfinished Business: Returning the Ministry to the People of God*. Rev. ed. Grand Rapids: Zondervan.

Otto, Rudolf. 1925. *The Idea of the Holy*, translated by J. W. Harvey. New York: Oxford University Press.

Palen, J. John. 1981. *The Urban World*. 2nd ed. New York: McGraw-Hill.

Parillo, Vincent N. 2007. *Strangers to These Shores*. 8th ed. Boston: Allyn & Bacon.

Paris, Peter J. 1995. *The Spirit of African Peoples*. Minneapolis: Fortress Press.

Peck, M. Scott. 1988. *The Different Drum: Community-Making and Peace*. New York: Simon & Schuster.

Perkins, William Eric, ed. 1996. *Droppin' Science: Critical Essays on Rap Music and Hip Hop Culture, Critical Perspectives on the Past*. Philadelphia: Temple University Press.

Perkinson, James W. 2003. Rap as Wrap and Rapture: North American Popular Culture and the Denial of Death. In *Noise and Spirit: The Religious and Spiritual Sensibilities of Rap Music*, edited by A. Pinn. New York: New York University Press.

Perry, Imani. 2004. *Prophets of the Hood: Politics and Poetics in Hip Hop*. Durham, N.C.: Duke University Press.

Peters, Ken. 2001. *Tupac vs. USA*. Dennon Entertainment.

Pinn, Anthony B. 1995. *Why Lord? Suffering and Evil in Black Theology*. New York: Continuum.

———. 2003a. Making a World with a Beat: Musical Expression's Relationship to Religious Identity and Experience. In *Noise and Spirit: The Religious and Spiritual Sensibilities of Rap Music*, edited by A. Pinn. New York: New York University Press.

———. 2003b. Rap's Humanist Sensibilities. In *Noise and Spirit: The Religious and Spiritual Sensibilities of Rap Music*, edited by A. Pinn. New York: New York University Press.

———, ed. 2003. *Noise and Spirit: The Religious and Spiritual Sensibilities of Rap Music*. New York: New York University Press.

Potter, Russell A. 1995. *Spectacular Vernaculars: Hip-Hop and the Politics of Postmodernism*. New York: State University of New York Press.

Pratt, Geraldine. 2008. Grids of Difference. In *Cultural Studies: An Anthology*, edited by M. Ryan and H. Musiol. Malden, Mass.: Blackwell.

Ramsey, Guthrie P. 2004. *Race Music: Black Cultures from Bebop to Hip-Hop*. Berkeley: University of California Press.

Reed, Teresa L. 2003. *The Holy Profane: Religion in Black Popular Music*. Lexington: University Press of Kentucky.

Ridder, Richard. 1983. The Old Testament Roots of Mission. In *In Exploring Church Growth*, edited by W. Shenk. Grand Rapids: Eerdmans.

Ritzer, George. 2000a. *The McDonaldization of Society*. Thousand Oaks, Calif.: Pine Forge Press.

———. 2000b. *Classical Sociological Theory*. 5th ed. New York: McGraw-Hill.

Rodriquez, Jason. 2006. Color-Blind Ideology and the Cultural Appropriation of Hip-Hop. *Journal of Contemporary Ethnography* 35 (6):645-68.

Romanowski, William D. 1996. *Pop Culture Wars: Religion and the Role of Entertainment in American Life*. Downers Grove, Ill.: InterVarsity Press.

Rose, Tricia. 1994a. *Black Noise: Rap Music and Black Culture in Contemporary America*. Middletown, Conn.: Wesleyan University Press.

———. 1994b. A Style Nobody Can Deal With: Politics, Style, and the Postindustrial City in Hip Hop. In *Microphone Friends: Youth Music and Youth Culture*, edited by A. Ross and T. Rose. New York: Routledge.

Schiller, Herbert I. 1989. *Culture Inc.: The Corporate Takeover of Public Expression*. New York: Oxford University Press.

Seymour, Jack L. 2001. Meeting God in the Peoples of God. *Religious Education* 96 (3):267-69.

Shakur, Sanyika. 1993. *Monster: The Autobiography of an L.A. Gang Member*. New York: Penguin Books.

Shakur, Tupac, Afeni Shakur, Jacob Hoye, Karolyn Ali, and Walter Einenkel. 2003. *Tupac: Resurrection, 1971-1996*. New York: Atria Books.

Shaw, Daniel R., and Charles E. Van Engen. 2003. *Communicating God's Word in a Complex World: God's Truth or Hocus Pocus*. Lanham, Md.: Rowman & Littlefield.

Shenk, Wilbert R. 1993. *The Transfiguration of Mission: Biblical, Theological*

& *Historical Foundations, Missionary Studies; No. 12.* Scottdale, Penn.:
Herald Press.

———. 1995. *Write the Vision: The Church Renewed.* Christian Mission and
Modern Culture. Valley Forge, Penn.: Trinity Press International.

———. 1999. *Changing Frontiers of Mission,* American Society of Missiology Series 28. Maryknoll, N.Y.: Orbis Books.

———. 2002. *Enlarging the Story: Perspectives on Writing World Christian
History.* Maryknoll, N.Y.: Orbis Books.

Slobin, Mark, and Jeff Todd Titon. 1984. The Music-Culture as a World of
Music. In *Worlds of Music: An Introduction to the Music of the World's
Peoples,* edited by J. T. Titon, J. T. Koetting, D. P. McAllester, D. B. Reck
and M. Slobin. New York: Schirmer Books.

Smith, Efrem, and Phil Jackson. 2005. *The Hip Hop Church: Connecting with
the Movment Shaping Our Culture.* Downers Grove, Ill.: InterVarsity
Press.

Smitherman, Geneva. 1977. *Talkin and Testifyin: The Language of Black
America.* Boston: Houghton Mifflin.

———. 1994. *Black Talk: Words and Phrases from the Hood to the Amen
Corner.* Boston: Houghton Mifflin.

———. 2000. *Talkin That Talk: Language, Culture, and Education in African
America.* New York: Routledge.

Snapper, Juliana. 2004. Scratching the Surface: Spinning Time and Identity
in Hip-Hop Turntablism. *European Journal of Cultural Studies* 7 (1):9-25.

Song, Choan-Seng. 1979. *Third-Eye Theology: Theology in Formation in
Asian Settings.* Maryknoll, N.Y.: Orbis Books.

Southern, Eileen. 1983. *The Music of Black Americans.* 2nd ed. New York:
W. W. Norton.

Spencer, Jon Michael. 1990. *Protest and Praise: Sacred Music of Black Religion.* Minneapolis: Fortress Press.

———. 1991. *Theological Music: Introduction to Theomusicology.* New York:
Greenwood Press.

———, ed. 1992. *Sacred Music of the Secular City: From Blues to Rap,* vol. 6,
Black Sacred Music: A Journal of Theomusicology. Durham, N.C.: Duke
University Press.

Spirer, Peter. 1997. *Ryme and Reason.* Miramax Films.

Stephens, Ronald Jemal. 1991. The Three Waves of Contemporary Rap
Music. In *The Emergency of Black and the Emergence of Rap,* edited by

J. M. Spencer. Durham, N.C.: Duke University Press.

Stovall, David. 2006. We Can Relate: Hip-Hop Culture, Critical Pedagogy, and the Secondary Classroom. *Urban Education* 41 (6):585-602.

Stulman, Louis J. 1998. *Order Amid Chaos: Jeremiah as Symbolic Tapestry.* Sheffield, U.K.: Sheffield Academic Press.

Thoennes, Erik. 2007. Laughing through Tears: The Redemptive Role of Humor in a Fallen World. *Presbyterion* 33 (2):72.

Tiersma, Jude M. 1999. Reading the Writing on the Wall: Missional Transformation through Narrative in Postmodern Los Angeles. Ph.D. dissertation, School of Intercultural Studies, Fuller Theological Seminary, Pasadena, California.

Tillich, Paul. 1955. *The New Being.* New York: Charles Scribner's Sons.

———. 1957. *Systematic Theology.* Vol. 2. Chicago: University of Chicago Press.

———. 1959. *Theology of Culture.* New York: Oxford University Press.

———. 1972. Paul Tillich in Conversation on Psychology and Theology. *Journal of Pastoral Care* 26 (3):176.

———. 1984. Beyond Religious Socialism. *Christian Century* 101 (22):686.

———. 1985. Personal Introduction to My Systematic Theology. *Modern Theology* 1 (2):83.

———. 1990. The Right to Hope. *Christian Century* 107 (33):1064.

Ting-Toomey, Stella, and Leeva C Chung. 2005. *Understanding Intercultural Communication.* Los Angeles: Roxbury Publishing.

Trapp, Erin. 2005. The Push and Pull of Hip-Hop: A Social Movement Analysis. *American Behavioral Scientist* 48 (11):1482-95.

Tyson, Christopher. 2003. *Exploring the Generation Gap and Its Implications on African American Consciousness.* Urban Think Tank.

Wade, Bonnie C. 2004. *Thinking Musically: Experiencing Music, Expressing Culture.* New York: Oxford University Press.

Watkins, Ralph C. 2003. Rap, Religion, and New Realities: The Emergence of a Religious Discourse in Rap Music. In *Noise and Spirit: The Religious and Spiritual Sensibilities of Rap Music*, edited by A. Pinn. New York: New York University Press.

———. 2007. *The Gospel Remix: Reaching the Hip Hop Generation.* Valley Forge, Penn.: Judson Press.

Watkins, S. Craig. 1998. *Representing: Hip Hop Culture and the Production of Black Cinema.* Chicago: University of Chicago Press.

———. 2005. *Hip Hop Matters: Politics, Pop Culture, and the Struggle for the Soul of a Movement*. Boston: Beacon Press.

Webb, Gary. 1998. *Dark Alliance: The CIA, the Contras, and the Crack Cocaine Explosion*. New York: Seven Stories Press.

West, Cornel. 1992. On Afro-American Popular Music: From Bebop to Rap. In *Sacred Music of the Secular City: From Blues to Rap*, edited by J. M. Spencer. Durham, N.C.: Duke University Press.

———. 1993. *Prophetic Thought in Postmodern Times: Beyond Eurocentrism and Multiculturalism*. Vol. 1. Monroe, Me.: Common Courage Press.

White, Russell Christopher. 2002. Constructions of Identity and Community in Hip-Hop Nationalism with Specific Reference to Public Enemy and Wu-Tang Clan. Ph.D. dissertation, University of Southampton, England.

Willox, Ashlee Cunsolo. 2008. The Cross, the Flesh, and the Absent God: Finding Justice through Love and Affliction in Simone Weil's Writings. *Journal of Religion* 88 (1):53.

Zanfagna, Christina. 2006. Under the Blasphemous (W)Rap: Locating the "Spirit" in Hip-Hop. *Pacific Review of Ethnomusicology* 12:1-12.

Index

CPSIA information can be obtained
at www.ICGtesting.com
Printed in the USA
LVHW011110100122
708184LV00009B/1287